UP POMPEY

UP
POMPEY

A Clueless American Sportswriter
Bumbling Through English Football

CHUCK CULPEPPER

Weidenfeld & Nicolson
LONDON

First published in Great Britain in 2007
by Weidenfeld & Nicolson

10 9 8 7 6 5 4 3 2 1

A CIP catalogue record for this book
is available from the British Library.

ISBN 978 0 297 85283 4

Typeset by Input Data Services Ltd, Frome

Printed and bound at Mackays of Chatham plc, Chatham, Kent

The Orion Publishing Group's policy is to use papers that
are natural, renewable and recyclable products and made
from wood grown in sustainable forests. The logging and
manufacturing processes are expected to conform to the
environmental regulations of the country of origin.

Weidenfeld & Nicolson

The Orion Publishing Group Ltd
Orion House
5 Upper Saint Martin's Lane
London WC2H 9EA
An Hachette Livre UK Company

www.orionbooks.co.uk

In memory of Louise, Florence, Jim and Ed

Contents

Pompey's Leading Characters during the 2006–07 Season   ix

1. Common sportswriter malaise   1

2. Fumbling around in daylight   9

3. 'F—ing move!'   17

4. Is that really Chelsea's pitch?   24

5. A 12-inch Digix in Camden   31

6. My very own relegation weekend   39

7. Sunday contempt   47

8. Media-inaccessible England   55

9. Two months to choose   62

10. Clueless   69

11. Knowing too much   76

12. Away fan   83

13. The best goal in my admittedly limited lifetime   90

14. I hear my people   96

15. Europe   103

16. Away fan extraordinaire   110

17. The distinct horror of rail replacement   117

18. An FA Cup debutant   125

19. Cheering for a toilet-seat thief   132

20. 'Have we just . . .'   139

21. New Trafford   146

22. Eavesdropping on trains   153

23. 'We were mental'   160

24. Chimes and mammals   167

25. Lonely walks he who walks to Plainmoor   175

26. A Blackburn fiasco   182

27. Never miss a chance to hang out in a pub with a blue bear   189

28. Betraying a kind Reading fan   196

29. Just disgusting   203

30. Rather hopeless   210

31. The greatest own goal in history   217

32. You have to be kidding me   224

33. Not-taken roads   231

34. Adopted   238

35. It's really the heart of England   245

36. Elvis and the Beatles   252

37. One goal from Europe   259

38. The whole meat raffle of it all   267

Pompey's Leading Characters during the 2006–07 Season

SOL CAMPBELL (Plaistow, London, England, 18 September 1974)
To seasoned observers, he's a respected veteran defender and colossal physical presence who alone has cleaned up many a threat and eased the worries of thousands of fans at Tottenham, Arsenal and Portsmouth. To a clueless American, he's pretty much Zeus.

KANU (Odessi, Nigeria, 1 August 1976)
To seasoned observers, he's a rubbery 6-foot-5 striker who's 'world-class on the ball' and who has graced winners of the Premiership, the European Champions League, the FA Cup, the UEFA Cup and the Olympics, and played for Ajax, Inter Milan, Arsenal, West Bromwich Albion and Portsmouth. To a clueless American, well, the way he presses himself against defenders to use his body as a barrier between them and the ball, he'd make a swell basketball power forward.

DAVID JAMES (Welwyn Garden City, England, 1 August 1970)
To seasoned observers, he's a respected goalkeeper of long-standing excellence infused with the occasional gaffe. To a clueless American, he's a thoughtful columnist in the *Observer*, and the Roman haircut long about autumn 2006 was unbelievably mod.

LINVOY PRIMUS (Forest Gate, London, England, 14 September 1973)
To seasoned observers, he's a commendable defender of limited gifts, a grinder who nobly worked his way up through Barnet and Reading (before Reading was Reading) and, with honest effort, overcame doubters. To a clueless American, he's a commendable defender of limited gifts, a grinder who nobly worked his way up through Barnet and Reading (before Reading was Reading) and, with honest effort, overcame doubters.

PEDRO MENDES (Guimaraes, Portugal, 26 February 1979)
To seasoned observers, he's a workaholic midfielder some might even spot as the indefatigable brains of the operation. To a clueless American, he's that gritty guy who scored that astonishing goal against Manchester City on 11 March 2006, and who fell unconscious after Ben Thatcher tackled him gratuitously, and who shook Thatcher's hand on the pitch four months later, and who shouldn't have shaken Thatcher's hand on the pitch four months later because Thatcher shouldn't have been in the league.

MATT TAYLOR (Oxford, England, 27 November 1981)
To seasoned observers, he's a left back and left midfielder noted for impressive rushes to bolster the attack and for goals of prodigious, even outrageous, length. To a clueless American ... when you're new at watching something and somebody gives you a 45-yard goal that rises like a shooting star and then dives like a swan beyond the goalkeeper's shoulders, you pretty much never forget that person.

BENJANI MWARUWARI (Bulawayo, Zimbabwe, 13 August 1978)
To seasoned observers, he's a striker of pace and of potency and of loads of goals still coming someday, whose transfer in January 2006 set the club record both for monetary amount and for attention from investigators of questionable transactions. To a clueless American, it's spine-tingling when the Fratton End sings,

'He comes from Zimbabwe/He's gonna score today,' not least because in America 'Zimbabwe' might get mispronounced so the song would go, 'He comes from Zimbabwe/He'll score, you wait and see.'

GARY O'NEIL (Bromley, South London, England, 18 May 1983)
To seasoned observers, he's a promising midfielder who turns up as if through cracks in the air with his knack for pesky goal-creation. To a clueless American, he's refreshing because he looks so gawky and geeky and there's always a millisecond of marvelling that somebody so gawky and geeky can dwell among the gods.

NIKO KRANJCAR (Zagreb, Croatia, 13 August 1984)
To seasoned observers, he's the stylish young midfielder with eyes on the sides of his head, the son of Croatia's national coach, the captain of the Dinamo club at the age of 17, and the reason for the most expensive transfer in the history of Croatian sport. To a clueless American, that goal at Fulham was just gorgeous.

LOMANA LUALUA (Kinshasha, Congo, 28 December 1980)
To seasoned observers, he's a fleet, if staccato, runner, with talents both for occasional goals and occasional forgetfulness that he's got team-mates out there. To a clueless American, he's that former child gymnast who does dazzling somersaults after goals but hasn't done any in a while because he hasn't scored any goals in a while.

NOE PAMAROT (Fontenay-sous-Bois, France, 14 April 1979)
To seasoned observers, he's a little bit of a Hercules, a strapping lad, a defensive bulwark and a daunting tackler, who came from Tottenham in January 2006 and scored at Emirates Stadium the following December. To a clueless American, he's proof of the existence of rugged French cowboys so often unacknowledged by ignorant American cultural jingoists.

DEJAN STEFANOVIC (Nis, Serbia, 28 October 1974)

To seasoned observers, he's a solid central defender, deft passer and 'great in the air', all grown up from skittish 1990s days at Sheffield Wednesday, and influential in the decision to replace Alain Perrin with Uncle Harry in late 2005. To a clueless American, it's still inscrutable trying to discern who might be great in the air or lousy in the air.

ANDREW COLE (Nottingham, 15 October 1971)

To seasoned observers, he's an ageing striker No. 2 in all-time Premiership scoring and the winner of every conceivable team honour. To a clueless American, he scored two goals but then left on loan to Birmingham in April, and must've been no more than a so-so acquisition because that's what everyone kept saying.

RICHARD HUGHES (Glasgow, Scotland, 25 June 1979)

To seasoned observers, he's a yeoman defensive midfielder who took the Bournemouth route to Portsmouth and openly roots for Scotland against England. To a clueless American, I'd barely notice him for long swatches of time and then he'd turn up in my sightline and I'd think, *Oh, he's out there*, which could mean he's a marginal player, or could mean he's a wonderful player, or could mean absolutely nothing.

GLEN JOHNSON (Greenwich, London, 23 August 1984)

To seasoned observers, including Sven-Goran Eriksson, this bale of speed and muscle leads all young English right backs in promise. To a clueless American, it's easy to envy his frame as he looks like a statue, just as it's difficult to envy his frame of mind (speeding in his Aston Martin, forgetting his passport for Chelsea's Champions League semifinal trip to Barcelona, trying to steal bathroom fixtures at the B&Q in Dartford) in which he sometimes seems to think like a statue.

1

Common sportswriter malaise

I came down with a dogged strain of common sportswriter malaise on the morning of Tuesday, 23 January 2001. It broadsided me in Florida, in Tampa, on the floor of Raymond James Stadium, an edifice named after an investment firm and set amid boulevards of soul-murdering strip malls. It struck during my 10th Super Bowl Media Day, an annual event that persists despite both reporters and athletes finding it loathsome.

As about 2,300 reporters surrounded two American-football teams – one, then a break, then the other – it dawned on me in a howling rush that I had spent a 14-year career immersed in a vat of drivel, banality and corruption, especially drivel. I had taken the only brain Mother Nature had granted me, and I had exposed it to almost 15 years of listening to stale and preposterous utterances from managers, athletes and sports-talk radio. It felt as if my brain had stored, as fluid, all the fibs and the grotesque marketing and the extravagant nonsense, until one day the organ simply overflowed.

Woozy, I fled up the stadium steps toward the free breakfast buffet.

I cannot recall the precise rote utterance by an athlete or coach or reporter that wrought this cranial convulsion. I wish I could, but I believe the human mind has a mechanism that represses things that aim to kill it. At Super Bowl Media Day, some reporters seek insight. Some seek piffle. All receive piffle.

There's such a debilitating barrage of piffle that it'd be yeoman to pinpoint particular piffle.

I know it wasn't when Baltimore Ravens linebacker Ray Lewis compared his double-murder charge and obstruction-of-justice guilty plea to the plight of Jesus Christ, because I weathered that session dutifully. I doubt it was New York Giants cornerback Jason Sehorn chatting with reporters about his marriage proposal to actress Angie Harmon on a late-night talk show, because I deeply feared that session and did not stray near. It could've been when, for the 1,000th time, across 10 Super Bowls, I heard somebody ask a player whether his team could handle Super Bowl distractions, followed by the 1,000th identical answer of, *Yes, we can because we understand why we're here*. No one had ever said, *No, I don't think so*, which would've been mildly intriguing.

I just know that everything around me felt so hackneyed and so marketed, every conversation so staged, that I could feel the last shreds of individual humanity draining from my system.

This malaise, epidemic among colleagues, had beset me only in twinges before. For years, I had stood in clusters of reporters listening to university basketball players recite the tired balderdash learned in sessions with university PR staffs, and every once in a while I'd feel a sudden flash commanding me to take my own pen and gouge out my own eyeballs. I'd heard almost 15 years of athletes claiming they'd succeeded even though nobody respected them. That must've killed 10,000 brain cells. I'd heard almost 15 years of coaches and athletes saying they took it one game at a time, as not a single contrarian in all that time ever dared to say he took it two games at a time. That must've killed 100,000 brain cells. I'd listened carefully to almost 15 years of retired athletes doing TV commentary during games and studio shows or on talk radio.

That must've made me an idiot.

Athletes crediting a deity for a fleeting game outcome or extolling a deity once in legal trouble ... Commentators extolling purity because some places look pure, even amid the phantasmagorical corruption of American *university* athletics . . . Athletes, managers and commentators saying it's not about the money . . . American Ryder Cup players playing 'for my country' . . . The preposterous refrain that the winner of a game *'wanted it more'* . . . *'We just have to focus'* . . . *'They really have athleticism'* . . . *'A quarterback controversy'* . . . *'The people who criticize me don't know me'* . . . Or, the post-arrest staple, invented by PR handlers: *'I made a mistake'* . . .

It just all crashed in.

Still, after some free-breakfast comfort food – eggs, sausage – the bug went into remission, and even after the dreary Super Bowl game itself – uninspiring Baltimore Ravens 34, uninspiring New York Giants 7 – I hopscotched a huge country without complaint, even seeing some poignant things.

At the Daytona 500 that February, the great driver Dale Earnhardt died on the final turn of the final lap, and I saw a vast track enveloped in a mourning love while a gnarled mechanic sobbed into a payphone. At the annual 64-team university basketball tournament that every March grips us so much that we overlook the phantasmagorical corruption, I saw the gorgeous San Diego by the Pacific. At the Masters in April, I saw a single golfer born to an African-American Vietnam War veteran and a Thai mother ensure that his Orlando coffee table could hold all four major golf trophies at once, proof that humanity, through careful parenting and tutelage, could tame its own beastly invention, golf.

Delights popped up as years galloped by. When the Boston Red Sox won the baseball World Series in 2004 to end an 86-year drought that had become a national cliché, I got goose bumps at the amphibious parade that ran on streets plus the Charles River, and I interviewed fans for whom the outcome had brought connection to deceased relatives they just knew had watched. At Athens 2004, I saw a female Korean archer score a mandatory 10 on the last chance. In October 2005, I saw a university football game between Southern California and Notre Dame that beat the best theatre ever made. I saw Roger Federer play tennis. I saw Tiger Woods often.

It's just that the remissions began thinning.

At the very sporting events that had filled the daydreams of my sunny Virginia childhood, I'd feel a fleeting and deadening sense of triviality, the sensation tripled during any assignment to any game in the National Basketball Association's droning 82-game regular season. With access to the very sportsmen I'd once yearned to meet as a child, I'd find myself wishing such access unavailable, the feeling tripled with Major League Baseball, home to the most over-interviewed athletes. I grew so weary of Lance Armstrong's defensive preening that his face on the screen triggered a neuromuscular response wherein I'd reach involuntarily for a remote control, even in a bar.

And university sport. Since childhood, I'd loved university sport, that American oddity featuring gigantic TV audiences and filled stadiums with 60,000 or 80,000 or in some cases 100,000 seats. I'd always perceived it as a continent of fine athletic drama dotted with episodic sleaze. Only after about 20 years of learning about universities slipping illicit cash payments to coveted high school athletes, furtively giving cars to coveted high school athletes, bribing the coaches of coveted high school athletes, treating high school athletes to weekends of lavish dinners and (sometimes) prostitution services on 'official visits', fudging the academic records of college athletes to keep them eligible, having tutors do the schoolwork of college athletes to keep them eligible, using corporate sleaze to wring ever more money from the sweat of unsalaried college athletes, and so on, my thick skull awakened to the thought that maybe it's a continent of sleaze dotted with episodic honour.

It got tougher by the year.

In 2002, we Americans endured another tired baseball labour strife that clouded the season with potential cancellation. We had a former Most Valuable Player estimate that half the baseball players took performance-enhancing drugs. We staged an Olympics in Salt Lake City in which a figure-skating judge with a fur collar admitted trading scoring favours. At least she's French, we thought – you know, not like us.

In 2003, we had a row over the Augusta National Golf Club's pitiable boys-only membership policy. We had a basketball player we liked immensely, Kobe Bryant of Los Angeles, arrested on rape charges. The No. 1 sports star of the year? That would be THG, the newly revealed performance-enhancing drug. To top it all, we had a grand American epitome in Texas: a shooting death of a university basketball player, followed by his coach's fear that past illicit payments to the player would get exposure, followed by the esteemed coach trying to persuade his assistants to brand the deceased as a drug dealer (thus explaining the good bank balance), complete with the coach saying, 'Reasonable doubt is there's nobody right now who can say we paid Patrick Dennehy ... because he's dead.'

In 2004, we had a big, tired hissy fit over Janet Jackson's nearly exposed breast in the Super Bowl half-time show, after decades upon decades of cheering cheerleaders with nearly exposed breasts. We had hockey player and eternal thug Todd Bertuzzi sucker-punching Steve Moore during a game, knocking him unconscious and fracturing a neck vertebra. The exhausted, please-don't-tell-me-any-more storyline of the basketball Los Angeles Lakers finally reached preposterous denouement, when the Lakers had to trade the most awesome bloody force in the game, Shaquille O'Neal, because he and Bryant could not coexist with him. We had a brawl in Detroit during which a fan threw a projectile at a basketball player and basketball players took to the stands slugging fans. I went eagerly to the Athens Olympics, and spent the first Saturday night camped outside a hospital with Greek reporters, awaiting in vain two Greek sprinters who may have faked a motorcycle accident to avoid a drug test.

In 2005, we Americans spent an entire autumn hearing daily if not hourly about one narcissistic football receiver in

Philadelphia. We spent our second straight summer in New York speculating about the intra-team compatibility of one profoundly dull baseball third baseman. I'd begun to realize a 21st-century maxim that may have nagged at many fans: sport sucks, but I'd hate to live without it.

Then came Friday, 17 March 2005, the nadir de nadirs, when I spent an entire day of this gift of a lifetime watching the congressional baseball steroid hearings.

There, you had a day-long view of a committee in Congress. Nobody should ever have a day-long view of any aspect of Congress, where we send some of our most heinous citizens so that we don't have to live among them.

And there, we also had a row of grotesquely coddled baseball players who should never speak on television for such duration in any culture concerned for its well-being. One wagged a finger at Congress and said he'd never taken steroids, when by July he would test positive for the steroid stanozolol even though it's remarkably hard to flunk such tests. Another, whose cartoonish muscles had abetted his then-record 70 home runs in the summer of 1998 that unleashed poetry about baseball's return to national glory, kept saying he hadn't come to talk about the past. ('Steroids is bad,' he said in his opening statement.) Another, invited for his alleged intellectualism and because he previously called steroids a problem in baseball, basically said he hadn't really meant steroids were a problem in baseball. Another claimed translation issues after spending years doing interviews in English. The most credible of all became the one on the end of the row, the handsome former player everyone resented, the first-time author whose just-released book regaled a naïve nation with glorious steroid tales such as players shooting up each other in their rear ends in restroom stalls.

Then, every once in a while, there would come an unspeakable moment in which one congressman or another would, before our very eyes, morph into blubber and start fawning over the presence of baseball players.

As the first edges of darkness clinched the day as spectacularly misspent, my Tampa malaise had set in again: *Wow. I think I might detest sport.*

From an upbringing decidedly anti-cynical, I had transmogrified into a threat to foist cynicism upon children in my newspaper's circulation area plus any finding me by accident on the Internet. With no right for complaint given all the crummy jobs in the world compared with mine, I figured I'd ride to retirement or death with flaring depression. On the plus side, I had drained some of my vast reservoir of gullibility and reduced the saccharine content in my copy. I'd begun to leave the house for sporting events fancying myself a chronicler of sin rather than feat, and reassuring myself it's important to cover sin.

It helped some.

Then in 2006, I happened upon a cure I'd never imagined and that my numerous ambivalent colleagues hadn't tried. I merely moved to another country for the oldest reason in the book – love – and alighted an ocean away from *SportsCenter* playing morning highlights that recur until you want to primal-scream. When Virgin Flight 46 from JFK to Heathrow landed, I would step out not only into another country, but the country with the world's most popular sports league, a league so dynamic it compels Bulgaria and Burkina Faso, stokes the curiosity of half of China and big chunks of Colombia, and prompts young men from Mauritius to think up Man United songs that denigrate Liverpool.

I would inhabit London, the central nervous system of Planet Earth.

After 18 mostly wondrous years covering five Olympics, 25 major golf tournaments, four Wimbledons, 11 Super Bowls, 10 Kentucky Derbys, one Sunday-night romp up the Champs-Elysées in July 1998 with a bunch of French people who might've abhorred football but seemed to enjoy winning, seven baseball 'World Series', seven American university football Rose Bowls, five Sugar Bowls, five Fiesta Bowls, three Orange Bowls, basketball from Hawaii to Alaska to Kentucky to Athens to Sydney, nine Indianapolis 500s, three Daytona 500s and one tractor pull, among other events, I found myself purged of free media credentials, free media shuttle buses and free media buffet lines. I bought tickets as do real people. I went to stadiums and sat as a fan among the completely irrational other fans. I breathed amid the wisest, savviest old fan culture upon the earth. I relearned arts forbidden in press boxes, including applauding, cheering and even jumping up and down like a buffoon.

Crucially, I came upon a league chock-a-block with facts I didn't know, legacies that hadn't grown exhausted and astounding fan noise I couldn't wait to comprehend.

I felt confounded at mysterious words such as 'Hotspur', 'Everton' and 'Sven-Goran Eriksson'. I pictured 'West Ham' as some gumdrop village somewhere in the countryside. I feared I would mispronounce the words 'Arsène Wenger' in public. I could not for the life of me define 'bung'. I had only just learned the home city of the mystically titled 'Aston Villa'. Only after marvelling at Gary Lineker's sublime TV talent did I learn he'd actually played the game and played it rather well, belying the grand tradition of former players as unenlightening cliché-spewers. I suddenly learned that in addition to the Premiership, the European Champions League and the FA Cup, clubs played for a fourth annual trophy formerly called the 'League Cup' but by now named after a beer.

I knew nothing of the specific fraudulence of any player or manager. I certainly knew no criminal records. I knew nothing of what constituted a banality by English sports-talk standards. It was like starting over.

It was like childhood, with beer.

2

Fumbling around in daylight

Months before relocating, I made an incompetent football vacation through England in late August 2005. Somewhere in my denseness, I yearned to join those Americans who exude uppermost coolness by holding their own in Premiership conversations (with sportswriters Doug Cress and Mike Penner the first I ever knew). Surveying the schedule from home in New York, I spotted a golden nugget even I could detect as enticing: Chelsea vs Arsenal on Sunday, 22 August.

I began making my plans for Highbury. Having read Nick Hornby's *Fever Pitch* in 1994 in a halting attempt at competence, I fancied myself almost debonair that I'd get to see Highbury soon. I told my chum Jerry, a New Yorker who started liking Chelsea before it became *Chelsea*, that I might even see Chelsea play at Highbury, what with everybody on vacation in August. I briefly liked myself.

Of course, as I rode in a taxi on FDR Drive along the East River in New York one day, Jerry telephoned with a polite bit of instruction. While American fixtures always list the visitor first – Washington at Dallas, Arsenal at Chelsea – English fixtures always list the home club first, thus the match would occur at Stamford Bridge, a place of which I'd never heard and which I'd certainly never read about in any landmark book.

It was such a grand beginning.

Upon arrival in London with nine allotted days, and dumb

as a bag of rocks, I found an atlas in my friends' living room and traced a map of England. Then I began doing the heavy research required to fill in 20 dots upon the map. I learned the location of the long-mysterious 'Aston Villa'. I found Wigan with dogged effort. I soon knew the answer to the befuddling question 'Where is Middlesbrough?' – becoming one of the first Americans in history with that distinction. I made little dots for previously mysterious places like Bolton, Blackburn and the briefly elusive Charlton. I woke on a Saturday, went for some spectacularly priced coffee and scanned the slate of matches.

Choosing Charlton to start, with tickets available for the monster clash with Wigan, I left Barons Court in west London around 1 p.m., rode a numbing sequence of Tubes and trains and incompetence through the inconceivably vast capital, and did reach Charlton's ground in south-east London by 4.15, or during roughly the 55th minute of the match. There, I learned two things about England.

It's capitalist, yes, but it does practise some limits. Despite available seats, the woman in the club office would not sell me a ticket even though I wished to pay full price to witness maybe 35 minutes – plus added time! – of the can't-miss glory of Charlton vs Wigan. Polite and even faintly pitying, she appeared as if she'd never heard such a request. That differed from the United States, in which any corporation would take most any chance to rip out the cash from your wallet, as well as the lining, the credit cards, the decrepit pictures of family members and the hide off the cover. In the United States, turning down money can result in a prison sentence.

And then, I learned that if you loiter outside a football stadium during a match, you might join some Asian tourists snapping photographs. This both mystified and delighted me.

I did get my first real-life peek at the Premiership, though, when a nice security guard let me place my left eye between two fence posts at the side gate. I saw a goalkeeper and decided he played for either Charlton or Wigan. Within moments, I walked away down Floyd Road among a flood of Charlton supporters mildly elated over their 1–0 win and feigned that I, too, had taken in the grandeur.

In fact, it would take me eight calendar days and four Premiership days to find my way into one football stadium. I would go to Stamford Bridge that Sunday, because as an American, I reckoned that if you're willing to pay enough and plunge even further into debt, you can get anything. I would turn down a sidewalk offer of a ticket for £48.50 because I feared it counterfeit, not really considering that if somebody wished to sell a fake ticket, they probably wouldn't bother with the 50p part. I'd resist the temptation to take a train to Sunderland way up in the north-east on the following Tuesday night. I'd turn up at Highbury for a Fulham match on a Wednesday night inanely thinking tickets available, and I'd marvel that I'd never, ever seen a stadium so intimately tucked into its neighbourhood, and I'd gaze at an elderly woman sitting in her living room blithely watching the news just barely across a narrow street from Thierry Henry.

But I'd not get in, of course.

Luckily, from one angle, I did get an excellent glimpse of an entire stand containing other people watching, so I got to see other people see Arsenal vs Fulham. They looked enthralled.

My Premiership wisdom accruing dramatically, I reckoned I might not get into Manchester United's Old Trafford that coming Saturday, so I took a Friday stadium tour in the rain. With eight fellow tourists, including a Hungarian father and son who repeatedly violated the tour rules and even walked out to the edge of the pitch at one point – I thought they might even practise some penalty kicks before the kindly female tour guide reined them in – I learned much. I learned that Sir Alex Ferguson has occasional quibbles with the press. (No!) I learned the fascinating fact that certain people apply for ambulance jobs so they can wedge into the rotation of those assigned to the stadium tunnel on match days. That alone calls for a football documentary if

not an original screenplay, perhaps with the title 'I Just Hope
They Learn CPR Along the Way'.

Mostly, though, I went mouth-agape at the Manchester
United dressing room. I simply could not believe it, and still
don't. It had nice hot tubs over in the distance, I suppose, and it
would've passed my mother's rigid cleanliness test, but it lagged
startlingly shy of the plush pro dressing rooms I'd frequented
with brain-deadening regularity in the United States. I might
even dare call it spartan if that would not offend Sir Alex
Ferguson. In fact, this dressing room would qualify as a tenement
next to the posh locker room of even, just for one example of
many, Florida State American football.

And Florida State is just a *university*, albeit one that grasps
the God-approved need of spending money on lavish locker-
room carpeting. Carpeting replete with huge Seminole insignia.
Huge Seminole insignia onto which you're not allowed to step,
even mistakenly. Step on it, and a student towel attendant about
half your age will come up and upbraid you.

Really.

But then, in our measured culture, we know that any new
baseball or American football stadium locker room must boast
luxury so that we can lure in more of the athletic gods who'll
bring us the methadone of victory. In the case of San Francisco
Giants home-run hitter Barry Bonds, our locker rooms might
have an easy chair for strategic napping, although the easy
chair might not be quite so swish as widely reported. Even the
bathroom stalls might be wide and comfortable enough that two
hunky star players can fit into one, so that one can inject the
other's rear end with a steroid.

A player's locker will have the amenities of a fine closet. It
will remind him yet again of his rightful place at the apex of the
cosmos, just in case he needs more reminding. It will feature a
shelf on which the god might store vital items such as his cologne,
his chosen religious ornament, his souvenir from the day he hit
that game-winning home run. It may have compartments for

the necessary and furtive storage of his performance-enhancing drugs. To the edge of the shelf he might tape photographs of his children or his wife or his mistresses in various away towns (the latter a slight exaggeration as he'd seldom showcase the mistresses to nosy reporters who never report on the mistresses anyway). His locker will boast little walls on each side, cordoning it off from the other lockers, plus nice hanging implements for his fine, fine clothes.

From what I could see, Manchester United players get a shared bench and a hook on the wall.

I do remember the hooks as red, so there's one decorative touch.

Standing in that locker room, jaw headed south, I just couldn't believe the athletes had not staged some sort of revolt as to these threadbare conditions. All that arrogance, all that self-centredness, all that certainty as to their indispensability – and I refer to Cristiano Ronaldo alone – yet no beef about dressing-room conditions?

It refreshed me and pointed again to the cultural importance of keeping locker rooms closed to the media. United States professional sports leagues have mandatory policies about opening their locker rooms to reporters for certain swatches of time both before and after games. This stirs more interest in the sport, and more interest stirs more money – and we have shown a certain fondness for more money. Thus do American athletes turn up constantly on TV, in front of their lockers, often shirtless or wearing only a towel, spewing rehearsed lines into gaggles of microphones as 20 reporters surround them and jockey for position and absorb the bony elbows of cameramen. We consider this normal. Perhaps if at Manchester United we saw Wayne Rooney on TV after each match, standing before his pathetic little red hook, the club would feel embarrassed and endeavour to do something to placate the poor tycoon.

As it happens, only tourists get to see this tidy slum, and

some of them barely notice as they're plotting their bid to skirt the rules and walk out onto the pitch.

It's just as well.

I wandered through the museum and learned that apparently Manchester United seems to have won the three most coveted competitions at the same time during the spring of 1999. I had not realized this even as a sportswriter, but that's forgivable given I spent May 1999 chronicling three-year-old colts.

Then I took my dressing-room astonishment and left the building, noticing some 'Die Glazer' graffiti just across the road and wondering why that hadn't been part of the official tour.

Later that Friday, I pored over the Saturday candidates for my Premiership debut and noticed the curiosity of two clubs who had just celebrated 'promotion' in May 2005, a concept literally foreign to myself and my culturally barren country with no relegation and no promotion. Wigan and Sunderland would appear on the same pitch, and as far as I could tell that pitch would be in the city of Wigan. I decided to celebrate their promotions with them.

So I debuted, at Wigan, on 27 August 2005, and while there's no need to insert violin music right here, I felt happy. No American I knew had ever been to Wigan. No American I knew had ever heard of Wigan. My parents and grandparents had told me umpteen stories through a Virginia childhood with nary a mention of Wigan. With Americans sharing a common inability to view a map and spot, say, Louisiana – this helps explain why it took us four days to get food to starving Americans after Hurricane Katrina – Americans certainly could not point out Wigan. Or even Preston. Let alone Bolton. I disembarked at Wigan and walked out of the becoming town centre toward the stadium, past the strip malls of outer Wigan.

I marched like a fiend to the JJB Stadium ticket window and thought it a mite intrusive both when the woman behind the glass asked for some identification and when my name appeared on the ticket. We never field such questions in the 50 colonies, and we buy nameless single-game tickets without anyone knowing our identity so long as we seem to have a modicum of apparent human features, such as a wallet and at least one hand for reaching into it.

I found it almost pushy when the woman asked, 'Home or away?' We Americans don't sit segregated. We get to revile others right up close. We do have away cheering sections for, say, college football, an enormous sport in our country, but they're not strictly demarcated. We reserve the right to go to Yankee Stadium in the Bronx and sit in the upper deck with hordes of New York baseball fans and pockets of Boston baseball fans, so that we can ruin a luminous Sunday afternoon annoyed at IQ-depleting 'banter' that ricochets, *for three to four hours*, between the majority New York fans and the minority Boston fans. This usually includes such profundities as, follow carefully, please: *Yankees suck, Yankees suck*. This makes us so proud and suspends our wonder at the trite inanity of our political debates. We reserve the right to pull for a home American-football team, then grumble because those three frigging away fans from two rows ahead kept standing up and cheering their improbable victory. This gives us a conversation piece at awkward family gatherings where we can use up some of the interminable time by explaining how we almost, *almost* told those clowns to shut up.

Come to think of it, stadium segregation is an ingenious concept, galvanizing competing noise and prolonging life in general. It must count among the reasons Britons live six months longer, on average, than do Americans. It is the handiwork of an experienced nation with an 849-year head start on our little concoction across the Atlantic.

On a sunny day inside the JJB, with the Premiership angels singing overhead in my estimation, I sat amid bafflingly large chunks of empty seats but smack next to one couple.

In America, it's considered proper to have a chat with two other people when you're, say, the only three people within a

15

large cluster of empty seats. In England, it's not.

So as the public-address speakers played pop music, I said to the woman next to me, 'Do you know this song?'

She looked dumbstruck by such forwardness and said, 'No.'

That concluded our afternoon's discourse.

3

'F——ing move!'

Kick-off approached at Wigan, and most of those nearby seats simply refused to fill. I thought it surprising that Wiganites would not revel in Premiership status after their inspiring three-decade vault through the concentric circles of lower leagues. I reckoned August must find most Wiganites on vacation, just another reason Wiganites and other Europeans outlive Americans.

Among the 17,222 others that day, three shaven-headed blokes did take the seats just behind me. They looked a bit scary to me at the time, but that's probably because in America our parents and our grandparents often condition us that life is a process which you spend in an incessant attempt to avoid getting mugged. My dear maternal grandmother, for example, might've unwittingly invented the concept of carjacking. Through the 1970s, whenever we'd leave her house in Virginia Beach, Virginia, at night, she'd tell us to make sure to lock the car doors because people tended to try to rip open your doors and steal your stuff when you idled at red lights. I would digest this advice despite never once seeing a single awake human at any traffic light in any of the eternally comatose Virginia cities – Norfolk, Portsmouth, Chesapeake – between her house and ours.

Besides, within the first minutes of action at Wigan vs Sunderland, one of these three blokes hopped up and down with his hand upon my shoulder for leverage, because Wigan had just scored through a penalty in the second minute after one Jason Roberts had gone down under duress from one Gary Breen. This began a long sequence of embraces with strangers in the football grounds of England. Whether I cared who won or not, whether I attended a match as a curious tourist or a wishing fan, I have hugged people I didn't know and never would see again, pretending to rise to their level of elation. In America, we'll chat with a stranger all game long, but we'd never hug them after a favourable play. We're simply too young as a culture to have evolved to that level of self-assurance. We stand off and high-five them, then we reach upward and downward to the other rows giving and receiving high fives, as if we had something to do with the act of exceptional talent that just transpired on the field. In England, nobody seems to chat, but many people do hug.

The sunny day at Wigan did bring Wigan's first ever Premiership victory, by that precarious 1–0 from the penalty. The day brought several first-time realizations. I never knew that husky male voices in football grounds croon the American ditty written either by Jimmie Davis and Charles Mitchell or by the Rice Brothers, 'You Are My Sunshine', once listed as Country Music Television's No. 73 country song of all time. This blew me away. 27 August 2005 did mark the first time in my life I had ever heard the word 'f——' matched with the word 'sake', and it came from a single throat that observed a referee's snap decision from a quarter-mile off and hollered, 'F——'s sake!' Despite roaming the globe a lucky amount, I had never known that f—— had a sake until alighting at Wigan. I suppose everyone and everything has a sake, so f—— deserves one as well.

And then, at the end of Wigan's victory at the dear old JJB, I heard a rendition of John Philip Sousa's magnum opus, 'Stars and Stripes Forever', the official national march of the United States by decree of our esteemed Congress, only with the lyrics rewritten so that the many words of the original song had been distilled to two, sung while pointing at Sunderland fans:

Going down, going down, going down,
Going down, going down, going dowwwwn ...

Thus did Wigan fans correctly forecast a relegation eight months out, while I felt reassured that after my homeland had gained so much energy from English imports like The Clash and the Sex Pistols and the Buzzcocks and the Buggles and the Psychedelic Furs and the Pet Shop Boys and the Beatles and David Bowie and Elton John and Rod Stewart and Oasis and Arctic Monkeys and the Smiths, and the Smiths, and the Smiths, my country had given the British Isles some songs to sing at football matches, especially at Anfield.

Wigan had proved a grand adventure, but I figured Newcastle might stir my senses even more. For one thing, the stadium held 52,387, I read, as opposed to Wigan's 25,138. I'd found an available ticket by dialling Newcastle United's number in proper sequence, showing unmistakable progress in accessing Premiership stadiums. I reached Newcastle on Sunday morning, awakened just as the train crossed the river into the station, a beautiful setting in a beautiful city. A nice day, and the visiting team would be Manchester United, who, as a new-found American expert on this stuff, I knew had won three titles in 1999, plus some other titles on some other occasions. The little chart I had made of every season since 1992–93, in fact, showed Manchester United winning eight times since the Premiership's inception. Bounding out into Newcastle for my first time, I proceeded to the gleaming modern stadium wedged appealingly into the city, and it took me only 35 minutes of circumnavigating the enormous structure to locate the proper gate for entry. After a beer and a revulsion at a meat pie I spotted going into a nearby mouth, I plopped down in the upper deck next to a freckled woman who looked about 30. Some reflex within me craved conversation, but she never once acknowledged my presence upon the earth.

Instead, I heard her utter only three things during the match.

The first: 'Move!'

From the upper deck, high above the city of Newcastle, she commanded her feckless Newcastle United players to move rather than standing around as spectators against the Manchester United defence. Her advice seemed sound, but it did conjure something I'd found achingly sad since 1995. One night then, in a basketball arena in Chicago, from the upper press box, I suddenly took notice of a middle-aged man in the upper rows, screaming at the referees. I became momentarily profoundly depressed, and I mean seriously, incontrovertibly glum. I don't know why I had never studied this kind of thing before then, but suddenly I saw the fanatic in all his twin strains of powerlessness. Not only did he cut a preposterous figure, mustering anger over calls he could not possibly see as well as the three referees granted access to the actual floor with the players, but he yelled at referees who probably couldn't have heard him in an empty coliseum and absolutely couldn't have heard him through the clamour of 19,999 other people. It's mind-boggling, yet commonplace, universal. This capacity to excoriate referees who can't possibly hear us might be one of the few things that bridges our troubling disparities as a planet.

The second thing she uttered: 'F——ing move!'

This proved beyond a doubt my theory that the Newcastle players could not hear her instructions. Sure enough, Newcastle did not f——ing move and did not f——ing score that day – an offside negated their one 'goal' – and even a know-nothing American could spot that Newcastle's best hope lay in a combination of hoping for a goalless draw and praying for a Manchester United own goal.

The third thing I heard her say: 'F——ing w——ers!'

That plaudit went toward the sliver of Manchester United fans over to our right in the upper deck, people who, curiously, could not hear her either. It also helped summarize my novice's afternoon. I had never – *never* – heard the English word 'f——' used in so many creative forms, despite prior residence in New

York, despite spending an inordinate chunk of life near sports fans and despite seeing almost every Martin Scorsese movie. At Newcastle that day, I heard it as a noun, verb, adjective, adverb, conjunction, preposition, pejorative, subjunctive, and maybe even a gerund. I heard it hollered without compunction within earshot of children, which would be taboo in the United States. Eighteen months later, two kindly lads who support Brentford would inform me that some English fathers teach their children that there's football-ground language and there's language for everywhere else, but at this point I felt stunned.

I might overstate, but Newcastle fans seemed to possess an uncanny, almost innate sixth sense. They seemed to spot doom just around every corner even when doom hadn't necessarily revealed itself to others. If keenly observant, you might even detect that they might have undergone some sort of phase, maybe even some sort of half-century, that may have included a certain lack of trophies. They embodied what the great English tennis sage and clothing designer Ted Tinling once said after Martina Navratilova blew a US Open final to Steffi Graf: 'At 4–2 in the second set, Martina saw vultures no one else could see.'

We do have alien cousins of Newcastle in the United States. We have fan bases which have remained nobly fervent even through the most prodigious title droughts. Despite our youth and inexperience as a nation, we do have people who have hungered even longer than Newcastle with its 51 seasons *sans* domestic trophy. The most famous cases follow baseball in Boston and Chicago.

The loud baseball fans of Boston famously waited 86 years between 1918 and 2004. The quieter baseball fans of Chicago's White Sox on the South Side of the city waited 88 years between 1917 and 2005. I felt certain that if the Chicago Cubs of the North Side, drought-stricken since 1908, followed Boston in 2004 and the South Side in 2005 with a title in 2006, it might signal Armageddon.

They did not.

21

I spent the last 20 days of October 2004 in Boston as the baseball Red Sox won their last eight games – against the hated New York, plus St Louis – to quench the 86-year drought. I heard great celebrations and great sounds and felt great goose bumps. I stood on the narrow road behind the stadium and watched it fill so swiftly with revellers that it truly frightened me. I interviewed bereaved relatives of lifelong fans who'd lived normal life spans but died during 2004 and never saw the moment.

I understood that Boston fans and Chicago fans and Newcastle fans participated in something weirdly privileged. By nurturing their interest and keeping it keen through a long wait, even by wallowing in their gloomy endurance – preening over it, in some American cases – they stood the chance of a pay-off that would trump any title by New York or Manchester United.

For that reason, plus the loveliness of the city in general, Newcastle United zoomed onto my list of prospective favourite clubs. When I'd learned that about 20,000 showed up just to watch Michael Owen sign his contract – they must have sensed that, while playing, he might actually move – that enhanced the appeal all the more. When I'd carefully studied the 1995–96 season, in which Newcastle led by 12 points in March but still did not win the Premiership in May, that added still more.

But on that first Sunday, in the 66th minute of Manchester United's 2–0 win, I saw something non-Newcastle that lodged for ever in my memory. I saw Wayne Rooney score. By now, I picture him making a bull-in-a-china-shop barrel up the pitch leaving Newcastle players – who couldn't or wouldn't move, anyway – strewn around like carcasses until he stood alone, scored deftly for a 1–0 lead and hurried over to a corner below the visiting supporters. In actuality, Manchester United goalkeeper Edwin van der Sar punted, defender Jean-Alain Boumsong failed to clear the ball, and Rooney scrambled to it and rammed it in past Shay Given. Pretty soon, Newcastle fans commenced filing out even before Ruud van Nistelrooy's add-on in injury time. They carried the distinct look of having seen this match before.

Only on Monday would I learn that TV cameras had recorded Rooney's celebration, and that some resourceful video-tape editors had slowed down the scene to allow for accurate reading of his lips as he shouted toward his admirers in the upper deck.

He called out to them, 'F—ing beauty!'

He thus garnished my Newcastle and Premiership debuts poetically, and sent me back toward the United States with a fresh array of f—ing knowledge.

4

Is that really Chelsea's pitch?

Ten days after moving to England in February 2006, I did go to watch the club called ChelseaTheyBoughtTheirTitle. Two generous lawyers invited me. I had heard much about ChelseaTheyBoughtTheirTitle, and marvelled that when people spoke of this club, they seldom settled for the terminology 'Chelsea', but always opted for the more demanding elocution of 'ChelseaTheyBoughtTheirTitle', almost as if they were manifestly incapable of pronouncing 'Chelsea' without affixing 'TheyBoughtTheirTitle'.

Chelsea would play some straggler from the south, Portsmouth. We had a Portsmouth in my home state of Virginia, close to Suffolk, Norfolk, Hampton, Windsor, Southampton, Sussex and Virginia Beach, as we're incapable of thinking up our own names save for the odd 'Virginia Beach', which we concocted on our own by standing on a beach, then noticing we were in Virginia. In the spectacular wastefulness of the teenage years, I'd spent many nights among friends in Portsmouth, the Virginia version, driving around and around and around and around and around with no destination, much like Formula One. I even lived in this derivative, Virginian Portsmouth for a year aged 17 when our parents moved us from adjacent Suffolk while they finished our new house. I spent much of the year wallowing in spite that they'd moved us 25 minutes from our buddies.

I often wonder why anyone has children.

For the 3 p.m. kick-off of Chelsea vs Portsmouth – if I'd gone alone one year prior, I might've mistakenly taken a train to Portsmouth – we met at 12.30. From the station the London lawyer, Duncan, an understated and kindly sort of about 40, began shepherding myself and Jerry, my great friend for 25 years, a New York lawyer, and one of a smallish assortment of Americans who prefer the Premiership to American sports. He led us through a maze of streets away from the Stamford Bridge hubbub, to a fine nugget of a pub I could not find again if you gave me three hours and one London A–Z already turned to page 99.

The pub half-teemed with Chelsea fans, but with the real deals, the long-sufferers, those who knew Chelsea before it changed its name to ChelseaTheyBoughtTheirTitle. These people had weathered lean decades before striking Russian oil. They had not just straggled in from Tokyo or Chicago or Mayfair professing satellite-TV devotion. Even Jerry had signed on in the 1990s, safely before the Roman Empire.

In a small ring of six Chelsea fans, then, I stood for more than two hours, talking, listening, learning and drinking enough beer to stagger a large farm animal. We chatted about the leaner Chelsea years, about the astounding fitness of rugby players, about some upcoming exposé of an alleged gay orgy among Premiership players, about the 1999 United States women's team drawing 90,000 to the Rose Bowl for the World Cup final, about how they'd love to have Wayne Rooney on their squad, about how most Britons can't abide American football's abundant halts. It was sublime, this pre-game. To a wayward sportswriter, these hours proved so magical, so alleviating of life's puny worries, that I realized at once I'd spent two decades missing something.

Now, American sportswriters do tend to arrive two or three hours before game time – or 30 minutes before if atomically inept like myself. We enter the press box. We put down our laptop bags. We convene in little groups. We gossip about other sportswriters or about things we know to be true of athletes or managers but can't get into the newspaper. We have a pre-game meal, often of food that will kill you faster than will other food – or, at Cincinnati's stadium during the 1990s, of food that might kill you before sundown. We drink sodas. We do not drink alcohol – it's forbidden – even though that would be one hell of a lot healthier than sodas. We're at work, so there's stress.

American fans, meanwhile, carry on a tradition akin to the venerable pre-game pub. It's called the tailgate, it's an extraordinary invention, and it's among the top five reasons for the United States to exist. It arguably trumps even the nation's grand achievements such as the interstate highway system, the university system, the washing machine, the skyscraper, the first flight, the first credit card and certain forms of the rabbit corkscrew. Tailgating finds its essence at university football games, finds its quintessence in the American South, and finds its epitome at the genteel and elaborate Grove, a patch of ground at the University of Mississippi, in Oxford, Miss., another city name we borrowed owing to the inability to think up our own.

I once saw West Virginians tailgating in a Holiday Inn parking lot just north of Detroit on a cloudy 23 December at 19 degrees Fahrenheit. Their bleak surroundings gave me a wave of sadness, but on closer inspection I spotted their grill and their hardiness and I felt a second wave, this of impression and awe at their refusal to let cold Mother Nature foil their tailgate. I branded them heroes as they tended to their sausages.

On autumn Saturdays all over a huge country, fans will drive into stadium parking lots some six hours or nine hours or, if blessed with sleeping quarters, 24 hours before kick-off. Almost invariably, a wife or two (or more) in garish school colours will bound out of the passenger seat. A husband or two (or more) in even more ghastly school colours will assist. A table will unfold and stand nobly behind the vehicle, and the wives will unveil their Thursday–Friday creations, masses of cold cuts, potato salad, finger sandwiches, barbecue. Sometime in these opening moments of the weekly symphony, a cooler full of beer might appear, or a separate table might buttress a bourbon bottle next to a vodka bottle next to a Bloody Mary mixer next to soda mixers next to, in some cases, a bottle of red wine just in case someone stops by with the really weird wish of protecting his arteries. There might be plastic glasses and paper plates and plastic cutlery. Many tailgate areas will feature a grill and the peerless smell of charcoal. Gristle will metastasize. Some tables might even boast a heated dish full of swimming meatballs, next to a tiny glass brimming with toothpicks.

If there's a heaven, it looks something like all of this. In heaven, everyone will have an automobile – fuel-efficient, of course – and everyone will pull up to an eternal tailgate with cold cuts and bourbon and what-all. Nobody will worry about the food's health effects, because everybody already will be dead.

In the moments before Chelsea vs Portsmouth, I realized you have to miss something in life, and I'd missed a thousand pre-game conversations, walking past a thousand pre-game tailgates toward the press box, gazing at their food, inhaling their smoke and squinting at the school colours on 50-year-old men who never got over the cruelty of having to *graduate* and, you know, *leave*.

Somewhere in the neighbourhood of page 99 in the London A–Z, I had a mild epiphany.

The so-called 'pre-game', I reckoned, usually beats the hell out of the 'game' itself, especially considering that during the 'pre-game', the 'game' still maintains all magical possibilities. So we may just have it backward when we frame things in terms of 'pre-game' and 'game', like some undercard leading up to some main event. Maybe in the grand scheme of life upon this violent and wretched planet, we should see the middling 'game' only as something that provides fodder for the next glorious 'pre-game', when again we can converse with old and new friends. If the 'pre-game' really pales next to the 'game', then why did we scramble from the 'pre-game' so late that day, that we'd missed the first two minutes of the 'game'? If the 'game' is so important, after all, then why do so many intelligent people on both sides of the ocean prepare for it by drinking themselves into a state where they'll be unable to remember two-thirds of it?

In fact, during the 'pre-game' of 25 February 2006, I learned from Duncan a sacred truth about 'soccer'. In the relatively limited 'soccer' I'd watched – World Cups and Olympics, mostly – I'd never once mulled the nugget Duncan spoke. Duncan explained that in his two adult decades attending football both at Stamford Bridge and at Chelsea away matches, only once could he recall arriving at his seat with a bloodstream uninhabited by beer products. And that particular game, he said, just looked all wrong, all horridly misshapen.

Never again had he erred so thoughtlessly, and never again would I endure one of my occasional beer-less football matches without wondering if they just looked wrong. Luckily, I remain for now too dim to tell.

So after the glory of the pre-game, we headed for the sigh of the game and somehow got through the gulag turnstiles of old Stamford Bridge, an obstacle common in English stadiums but bewildering to an American accustomed to traversing little toothpick turnstiles. Having revelled at Wigan and Newcastle in that little slice of magic you feel from that first view of the green pitch, I entered Stamford Bridge to find . . .

The pitch . . .

The pitch . . .

The pitch looked like some forlorn, abandoned field in east Texas. Mud ruled. Whatever grass dared to pop its merry head above the surface of the earth seemed to have undergone a trampling from some urban herd of cattle. It became possible, when beholding this pitch, to feel sorry for the blades of grass that jutted to the surface. They'd come out on a Saturday and they'd found no friends. Some convened in wee clumps. Seemingly half the money in the world couldn't beat the English winter and the Champions League obligations in the great race to destroy or preserve a pitch. ChelseaTheyBoughtTheirTitle, this palace of talent and fine divas, mauling the league toward a second title, had a decrepit pitch, if only for a few weeks.

That's what I remember about this mundane match amid ChelseaTheyBought's march toward a second straight Premiership title, because I just kept looking at the pitch. I'm sorry. I do know that the perfunctory 2–0 win over Portsmouth gave ChelseaTheyBought three points, making 69 points for the season with a staggering 15-point lead and 11 games remaining. I know that the Chelsea manager, whose name I mispronounced by using an 'H' sound on the first letter in 'José', inserted Eidur Gudjohnsen in the 60th minute, and that Jerry said he liked this Icelandic bale of energy, and that I marvelled to myself at a league with Icelanders, given our startling lack of Icelanders back at home.

I remember our stadium section seemed infested by tourists such as, say, us.

I really felt no sense of Portsmouth, that they held 19th in the table, that they did not so much teeter, as hurry, toward relegation. I knew neither that Portsmouth had lost in January 5–0 in Birmingham, nor that it was rare that season that somebody would lose 5–0 to Birmingham. I just know that I felt the vague sense of malaise that used to brush up against me during the 1990s.

In that time, as a sports columnist in Lexington, Kentucky, I followed an American sport dynasty, University of Kentucky basketball, during one of its heydays. Roughly 15 times per winter, the schedule would bring a perfunctory game. Kentucky would play, for example, the University of Georgia. Now, when waking that day, you'd know Kentucky would trounce Georgia. Walking to the arena, you'd know Kentucky would trounce Georgia. Inside the arena, Kentucky would trounce Georgia. And afterward, we'd conduct forgettable interviews to glean forgettable quotations about how Kentucky had trounced Georgia.

Yet still, despite only a 0.0001 chance of any surprise or intrigue, that arena would fill to 24,000. People who knew full well Kentucky would trounce Georgia would pay good money to see Kentucky trounce Georgia, then listen to radio shows detailing Kentucky's trouncing of Georgia. It's the same with Chelsea vs Portsmouth circa February 2006, and it's the same all over the world. This kind of sleepwalk occurs especially in sports in which some clubs have money advantages, such as American baseball or the Premiership. Even I knew Chelsea would beat Portsmouth by about 2–0, and so I went and watched Chelsea beat Portsmouth by 2–0.

In the numbness of predictability ever more common to sport as it becomes ever more business, the day winds up living on only in other ways. There's the marvel of talking to people from another sports culture in a pre-game pub. There's the beer, the elixir of choice for a country 849 years older than my own as the most effective way to cope with the daily horror of life. And there's Duncan's wisdom about how a game might look wrong if not mixed with said beer.

And there was that pitch.

5

A 12-inch Digix in Camden

As an arriviste, I knew it'd be gauche to glom onto the glory of any of the four kingdoms of the Premiership.

I couldn't choose Chelsea as my club in the year 2006, for that would show all the maturity of this nine-year-old kid from my childhood who chose as favourite teams the Florida-based Miami Dolphins (American football), the California-based Oakland Athletics (baseball) and the North Carolina-based North Carolina State Wolfpack (university basketball). Why such geographical disparity? Because those teams happened to win the titles when he was nine.

Likewise, I knew I'd loathe myself as one profoundly dull individual if I chose Manchester United, which by now would resemble rooting for Wal-Mart. If you didn't join the crowd pre-Ferguson, you're lapping at the shores of shady.

Further, I could not choose Arsenal, even though to those Americans with the first clue about the Premiership, Arsenal's the coolest of the kingdoms. First off, it's the best club name in the world, better than any of ours, even with our 300 million citizens and 12 million illegal residents and 3,718,695 square miles. As a special bonus for Americans, the name 'Arsenal' conjures weaponry, and we adore weaponry, reserving our highest presidential-approval ratings for presidents who bomb the hell out of some fourth-rate military power. Our major clubs tend to go by the name of the city in their address or, for an extra splodge of good and dreary marketing, their states. See Arizona Cardinals of Phoenix, the Florida Marlins of Miami. And then there's Arsenal's typical style of play, which sometimes deserves, as accompaniment, Mozart. I've heard many people regard Arsenal as a second-favourite club, in direct violation of the teachings of my football guru Tom. My football guru Tom, half-English, half-American, thus uniquely suited for football guru-dom towards an American, cherishes Liverpool. As a young man he discussed with his own father how Liverpool victories enhanced existence with an almost mysterious profundity. He recalls actual physical illness upon Arsenal's famous added-time goal of May 1989. His nimble memory bank can link certain Liverpool victories to certain life crescendos, such as meeting his marvel of a wife, Marion. He has taught his four young children that the words 'Manchester United' constitute profanity. He has reminded me of my football duncehood by dutifully instructing me of my chronically clunky word choices, such as my references to goalkeepers' 'blocking' shots. And he says it's impermissible in England to have a second-favourite club.

Still, I knew Americans who chose Arsenal in 1995. By signing on in 2006, I'd not only qualify for JCL status (Johnny Come Lately), but I'd have missed three titles, including an almost inconceivable unbeaten season. There's little so unctuous as retroactive gloating.

As well, I could not quite choose Liverpool, even though among the four mastodons it seems to have the biggest heart. It floors me to this day that two New Yorkers, Richard Rodgers (1902–79) and Oscar Hammerstein II (1895–1960), sat down in the mid-1940s and wrote the closing number for their 1945 Broadway show *Carousel*, and that 60 years later in Istanbul, Liverpool players 3–0 down at half-time in a Champions League final got motivation from hearing their fans croon to their players this 'You'll Never Walk Alone'. It gives me a chill even now. Moreover, I felt the Liverpool tug from the Liverpool influence of having a Liverpool football guru, in the way parishioners often tilt towards the worldviews of beloved pastors.

On 25 March 2006, I took the four-hour train from London to Liverpool just to be in the midst of Liverpool vs Everton, even though the sweet woman on the telephone the previous Monday had ushered me through the two-part dance that's downright mystifying to an American: she said they had tickets available, and she said she could not sell me one because I lacked a ticket-buying history. (What an affront to the ruthless churn of capitalism.) So I took the excited walk toward Anfield that day, and I hung out in various pubs around Anfield through Liverpool's 3–1 win, and I waited post-game like some crush-struck teen for the players to emerge, pretending I belonged, and before all that, I stood pre-game for 30 minutes at the Hillsborough memorial, and I watched an elderly man with a cane hobble pretty adroitly toward the stadium gates, halt, turn and touch a name among the 96 fallen before ambling on in. I easily could've chosen the Liverpool of my football guru Tom, but offspring must claim their own identities to sustain the evolutionary progress of life.

I sought some version of *it*, you know, *it*: the real, organic English football experience, and if *it* didn't exist any more in an era of gargantuan TV contracts, then something with shades of *it*.

Two weeks prior, on 11 March, I had piddled around on a Saturday night while *Match of the Day* played as background on the 12-inch Digix TV in the basement guest room in my friends' Camden house. At the time, I thought *Match of the Day* just some nifty highlights show rather than the venerable weekly religious service of a great nation. I couldn't have stated the surname 'Lineker' if necessary to win the Lotto, and I certainly couldn't have spelled it properly, if indeed I just did.

Suddenly, though, I heard this great crowd noise blaring from the set. The noise so clearly unleashed by what happened shockingly in the 93rd minute of Portsmouth vs Manchester City gave me goose bumps even through the screen of a 12-inch

Digix in Camden, even though I knew *nada* about either squad except that Portsmouth wore blue and had played on brown sod at Chelsea. Why bother with sport? Here's the No. 1 answer: because you might hear this kind of noise. It might swim through your ear canals and rustle your soul and electrify your skin and maybe even prolong your life.

For myself, following sport is largely about the hunt for that noise.

The noise Fratton Park forged from Portsmouth vs Manchester City on 11 March 2006 can prove elusive in the world. It requires a whole bale of ingredients. You need a crowd that cares more deeply than most. You need an intricate set of sporting circumstances. You often need some sort of shocking turn in the game or race. A comeback, maybe. Sometimes, a drought will help, as in: imagine the noise coming someday when the parched finally behold a title at St James' Park.

Sometimes, you can go a long way but still miss the noise out of your own chronic ineptitude, and it can bother you for the remainder of your life. I know. In one of the most famous home runs in baseball history, a hobbling Kirk Gibson of the Los Angeles Dodgers blasted a shot off one of the most impenetrable ninth-inning pitchers in history, Dennis Eckersley of the Oakland Athletics, in the first game of the 1988 World Series. It turned a sure 4–3 Oakland win into an indelible 5–4 Los Angeles win. It's *still* shocking. And myself? Rather than keeping my very own press-box seat with ideal view, I rushed downstairs early to beat the elevator rush so I could wait just outside the Oakland locker room to hear the winning pitcher's comments. The noise in that stadium must've been something. I wish I knew. Similarly, many observers equipped with ears claimed they'd never heard stadium noise to rival the night in Sydney when Cathy Freeman won the Olympic 400 metres. And myself? I had the ingenious and contrived idea of watching the race from the Sydney park where aboriginals had set up shop for the Olympics so as to make known their mistreated plight. That noise sure sounded like it might've been something through the dilapidated TV in their tent, and one or two of the over-interviewed viewers even seemed mildly inspired.

On *Match of the Day*, I missed the first playing of Pedro Mendes's searing goal at Fratton Park because I'd been unpacking a suitcase. The noise alerted me to watch further replays. Crowds usually disappoint with the general human incapacity to sustain noise, but this noise had serious sustenance. You could hear that the Frattonites had begun chanting, 'We are staying up, we are staying up,' and even I could discern what they probably meant. The show cut from the Fratton Park scenes to the *Match of the Day* panel, and I remember their grins at the Portsmouth exuberance, grins not of belittlement but of impression, so much glee emanating from 19th place.

Portsmouth, after all, had not won in the Premiership in 2006. They had arrived at 11 March with a measly 17 points from 27 matches since August. They had navigated the Premiership for three straight years, with a fourth apparently not forthcoming. That 5–0 loss to Birmingham had brought the requisite Grand Canyon of nadirs. That eyesore had given way to more benign losses to Newcastle, to Manchester United, to Chelsea after a gritty effort on a crummy pitch, and to Aston Villa. A February draw with Bolton had brought the lone, lonely point of the calendar year.

Well, a second point did beckon against Manchester City. Portsmouth had drifted into this apparent 1–1 draw with spirited play but squandered chances. Pedro Mendes had scored at 60 minutes with a curling projectile from 25 yards. Manchester City's Richard Dunne had headed in a Joey Barton corner in the 83rd minute. Time had waned. Added time had drained. Fratton Park had plunged headlong into that Zantac time '90+3'. Manchester City had almost finished clearing a corner. And Bradley Wright-Phillips had hustled toward the ball to clear it further and secure the draw.

Even a year on, I still cannot quite grasp just how Mendes

flicked the ball away from Wright-Phillips and maintained control. It still seems partly magical every time I watch it on YouTube.com (after which I give thanks for the parents of the inventors of YouTube.com). Every time, Wright-Phillips, from the hubbub around the goal, rushes out toward the ball. Every time, Mendes, from about the halfway line, rushes in. Every time, they converge about 40 yards from the goal. And every time I click 'Play' or click 'Watch Again' or click 'Watch Again' again, it still baffles me how Wright-Phillips goes from further in than Mendes to further out, Mendes goes from further out than Wright-Phillips to further in, and the ball decides it wants to hang with Mendes.

Every single time, then, Mendes cocks his right leg and sends the ball blasting to the top left corner of the net. The ball smooches the net cords and bounces down. Goalkeeper David James, soon to join Portsmouth, kicks it upward in disgust. Mendes rushes to the front row of fans. A security guard urges Mendes to hold off but seems to smile. The place absolutely reverberates with a bedlam almost unattainable upon the earth.

Even as somebody who couldn't get to Portsmouth without a map and certainly couldn't name any of its players, I had this thought: *Oh, to have been in attendance.*

Sitting over in America flipping TV channels in many a wee hour during a misspent life, coming across recorded Premiership matches that filled hard time on cable channels, I always did marvel in brief spurts at English football crowds, before I'd flip on over to some brain-deadening tedium like *Eyes Wide Shut.*

Three things always struck me: singing, creativity and endurance.

The very idea of tough, gruff, blue-collar men singing throughout a game remains alien to Americans. It probably relates to our youth and masculinity issues as a nation that we often rate singing as just a mite fey. We don't sing much at football stadiums or all that much in general, and it just might help explain why we're so stressed. 'When you sing, your consciousness is raised,' Frosty Westering said one day in September 2003. Frosty, then 75, coached small-college American football at Pacific Lutheran University in Tacoma, Washington state, near Seattle, three hours below Canada. By one of Frosty's unusual credos, his players sang habitually – before games, after games. During my three-day visit as a reporter, three of them gave me a ride in their pickup truck while singing 'Leaving on a Jet Plane'. That would sound kooky to some Americans, but then there's this other thing: Frosty had four *national* championships in the small-college divisions, not that he cared all that much. During warm-up exercises before the national championship game in December 1999, his players actually sang 'The Twelve Days of Christmas'. Imagine warming up for a title game, hearing the other side sing 'The Twelve Days of Christmas', then proceeding to get run over, annihilated, *totalled*, by 42–13.

So the singing in England grabbed me especially after my Frosty experience, as did the chanting, even though I never could understand any of it through the TV and can't understand four-fifths of it from my seats in the stadiums themselves. The very idea you could start up a brand-new chant based on events you've just witnessed – *brand-new!* – then have that chant infiltrate your section, then have it spread to the entire stand or even throughout the stadium, just boggles the American mind. I'm sure it has happened here and there in the New World, but I'm also sure it hasn't happened much more than here or there.

I mean, we're still doing the *wave*.

Third, I always marvelled at the stamina of English cheering. In some stadiums – Anfield, for one, and in other European nations – it seemed to carry on all the time. As a nation more than eight centuries behind evolutionarily, and with poorly developed lungs as a result, we seldom approach such durability of noise, and then only in university arenas, almost never at professional events. And while we do manage the occasional memorable crescendo, I'm pretty sure we've never had one stem from next-to-last place as at Fratton Park, a situation that would've coaxed only about 5,000 Americans to the stadium to begin with.

Yes, Portsmouth had barged right onto my shortlist. Not that they cared.

6

My very own relegation weekend

Despite our wealth of sports leagues, we lack any relegation process in the United States, and that's probably among the reasons we rank 48th in life expectancy, 10 spots behind the United Kingdom, just to name one of many superiors. Relegation, a balm for tedium, surely prolongs life. Whoever invented relegation deserves such esteem as to rank one-quarter of the way to Dr Jonas Salk in the pantheon of humanity. While Dr Salk found a way to enhance life for those who might have gone paralysed otherwise by discovering a polio vaccine, the inventors of relegation found a way to resuscitate cities, towns and villages that would lie dormant, as do many in, well, the United States.

In the closing weeks of American baseball seasons (September), basketball seasons (March and April), and sometimes even NFL seasons (December), our woebegone clubs usually go unnoticed except by next of kin. Like plankton or a decrepit tyre, they have sunk to the bottom to remain unseen for ages. Anybody who actually knows whether they occupy fourth or fifth place counts as exquisitely observant, as an eccentric social outcast, or as someone who writes about sport for a living, thereby often qualifying in both categories. Some clubs, like the Colorado Rockies of baseball, languish in the dungeons for so long that it's perfectly possible to forget they exist. It's a rite of Americana that in the stadiums of perennial competitive sediment such as Tampa Bay (baseball) or Atlanta (basketball) or Kansas City (baseball), among many others, you'll see small, telltale clumps of fans sitting around large swatches of empty seats.

Why do the people in these clumps attend these games? They might've got drunk and accidentally bought season tickets six months prior. They might've relocated from the city of the away team and come to support their old favourites. They might be the centrefielder's cousin's dentist's niece. They might be doting parents whose eight-year-old son supports the visiting New York Yankees because he has seen the Yankees on TV 73 times and has detected that the Yankees win all the time whilst the home club wins about 40 per cent of the time at best, so he has begged his beleaguered parents to take him to see the Yankees. They might've got free tickets because they won – and thus lost – a raffle at work. They might be old men who love baseball because, as the peerless American sportswriter Dan Jenkins put it, baseball supplies ample breaks and old men do have to piss a lot.

Or they might simply have succumbed to the tedium of 21st-century American life and opted for the stadium because it was the only thing left that didn't look like a chain store in a strip mall.

They might be asleep. They might be comatose. They might be deceased.

A snapshot of these souls registers immediate meaning in the skull of a born-and-raised American. It's the dregs of the season. It's the imbalance of the baseball salary structure that sends a franchise lacking a huge cable-TV contract, like Florida's Tampa Bay Devil Rays, floating to the bottom for every single season of its existence save for 2004, when it finished next-to-last and only the awake or the deranged noticed.

Even while it's a boring capitalist system that leaves Tampa Bay adrift, it's a deadening socialist system that allows a franchise to finish last year upon year upon year yet remain in the league. It tells the Detroit Lions they're still a National Football League franchise, against all human rationale and national honour.

From time to time, a snide American sportswriter here and there has noted that a certain American club here or there merits relegation – cheap laugh, if that – but there's never been any real push to implement relegation. In fact, as John Kerr, the soccer coach at Harvard University, and the first American to appear in the English top division (four matches for Portsmouth in 1987–88), explained to me on the telephone one day, relegation would be impossible in the United States because of the country's sheer size, the logistics, the costs.

Imagine, then, the pleasant shock of alighting in England one late winter. Imagine you've just jetted in from some deprived planet with no relegation. Imagine thinking relegation rather cute, nothing more. By April, you see the front of a newspaper section, and you see a little box containing the top of the table, but next to that, a little box containing the bottom of the table.

Huh.

Relegation, it turns out, is not some scarcely followed gimmick, but an entire, consuming, year-long emotional construct. Relegation is so many things. It's a hobgoblin whose leer from the shadows casts melodrama over an entire season, as with West Ham in 2006–07. It's a magic potion that lures the eyeballs to the bottoms of tables just as much as the tops. It's a phenomenal beast capable of wreaking fear, envy, shame, insecurity, desperation, horror, humiliation and class resentment – in other words, just about everything that makes sport worth the time.

As a bonus, the chase for 17th place can give everybody something to do when the chase for first yawns.

As a second bonus, relegation can help you sometimes if you've just arrived in a new country and you're completely wretched at decision-making and you're worried that choosing one of the 16 underling clubs would mean not getting to choose any of the 15 others.

Having seen the player who turned out to be Pedro Mendes score that cracking goal on TV in March, having heard the

Portsmouth fans, having gained goose bumps through a TV's small speaker, I decided to devise my own relegation weekend.

On the morning of Saturday, 15 April 2006, the first table-bottom I'd ever studied carefully looked as follows:

15. Aston Villa – 36
16. Fulham – 36
17. Birmingham – 29
18. Portsmouth – 29 (trailing on goal difference)
19. West Brom – 28
20. Sunderland – 12

With my new-found knowledge and wisdom, I carefully deemed it pointless to watch Sunderland and congratulated myself on my astuteness, for I had learned such intricacies in only *two months*. I knew I had to concentrate on places 17 through 19 with one eye cocked toward Aston Villa just to make sure it cleared.

On Saturday afternoon, 15 April, I would debut at Fratton Park for the visit from Middlesbrough, sitting 14th. I would let Portsmouth Football Club charge my credit card for the first time, as if to thank them for the inadvertent goose bumps of March. On Sunday, 16 April, I would turn up at Villa Park hoping to see Aston Villa and Birmingham gathered on the same pitch, resorting to an inane American optimism that somebody would let me in. On Monday night, 17 April, I would go to West Bromwich Albion for their match with eighth-place Bolton.

Now, in the United States, if on three successive days of a holiday weekend you went to see the 18th-place team play the 14th-place team, followed by the 17th-place team playing the 15th-place team, then the 19th-place team playing the eighth-place team, and if you had no prior allegiances to any of those teams, and if you spent Premiership-level money on tickets and train-level money on trains, and if you even stayed in a hotel one night, people might call you names.

'Loser' comes to mind.

Meanwhile, in older, wiser England, blessed with its greenery, its pubs and its relegation, I recorded more goose bumps per hour than during any 10 New Year's Eves, without even getting any at West Brom.

First, on Friday I called Fratton Park, where tickets remained for the Middlesbrough clash. I admitted to being an American tourist, and the woman on the phone half-apologized in advance for the stadium. This struck me as a cultural difference, coming from a country in which we bathe in nostalgia and revere grimy old stadiums where, to quote Boston radio guru Eddie Andelman on baseball's Fenway Park, the last strains of bubonic plague adorn the men's-room walls. In this woman's voice, I heard no pride in resisting the urge to go posh.

Studying a bit, I learned that Portsmouth harboured perhaps the most bizarre manager story I'd ever heard. Apparently, and you just won't believe this, they had a manager who once quit the club in 2004 and went to manage their most reviled rival, their very Lucifer, Southampton, then 12 months later, in a staggering turn of sporting history, *returned*. I figured I might encounter the single most bewildered set of fans on the planet. Come Saturday noon, I boarded the South West train and headed south.

Having been only to St James' Park, Wigan and Chelsea, but having seen plenty of other stadiums from the outside and peeked through their gates at slivers of grass, I felt astonished at the sight of Fratton Park. Here it graced the Premiership, yet there are Texas high school football teams with grander stadiums – in fact, many Texas high school football teams, what with Texas being altogether insane. Circumnavigating the stadium, idling around lost as per usual, trying to find the office where I could collect my ticket, I passed through a brick-walled alley so shock-ingly narrow it'd present great inconvenience to any sumo-wrestler Portsmouth supporters, who'd have no choice but to walk the other 98 per cent of the way around the stadium. From the outside, the whole place actually resembled a ramshackle rodeo ground my father and I visited in Cody, Wyoming, on a vacation in 1999.

I loved it.

Inside, of course, the pitch looked green, and there's nothing like that green. Those of us in the South Stand settled in close together and rubbed elbows plus the occasional triceps or shoulder blade. A kid three seats down had a stadium meat pie, and I briefly studied this alien creation which contained some sort of horrifying brown liquid that appeared quite possibly radioactive. I thought I'd retch. Eighteenth in the table by then, and the section crammed, no seatbacks visible. Three women sat to my right and never spoke to me; to my left, a row of men who never spoke to me.

The atmosphere simply excelled. Eighteenth place sounded like second. The fans made the sound of the Pompey chimes, which even I knew from some light reading dated back to the 1800s. They continually chanted something like 'Blarney', or 'Blurney', or 'Blarmy' – something I couldn't glean and felt too embarrassed to learn by asking, so I checked my programme to see if they had referred to one player's surname. I couldn't figure it out.

I had stumbled into the latent stages of a whiplash resurgence. At the end of December, Portsmouth sat 18th, with 17 points. At the end of January, Portsmouth languished in 19th, with 17 points. On the morning of 25 February, when I barely noticed it at barren Chelsea, it seemed even more hopeless, time expiring with 18 points, to 20 for Birmingham. Then came Mendes's goal at Manchester City – and immediate, absurdist, wondrous cries about staying up – but then, with Mendes's goal as fulcrum, a win by 4–2 at West Ham, a win by 3–1 at Fulham, a 2–2 draw with Blackburn, and a pinch-me 1–1 draw with Arsenal three nights before my debut.

That meant 11 points from five matches, a resurrection from bleakness to within a shout of 17th place, with the Middlesbrough tussle as riveting a sporting event as graced the planet. Eighteenth versus 14th, and riveting: simply unfathomable to a Yank. The first half went goalless, but somebody named Gary O'Neil scored in the 54th minute after somebody named Benjani Mwaruwari rampaged up the right and slid him the ball, but it's the remainder that'll lodge in my memory. For those last 10 or 15 minutes, as I recollect, the Middlesbrough menace threatened the Portsmouth goal with repeated flurries. Greenwich Mean Time inarguably slowed. Seconds dawdled, then crawled, then moved like sludge as the ball ricocheted hauntingly around the Pompey box and the woman next to me screamed, 'Get it out of there!' Even having stumbled into this scene in April 2006 all detachment and no clue, I became almost unbearably nervous.

Through all of this the stadium itself, with a clever malice, offered no digital clock, at least not one that I could locate despite looking around repeatedly. Only one anachronism of a clock – with hands! – garnished the façade over to the left at the rowdy Fratton End, and that thing didn't tell us much and seemed even to delight rudely in my unawareness of how much time actually remained. Once I thought I saw it smile like the devil. I thanked goodness I'd never left my seat and held my water and avoided the bubonic plague, not only because about 15 other people would've had to stand to let me out, but because I'd have come back even more baffled.

I suffered for my prospective future squad.

Finally, about seven hours later in my estimation, the referee blew a whistle, and Portsmouth had leapt to 32 points, clear of Birmingham by three and firmly into 17th place. I joined my new stranger friends in a rousing rendition of 'We are staying up! We are staying up!' I felt semi-Himalayan goose bumps. I remained at my seat and watched the players into the tunnel. Then, as I walked toward the aisle, I saw two children, a boy and a girl, each probably 11 or 12, descending, no, bouncing down the stairs to the right. I shall never forget them. 'We are staying up! We are staying up!' they shouted in a delirious two-voice chant.

In the United States, we don't have children beyond the age of 10 all delirious over late-season forays into 17th place. If we did, we'd probably recommend their families get a visit from Child Protective Services.

7

Sunday contempt

Naturally, we're inured to longer trips in the United States, partly because we're geographically huge and partly because longer trips help us fulfil our God-given duty to squander oil products at a pace exponentially more rapid than any other countries. I once saw a basketball game in Mississippi on a Saturday and an NFL game in Green Bay, Wisconsin, on a Sunday. It's believed to be the only Mississippi–Wisconsin weekend in United States history, and I'm deeply proud of this honour. Another time, because the office begged when it really didn't have to, I flew 90 minutes from New York to Indianapolis on a Saturday morning, drove three hours north from Indianapolis to South Bend, Indiana, saw an American football game between Notre Dame University and the United States Naval Academy, returned to Indianapolis by 2 a.m., woke by 6, caught a 20-minute flight from Indianapolis to Cincinnati, Ohio, connected to a five-hour flight from Cincinnati to San Francisco, took a one-hour taxi (traffic) across the San Francisco Bay to Oakland, and saw a Sunday-afternoon NFL game between the New York Jets and the Oakland Raiders.

Covering an afternoon basketball game in Nashville, Tennessee, then driving four hours through wee-hour snow flurries to St Louis for an NFL play-off game, when the boss didn't even ask for the play-off game?

Really, who wouldn't?

It's always a bit of a geography lesson, then, when you mention to an English fan your Saturday at Portsmouth followed by a Sunday at Aston Villa. Seems it's just not done all that much. Throw in the fact that Aston Villa would oppose Birmingham in a derby on Sunday, 16 April 2006, with tickets profoundly unavailable to the tourist, and such a weekend seems downright misguided.

Luckily, I major in downright misguided, so I rode the Sunday-morning train to Birmingham, watching bald guys drinking cans of Carlsberg and marvelling at how, through long evolution, English stomachs had come to consist of corrugated steel. Approaching Villa Park in a taxi from the city centre under a partly sunny sky, I knew I'd probably add to my growing list of games experienced from outside stadiums. Yet again, I'd stand in a parking lot wondering what had happened to cause that crescendo I just heard, or stand in a pub among strangers wondering why I didn't just choose a pub among strangers half a block from home. In my grand tabulation of matches experienced from outside the stadium, I already had Charlton, Stamford Bridge, the old Highbury and Anfield.

Add Villa, and I'd have only 15 parking lots to go for an even 20.

But we have this wonderful, horrible saying in America, and it goes like this: You never know. So on I went. Sure enough, when I proved unable to ask directions on account of maleness and took 25 minutes to circumnavigate the stadium and find the ticket office, the security guard at the door explained I could not purchase any of the remaining, available, unused, advertised tickets. He explained Aston Villa vs Birmingham is a 'derby' – he bafflingly pronounced it 'darby' – and you must have a ticket-buying history with the clubs. He recommended a pub up the street. It didn't even help when I showed him my United States passport, hoping in vain to convey runaway ignorance and exact some pity.

Thirty minutes to kick-off, and I believe I took on a bit of a forlorn look as I trudged back into the parking lot, when just then I heard a whistle from behind. I ignored it, presuming the whistler aimed elsewhere, but then the whistler whistled again.

I turned to see an approaching brother and sister, ages 22 and 21, with faces profoundly unvisited by the ageing process. They said their father's business trip had prevented his attendance, and that they'd sell me his ticket for £20, provided I was not a fan of Birmingham City. I said that until recently I'd lived in New York, New York, and had not known of the existence of a Birmingham City, and that I certainly did not wish to adopt Birmingham City on a sudden whim while standing among thousands of home fans at Villa Park. They grinned, took my £20 note and walked me around the stadium toward the Holte End, asking me questions about New York. They said their parents had taken them maybe four times to America, but always to Orlando, and I found these youths so decent and polite and exquisitely parented that I considered not even one single wisecrack.

Thereby did I enter the Holte End for a match between Aston Villa and Birmingham City with little to no idea as to the severity of the contempt therein. I mean, we Americans have rivalries. We have had, through the years, the Washington Redskins vs the Dallas Cowboys (NFL), the Oakland Raiders vs the Denver Broncos (NFL), the New York Yankees vs the Boston Red Sox (baseball), the University of Florida vs Florida State University (American football), the University of Kentucky vs the University of Louisville (basketball), Ohio State University vs the University of Michigan (American football) and then, the most beautifully, irrationally contemptuous of them all, the University of Alabama vs Auburn University (American football). We boast frothing contempt in almost all the 50 states. We know the value of a good, controlled, in-stadium hatred. Even while we feign gentility and perspective, we know a stadium improves on any day when it's seething, roiling and curdling with disdain.

I'd seen disdain.

I'd just never seen ... oh ... my ... god.

Aston Villa 3, Birmingham 1, even with its insignificance to the Premiership title, with its 16th place defeating 18th place, bolted into my all-time top 10 sporting events. It's up there in the neighbourhood of Rulon Gardner, the ninth child of Wyoming dairy farmers, defeating Hercules from Siberia in the Graeco-Roman wrestling at Sydney and then telling us that moving Aleksandr Karelin was like moving a cow. It's not far from the 2000 Super Bowl between the St Louis Rams and the Tennessee Titans, or the 2001 Wimbledon final between Goran Ivanisevic and Pat Rafter, or two famous basketball games in 1992 and 1998 between the University of Kentucky and Duke University.

In the Holte End that Easter day, wave upon wave upon wave of goose bumps washed over me, especially after half-time. The noise made echoes, and I'll never forget feeling the entire stand inhale during those pregnant milliseconds that precede most goals and help make football uniquely orgasmic. By that, I mean the millisecond just after the seasoned spectators have made a realization. They have realized their side will score, but they have not yet had the time to exult. They're inhaling, I suppose. There's that moment tucked in there, and I find that moment almost peerless upon the face of the earth, not least because you know euphoria's coming in the very next moment.

From the first half, we had only a Villa goal, at 10 minutes, in the opposite goal, after which the brother in the brother–sister tandem grabbed me, hugged me, hopped up and down while I stood like a log and then apologized to me, for I must've looked startled. Then we had a Birmingham equalizer. Twice after half-time would come the magical mass inhalation. It cropped up in the 56th minute just as Gary Cahill hurled himself skyward, contorted himself parallel to the ground, stretched out his right leg and yanked the ball toward the opposite corner of the goal. And it materialized again in the 78th minute, when Juan Pablo Angel fed Milan Baros unmarked on the right, and

Baros blasted a shot. Both times, I felt the quirky silence followed by an outpouring that would blow the doors off a house. The back of my neck exulted.

All along, I kept hearing things about this guy Steve Bruce, and while I'd never heard of Steve Bruce until the previous month, I got the distinct impression he might rank among the worst people in global history.

And the songs.

I'd just never heard such a range of songs. To a Briton, they probably seemed antiquated, but I knew not whether they were old standbys or instant creative concoctions, so I just found them incredible, even if I understood only about 37.5 per cent of the lyrics. Added oomph fuelled the songs, as clearly the Holte End knew that Portsmouth's 1–0 win over Middlesbrough had pushed Pompey to 32 points and shoved Birmingham firmly into the relegation zone at 29. On that day, I learned of yet another of relegation's knacks: how it ladles upon a match an entire new layer of songs.

To 'Guantanamera', the song about the Cuban peasant girl from Guantanamo and the emblem of Cuban patriotism written probably in 1929, we had:

> *Down with the Baggies,*
> *You're going down with the Baggies ...*

I gathered the word 'Baggies' might have something to do with West Bromwich Albion.

To 'Roll Out the Barrel', the concoction begun when Czech musician Jaromir Vejvoda wrote the music in 1927, we had:

> *Down with the Baggies,*
> *Down with the Baggies, you go ...*

That one managed to mesh an abiding loathing with playful mirth, and I loved it thoroughly, even though the worst thing I

51

could say about Birmingham was that its name's not as pretty as Aston Villa's.

Later on, the Holte End opted for a version of Vera Lynn's 1939 ballad penned by Ross Parker and Hughie Charles:

> *Someday we'll meet again,*
> *Don't know where, don't know when . . .*

I found this almost staggering. The Holte End, as lounge act. Imagine.

But at maybe the 71st minute a ditty latched itself doggedly onto my memory, not to unfasten any time soon, odd given I couldn't understand the lyrics. Suddenly, before my very ears, the Holte End crooned a phenomenal version of the Monkees' 1967 hit 'Daydream Believer', one of the few songs I'd actually liked from the ballyhooed 1960s that preceded my adolescence. I asked my host for the lyrics that we'd just heard but the Monkees never imagined. Maybe two or three times, he repeated to me the phrase 'sad bluenose bastard', but I just couldn't understand him, and so, with his hand shaking a bit – he's a nervous spectator who doubles over and smokes during matches – he carefully spelled it out:

> *Cheer up, Stevie B,*
> *Oh what can it mean,*
> *To a sad bluenose bastard,*
> *And a s—— football team . . .*

I felt retroactive goose bumps.

I felt awe.

I'd spent my life in stadiums, but I'd just never . . .

When I returned to my flat, I hastily emailed those lyrics to about 20 American sports friends. Many wrote back amazed. Others wrote back envious. It probably seems mundane to the average Premiership fan, but everyone deserves a religious experience at their first hearing of 'sad' combined with 'bluenose' combined with 'bastard'. After about 35 years of studious attention to American sports (as we call them, with the 's' always added), I felt I'd wandered into a new realm, in which teams could get relegated and fans who dislike them could make up songs about it, even to 'Daydream Believer', a Monkees song that during my teen years became a remake by Anne Murray.

Exiting Villa Park, we saw police chase some would-be brawlers across a field, the lone moment of near-violence I've seen even as I hail from a country in which many still think it's somewhat dangerous to attend English football. (Note: it's among our vast national reservoir of misconceptions.) I felt actually intoxicated, but by oxygen alone. Owing to the cruel but understandable English stadium policies, I'd been unable to have a beer at my seat, reason enough for colonies to secede from a motherland had we not seceded already. Or, viewed differently, who needs beer when you have relegation and 'Daydream Believer'?

After all, only relegation could've brewed that scenario from May 2005 at the Hawthorns, of which I learned the next night. Just before West Brom and Bolton played a goalless, thrill-less and largely songless Monday-night draw that completed my relegation weekend, a kindly man of maybe 60 began edifying me by answering my questions. This occurred in the concession area as I drank a beer and he ate a terrifying meat pie. He explained to me that 'Baggies' came from West Brom players wearing baggy shorts beginning about a century prior. He said that in all his days attending football matches, one of the best had to be that day in May 2005, when West Brom played Portsmouth on the final day of the 2004–05 season, and West Brom won to secure the coveted 17th place, and West Brom fans cheered, but Portsmouth fans also cheered, because West Brom's win shoved Southampton into relegation, a story that supplied my first inkling that Portsmouth fans might rather dislike Southampton. He said of football, 'It's really the heart of England.'

Then, after some time and a bit of familiarity and comfort, he gently said, 'If you don't mind my asking, what is your opinion of your current president?'

8

Media-inaccessible England

The transition from one national sports culture to another requires time. Luckily, there's no therapy involved, and the medication costs only £2.80 per pint even though they have to import it from Belgium.

Still in observer mode, I'd begun to notice some things.

Foremost, I'd never lived in a place in which a team could win more than one thing in one year. In the United States, we keep it simple, probably because we're a young culture with still-forming brains that become further impeded whenever we hold congressional steroid hearings. If you play in the NFL, our biggest league by far, 32 teams pursue one Vince Lombardi trophy, which goes to the winner of the Super Bowl and gets its name from a great 1960s coach who fulfilled many of our national militaristic quasi-pathological fantasies by screaming at – and scaring the hell out of – his players. In baseball, in basketball, in ice hockey, in Major League Soccer, you play for one title. They give second-place trophies, yes, but those often come equipped with public sneering.

I'd just about grasped the idea that Premiership clubs play for up to three titles – the Premiership, the FA Cup and either the Champions League or UEFA Cup – when Jerry informed me there's a fourth. I'd never once heard of this fourth cup named the 'League Cup' and named also after a beer, and almost immediately upon arrival in England in February saw

Manchester United and Wigan on TV playing in the final of this fourth cup named the 'League Cup' and named also after a beer. Some observers made light of the fact that Manchester United might not boast about winning this cup, being Manchester United and all.

By April 2006, I still had never once heard about the Intertoto Cup, and it would be a year before I would start to read about Blackburn pursuing a spot in the Intertoto Cup and even then, I simply could not believe yet another cup lurked out there. I could not comprehend the Intertoto Cup and decided to allow it more time. It may require even another year, absorbing the vagaries of the Intertoto Cup.

Plainly, it's a bit harder being a big-time manager or coach in England than in the United States. In addition to the usual issues all managers face, the English manager must dabble in energy conservation as he attempts to win two or three or four trophies at once. In filling out his teamsheet in a given week, he might have to sacrifice Wednesday night for Saturday afternoon or Saturday afternoon for Wednesday night. In the case of that decent sort Steve Coppell at Reading, he might even come right out and state misgivings about achieving the amazing feat of a UEFA Cup qualification from the first Premiership season, worried it will dilute Reading for other pursuits.

Having read that, I almost tumbled out of my train seat and into the aisle, for we just don't dwell in that kind of realism in the United States. We'd expect our coach to say something along the lines of, 'We'll worry about that when we get there, and if necessary we'll recruit some ragtag players from the area, coach them into shape, upset four superior teams on the path to a storybook title and become a really bad sports movie about the value of hard work that's really trite and clichéd but does well at the box office.'

English realism vies right up there with multiple trophies among jolts to an interloper. Only two days into my entire Premiership indoctrination, on a train from Wigan to Newcastle,

I read the following quotation from Sam Allardyce of Bolton: 'Our target is sustainability, to become a Premiership fixture like Charlton. We don't want to get to the next level because we know we can't, we're not daft. We could have finished fourth last year and missed maybe the only chance we'll ever get.'

We'd pillory somebody making such a statement for its failure to trade in daydreams. As an American, I had to read it thrice to digest.

I'd begun to take note of the phenomenal English loyalty, the phenomenal English eyes and the phenomenal English stomach.

I'd seen plenty of fan loyalty to American clubs, just not quite the same depth of loyalty as in England. Somewhat more than Americans, English fans seem to have their club insignias swimming in the bloodstream, perhaps affixed to the platelets. Where the idea of having one's ashes scattered on one's favourite pitch seems reasonably normal in England – the subject came up as part of my tour of Old Trafford – it's a concept present but not prevalent in the United States, even if we did trump England when a Philadelphia fan ran onto the field to scatter his mother's ashes *during a game*. English loyalty to club is so profound that England seems to have far fewer people who rather like this club or rather like that club or rather like that other club over there. My football guru Tom makes it sound as if having a second-favourite club consigns one to pay added Council Tax.

In English eyes, meanwhile, I detected telescopic strength, as if it correlates with beer consumption in parents. From even half a stadium away or more, these evolved lenses could spot perceived handballs in a benevolent attempt to assist the referee with his work. At times early on I thought the English felt it some sort of duty to go to the stadium and point out the handballs, to assist this beleaguered referee with his thankless work. I found this a routinely beautiful commitment to civic service.

And then, while I'd witnessed the strength of American stomach linings, as at car races and the Kentucky Derby (whose official drink is the glorified glass of bourbon called the mint julep), and while I'd witnessed in short bursts the sturdiness of English stomachs, I'd just not had the extended, day-to-day look at the true, Herculean measure of English stomachs. I'd not lived and travelled and followed football among these mighty organs, not comprehended their true durability against the torrent of challenging products and shocking mistreatment that come their way.

Still, the paramount cultural difference between following American sports like a ravenous hyena and following the Premiership like a ravenous hyena would be, weirdly enough, media access to players' dressing rooms for pre- and post-game interviews. American reporters in the big three sports have much; Premiership reporters have little. It causes a fundamental distinction in the sports-following experience. American fans watch athletes with great personal familiarity (even when misconstrued); Premiership fans watch their athletes with a certain mystery.

This makes the two lands just *sound* different: one chirping with athletes' voices, the other less cacophonous.

By the end of the 2005–06 Premiership season, I realized I'd never heard Wayne Rooney's voice, having sat too far away to hear him yell 'F——ing beauty' at Newcastle and having heard only others speak incessantly about his frigging metatarsal. When I thought about this, it startled me, for I'd come from a chatterbox culture in which you might absorb a quotation from your favourite athlete every single day for six months during the season, either by hearing it on TV or radio or reading it in a newspaper. Where they're always talking to us even if they're annoyed at the prospect. Where it's perfectly normal to sit with your breakfast cereal watching the morning highlights shows and think nothing of the fact you're watching an athlete standing in front of his locker shirtless, trying to say as little of significance as possible into a phalanx of maybe 10 microphones. Where brave beings known as 'sideline reporters' interview coaches even as they head for half-time, and even though the coaches never say anything remotely curious, the custom persists like gout. Where, in certain circumstances, players receive fines for skipping media sessions. Where signs adorn the walls outside players' dressing rooms, restating league rules about the necessity of letting in the reporters about 15 or 20 minutes after a game.

In baseball, the American reporter will have about three hours of access to the dressing room before games and roughly another hour afterward for the rehash of feats and blunders. That doesn't count play-offs or big-media games, in which there'll be organized pre-game and post-game press conferences (often transcribed and printed) in addition to the dressing-room access. For the NBA (basketball), the reporter will have pre-game access, post-game access and daily post-practice access during the season, even though he or she seems to have less access than he or she did 20 years ago, prompting him or her to pine away for bygone days. An NFL reporter suffers by contrast, because that reporter has only post-game access on Sundays, then some practice-time access during the week, varying slightly based on teams, and with some stars providing no access at their lockers but giving deeply unsatisfying 10-minute access in a press-conference setting. That doesn't include Super Bowl week, where the two teams combine for a one-hour session with selected players on Monday, three-hour interview sessions with all players on Tuesday, Wednesday and Thursday, and another hour with each coach on Friday.

Daily access to the coach or manager is a national given, written into the Constitution by the Founding Fathers in 1787. In general, coaches and managers appear on TV more than the president, a fact that always pleases about half the country. Players often hide in training rooms fixing phantom injuries just to avoid the ubiquitous media. Even the 119 big-time universities have regular weekly coach press conferences for football and basketball, regular coach-and-player post-practice access on Monday through Thursday, and multi-person media-relations staffs. That doesn't include championship events, which involve daily access with players and coach sitting at a long table in front of a room of reporters.

This regular national flood of access led us to one of our manufactured national crises, simmering for years but reaching its hysterical apex in the early 1990s. Then, we had a dreaded 'national conversation' because, of course, that blob of reporters bolting through every game began to include more and more women entering domains where men change clothes. We hemmed. We hawed. We argued. We shouted – especially on talk shows. We remembered our Puritan roots and all the joys they had brought us, even though we couldn't really think of any. We had some athletes who pleaded religious convictions and asked to meet women outside in the hall for interviews, but that didn't work. We had some athletes who saw women and *then* got undressed. We had some athletes who said and did lewd things to women. We had one legendary woman who, responding to a lewd gesture, said to an athlete, 'It looks like a penis, only smaller.' We had elected officials suggesting new laws, a true horror. We had fans perceiving athletes as victims. By now, we still might have beautiful female reporters getting asked out by athletes or athletes' wives staring contemptuously at beautiful female reporters, but the whole thing has subsided to normalcy.

All along, through the whole fatuous ordeal, there existed the easiest solution in dilemma history.

Ancient civilizations called it the 'towel'.

So imagine my surprise at the sound of England. From time to time, here's a Premiership player speaking after a match, seeking and achieving banality. More often, we hear from zero of them. Here's the manager, usually reliable for TV-camera commentary, then maybe press-conference commentary, but certainly no second round of questioning in the dressing room while surrounded by 15 reporters and doling out the better stuff. Here's an interview in a newspaper, every once in a while. Here's Sir Alex Ferguson opining that England's national team play timidly because they fear derision from the English press, when in fact added access might blunt some of that derision, because you're less apt to deride somebody you know a bit.

And then, here comes a fine trickle of summer books, in which the players get to tell their side. In fact, here's one book in which a Premiership player provides a melodramatic account of the day he learned one club wanted to offer him £55,000 per week, rather than £60,000. He recalls how he gripped the steering wheel of his luxury vehicle, trying to cope with the horrifying news: 'I was trembling with anger.'

Never mind the fact that if he finds £55,000 per week unmanageable, it's a really bad idea to give him £60,000 per week. I believe this inane passage from Ashley Cole's book alone, on balance, might justify the English approach of limiting player availability.

9

Two months to choose

While still in lame deliberation as the season waned, I found new understanding of the Premiership ... in Colombia. You can hear all about the foremost league's global tentacles, but there's something about seeing them up close. At a dinner in Bogota on an April vacation, one of the fellow diners heard 'England' and asked immediately if I'd ever seen Aston Villa play, and I briefly found that odd until I remembered the Aston Villa squad features the Colombian Juan Pablo Angel. On TV on a Saturday morning, I quickly came upon Arsenal vs Tottenham, which wowed me more in this completely exotic place than it ever did in the United States. And at a family party in a *barrio* near the airport in Cartagena, on Colombia's north and Caribbean coast, I ate *sancocho* and drank beer out of little green bottles and saw something unforgettable to myself: six boys, probably 14 or 15 years old, out in the dirt street, in a neighbourhood in which the electricity later would go out because a storm happened to brush by meekly. They had nothing to carry them through the humid afternoon except six pairs of shorts and one football, no shirts, no shoes, and no posts, so they used rocks. Still, they had themselves a fine Sunday, swaggering over their goals and cooing at bypassing girls and maybe even pretending to be Juan Pablo Angel, while I thought of all the childhood Sundays I had spent loaded with options yet choosing to sit in the air conditioning, affixed to the couch like a trapped muskrat.

Meanwhile, on Saturday, 29 April 2006, at Wigan, my old haunt, Portsmouth won 2–1 thanks to Matthew Taylor's penalty in the 71st minute and finished yanking survival from the oesophagus of relegation. After accruing 17 points in their first 27 matches, Pompey had hogged 20 from their next nine. The pitch at Wigan teemed with a 17th-place celebration of some 2,000 Portsmouth fans, quite a total given Wigan's geographic presence up near Iceland. Pundits called Taylor's goal a 'multi-million-pound penalty', called the Portsmouth manager 'Harry Houdini', quoted owner Milan Mandaric saying, 'In my seven years at Portsmouth Football Club, this has to be the most emotional moment.' In yet another of life's blunders, I missed it out of indecision, yet I felt some sort of kinship with it, as if that might be the *it* I sought. It certainly had a chance to be *it*.

As a new season began, I made a self-imposed club-choice deadline of 31 October, and set about testing the persuasive first impression of Portsmouth, born of Mendes's goal and of having once lived in a Portsmouth, albeit spending that time irked at my parents. I had it down to Portsmouth, Aston Villa, Newcastle, with outside chances of Reading, Tottenham, maybe Everton. I wanted to take the decision as seriously as a clueless interloper could take it.

Portsmouth had attributes besides Mendes's goal and a sister city in Virginia. I found the nickname 'Pompey' appealingly plucky, and I liked the presence of about 12 explanations for the nickname's origin. I liked that people chanted the same 'Pompey Chimes' that fans had chanted 110 years prior, so that I might one day chant the 'Pompey Chimes' and imagine it's 1898 and everybody's wearing only black-and-white clothing, thereby connecting me to history. Further, it dawned on me through careful research that Portsmouth's a seafaring town with a navy heritage. Not only had I come from a seafaring (if sleepy) metropolitan area with a navy heritage, but the idea of Portsmouth made me think of my maternal grandfather, a tugboat captain with a gruff demeanour and a big heart and mammoth forearms. He'd tell my brother and myself these wondrous stories from navigating the Chesapeake Bay, wondrous not least because he knew how to wink, and even as tykes we could sense the high percentage of fiction. I still remember the boat hit by a German vessel during the war and 'sawed half in two', and how he held on to the railing of his half so tightly as it bobbled, barely afloat, that his fingerprints remained in the metal even to the day of the tale. Opposing fans might mock Portsmouth fans with the 'Guantanamera' version 'Town full of seamen/You're just a town full of seamen', but that'd make me all warm and fuzzy.

Studying the season's early stages and roaming some, I noticed that Aston Villa had hired Martin O'Neill, whose BBC World Cup commentary I'd found salient and unafraid and instructive, even giving me the I'd-like-to-play-for-that-guy vibe, a vibe that seldom visits sportswriters, who know too well how the coach species bears striking resemblance to that of the cobra. By contrast, O'Neill seemed rather a sage, learned professor of football. But then, you can't choose a club for one manager, I thought. I saw a match at Reading because I wanted to see how the first crest in the top division in 118 years of existence might look, and it was good enough and spirited enough but not grimy enough. I sought more soot. I cast a studious eye on Newcastle, accursed, still digesting Michael Owen's gruesome World Cup injury, but the storyline seemed rote to me after a childhood and early adulthood listening to wailing accursed baseball fans in Chicago and Boston. I liked 'Tottenham Hotspur' because they figured in one of the great and charming mysteries of English football – why do some clubs have names such as 'Tottenham Hotspur' and 'Bolton Wanderers' or 'Blackburn Rovers', but others have only 'Portsmouth' or 'Everton'? – and I did feel a certain sympathy when Tottenham missed out on the Champions League because their players got food poisoning from a Marriott buffet, but they just didn't quite click.

Strangely, I got an added Portsmouth tilt from a gory incident very early in the new season. On Wednesday night, 23 August at Manchester City, in only the second game of the 38, Mendes futilely chased a ball as it scurried out of bounds, five minutes after the half-time break. The play had died. Mendes merely would retrieve the ball. Then, sickeningly, as Mendes neared the line, here came some Ben Thatcher, the first I'd ever heard of him, flying toward Mendes. Not content with a gratuitous tackle, which would've been merely stupid, he rushed in with a venom suggestive of some steroid rage, throwing a forearm to Mendes's head that knocked Mendes unconscious. Mendes remained unconscious as he rode off on a stretcher. He had a seizure. He received oxygen. Gary O'Neil called it 'the worst thing I've ever seen on a pitch'. Mendes woke in hospital on a drip. Thatcher apologized by writing a letter, which beats a phone call or media interview, but he received a paltry eight-game suspension. He wouldn't have seen the light of the pitch for two seasons if I ran the league or the world.

I run neither, but seeing this play every half-hour on the sports channel had the unintended effect of endearing me further toward Mendes and Portsmouth. At the same time, I tried to ignore that Pompey opened the season with five straight clean sheets, crushed Blackburn by 3–0 and Middlesbrough by 4–0, and hurried on to an eye-popping first place by 17 September, with 13 points to 12 for Manchester United and 12 for Chelsea. I didn't want to choose a club based on one luminous month and, besides, my football guru Tom had warned me of the triviality of early tables, a notion bolstered by manager Harry Redknapp when he said, 'We are trying to finish above our highest previous finish in the Premiership, which is 13th. We've had a good start but we're not getting carried away.' I tried to ignore the start, but probably failed.

Even the BBC *Panorama* football corruption special of 19 September 2006, which implicated Redknapp, deterred me only momentarily. For one thing, the whole ruckus taught me the definition of the word 'bung', unquestionably fulfilling a public duty toward uninitiated residents from far-off lands. I came to understand that a 'bung' amounted to a sort of illicit payment, and having come from a land of plenty that abounds with illicit payments in the field of university athletics, I felt a moving and emotional bridging of the cultures. I came to perceive our similarities as greater than our differences, and gained new-found hope for the world.

The programme showed Redknapp having an allegedly illegal conversation with an agent about a player from Black-burn. Luckily, by moving, I had emptied my tank of misgivings and started anew. Returning to fandom in a new country, I could reactivate my fanatic's rationalization gland and use the first of my fresh set of available rationalizations. I simply reasoned that I still could lean Pompey through my old saw of remembering that following sport means following sin. Weary from my homeland, I knew sports fandom had grown ever more confusing.

Besides, in a way, Redknapp reminded me of a horde of gloriously sinful great-uncles from my mother's side, who drank straight whiskey and swore in perpetuity and brawled in saloons and made excellent company whether or not Redknapp did any of the above. Harry even *looked* somewhat like they once looked.

Pompey had begun cooling off in late September, but I eyed the long term, the rest of life, the till-I-die, wherever I might reside – and the crowd and details of Pompey promised the best potential for recurrent goose bumps. From late September to late October, Portsmouth lost to Bolton, lost to Tottenham, beat West Ham, lost to Chelsea, beat Reading and collected one new fan, one more obscure droplet in the vast harbour of fandom.

With a fresh coat of Pompey, I headed for Fratton Park on 4 November for the match with Manchester United. I knew full well that the match would take place up north in Manchester, but I wanted to see if Portsmouth during a match felt anything like the Washington, DC, area, known to resemble a ghost town while any NFL Redskins game appears on television. I made a ceremonial walk to Fratton Park, past the arterial devastation of the KFC and the McDonald's, through the crosswalk, past the Safe Storage, to the edifice.

As the match began up north, I walked through No Sumo Wrestlers Alley to the Pompey store, listening to the match on the broadcast in the store as the only patron. Armed with a list of Pompey pubs I'd actually looked up and printed in a lapse into efficiency, I walked all over the neighbourhood, often alone in entire blocks of terraced houses, terraced houses being rather exotic to us Americans in our idolatry of lawns, which play an invaluable role in our employment of 12 million illegal immigrants. I wanted to feel the barrenness during a match, to sense everybody inside watching the match. Yes, it did seem beautifully barren, even if I lacked the first clue whether everybody was inside watching football or inside cleaning out the refrigerator or gone off to some horrendous mall.

The first three Pompey pubs I chose practically echoed with emptiness, for while they had TV in two cases, they lacked the proper cable package to air the Premiership, alerting me again to one American superiority: almost never does a sporting event appear on some channel outside the basic cable package. Finally, I found the Devonshire Arms, which had the game but proved so packed I barely could wedge in. More, I definitely could not fit in. I felt embarrassed, even presumptuous. Wearing black as usual, I thought everybody looked at me as if I didn't belong, even if nobody even so much as looked at me. How dare I take up rarefied space. Here a pub teemed with people who'd emerged from the birth canal tattooed with the sprightly blue-and-yellow Pompey insignia, people who in some cases had stuck close through the horrid late 1970s, or 15 straight second-division seasons between 1988 and 2003, people who loathed this Southampton. To myself, Southampton remained an American high school football dynasty from the boondocks on the other side of the boondocks near my hometown. I hated neither that

Southampton nor this one. By the time I looked up, Manchester United led 3–0. Nobody much groused. Everybody pretty much seemed realistic.

10

Clueless

The transition from silent objectivity back to irrational fandom requires time and metamorphosis. Luckily, as with changing national sports cultures, there's no therapy involved, and the medication costs only £2.80 a pint even though they have to import it from Belgium.

There's a slow moulting of two decades spent in American press boxes where an announcer always intones, 'Attention ladies and gentlemen, a reminder, this is a working press box and there will be no cheering allowed.' After sitting quietly through athletic drama for 20 years, jotting down stuff with a fervour, never breaching decorum except to giggle with your buddy Joe through an Indianapolis 500, where the event's so loud that nobody can hear you anyway, the body forgets how to cheer. When you observe people as they do cheer, they start to seem unhinged.

So I rode the South West Trains service the 90 or so minutes from London Waterloo south to Fratton Park on Saturday, 11 November 2006, wondering if I could summon the motor-sensory skills required to clap, and pretty certain I'd lost altogether the capacity to clap while jumping up and down. I had been a spectator in seats outside the press box precisely twice in the previous 10 years, including once at a classic NBA play-off game with four lead changes in the last 13 seconds while I stood there, arms folded, analysing. The train rolled in toward

Fratton and through the train window on the left I beheld again my new football home in all its mighty greyness. There it stood, as it had since 1898 when five Portsmouth men hatched the club from the vestiges of the local Royal Artillery club. It looked either majestically dingy or dingily majestic.

As Portsmouth were fixed to play Fulham at 3 p.m., Pompey stood fourth in the table, with its 19 points trailing only Manchester United (28 points), Chelsea (25) and Bolton (20), but my football guru had instructed me of the meaninglessness of early-season tables. Fulham stood somewhere else in the table, apparently. Of all the top-division clubs in England at that moment, I'd probably heard less about Fulham than any. I'd never heard an American discussion of Fulham. I'd never heard of an American who knew of the location of the Fulham club, and while I figured out within weeks that Fulham sits in London, I had no clue where in London. The name Mohamed Al Fayed rings familiar to Americans because he lost his son in the same accident that killed Diana, Princess of Wales, but it took me months to routinely connect Mr Al Fayed to Fulham, even though Mr Al Fayed owns Fulham. By 11 November, I knew no Fulham history except that Fulham employed two American players then – and three by now – but that counts as Fulham trivia, not Fulham history. I had no thoughts about Fulham except that as an instant know-it-all American I reckoned that it probably should lose at Portsmouth.

On a mostly cloudy day at Fratton Park, I made it through the gulag turnstile and took my seat in the Milton End stand behind one goal, which seemed far less rowdy than the opposing Fratton End behind the other. The great thing about the Milton End, though, is that you can hear the full brunt of the Fratton End, loudly enough that even an American can understand one cheer in 10. As I heard their indecipherable chants and wondered if there existed some sole person up there initiating them, I also heard two fabulous sounds that distinguished Fratton Park for myself: drums and a bugle.

Now, I once did attend the venerable beach volleyball competition on Bondi Beach at the 2000 Sydney Olympics, and while I don't remember who won or who played, I'll always remember that a lone Brazilian fan had brought along a trombone. These are the people who supply life with verve, I thought, these people who, before leaving the house or hotel room in the morning, remember to bring along a trombone. Sunglasses. Sandals. Wallet. Keys. Trombone. Well, at Fratton Park, they had two drummers that I could barely see way across the pitch in the Fratton End, plus one guy playing a horn. The combination sounded just a little like Friday nights in autumnal America, when people gather beneath lights for high school football games while the student band plays. I always loved Friday nights in autumnal America, so I loved that sound, but in the Fratton sound I relished something else. While the drummers' energy never seemed to waver as they lent the match a fine samba, I fixed my ears upon the bugle player. He could play along for a while, hitting the early notes in any song with gusto, but then he'd seem to go breathless, the last notes barely trickling out in tiny bursts.

It sounded as if, at some point, on cue, somebody would begin to strangle him.

It sounded as if the bugle itself would develop some sort of clot along the way whereupon it would begin the irreversible process of croaking, spewing only bits and pieces of sounds in its final gasps before bugle death.

It sounded human.

I decided I liked Fratton Park's humanity, especially that horn's distance from perfection.

I sat next to an elderly man who smiled at me once but never spoke. A few empty seats dotted the area. Portsmouth, fluid in attack early in the season, kept an abiding threat upon the Fulham goal, but the Finnish goalkeeper Antti Niemi kept rebuffing my adopted mighty blue squad. For some reason, the Portsmouth fans reserved a special loathing for him, shouting some sort of epithet I couldn't quite translate. As Portsmouth's collection of *almosts* piled up, I'd act out disappointment from time to time in a sophomoric attempt to fit in until I realized nobody cared, so I quit the tack.

Gary O'Neil's narrow miss at 52 minutes epitomized Portsmouth's frustration, but by that moment I had a little problem. Near the end of half-time, I'd walked up the steps and along the outside fence to the men's room, and I'd waited in line at one of the few places on earth with a shorter queue for the women's-room. I'd finally made it into the inner urinary-trough sanctum when play began again. While still in this rustic outhouse, where I did not spot any visible strains of bubonic plague, something happened to elicit a groan from the audience, followed by a silence. Too inexperienced to realize that a Fulham goal would've loosed a fair amount of sound from the nearby away section, I thought this sounded like it could've been a Fulham goal.

Now, I'm from the state of Virginia, where we believe – or at least believed, in my childhood – in not making nuisances of ourselves. We're a genteel, meek bunch, known for statesmen (eight presidents, none lately), keeping mostly quiet. Usually, we Virginians can't stand standing out. We'd never ask for any of your food even if starving, and we might not even ask a stranger whether Fulham just scored or not. It's inexplicable and even unbelievable yet true, and it's surely the familiar old impulse that prevented me from asking any of the strangers around me whether a Fulham goal had occurred. I might've feared they might laugh at me. Not only did I not inquire, but of course I saw no scoreboard, nor did I or anyone else pivot to check the gigantic new video screen just about 10 rows behind my shoulder blades, for apparently it malfunctioned that day.

That's how I reached my inconceivably inept status of the 57th minute, when Fulham's Claus Jensen launched a corner that team-mate Zat Knight headed, whereupon it deflected off

Portsmouth's Dejan Stefanovic and into the goal. Then and there, I believed the score might've just become 2–0, and I spent the next 17 minutes alternating between thinking that the match had become rather hopeless or that the match still hyper-ventilated with doubt. My later research indicates that Uncle Harry changed to a more attacking 4-3-3 formation, but I couldn't have discerned that had he changed to a 2-2-2-2-2. Uncle Harry summoned Andrew Cole in the 66th minute, but I wouldn't have noticed had it been Pelé.

I did sense that when Portsmouth finally did score after so many threats, the method made sense. We – no, they, for one must earn one's 'we' – sort of got tired of peppering the goal and finally just crammed in the ball. At the far end of the pitch from myself, O'Neil propelled a corner from my left and Niemi's right, and while 'propelled' probably falls shy of acceptable parlance, the thing just looked propelled. The ball went into the box in front of Niemi and began caroming around while a Portsmouth team meeting gathered in front of Niemi. Eventually, Cole scored. Fulham's manager complained about something.

I applauded, turned to the old man next to me and expressed undeserved relief, but I still did not know the score for sure. Either Cole had just made it 1–1 or he had halved Portsmouth's stark deficit. That meant that when Lomana LuaLua almost scored at 85 minutes, he either almost won the match or almost forced a draw.

Either way, I wished I could see LuaLua score. In the previous spring, he'd become one of the first Premiership players I re-cognized. I loved his name. I loved that he'd grown up practising gymnastics at an army camp in the Congo on the edge of Kinshasa, often on buried truck wheels that passed as a spring-board. I loved that he'd practise backflips off high walls, because I'd have never had the stones to do that. I learned snippets about LuaLua, such as that he left 100,000 Congo fans waiting to see him play in an African stadium because he'd forgotten to renew his passport back in England, or that he'd cleaned toilets in a McDonald's. And I loved that he'd punctuate goals with fabulous somersaults, until one day in April 2006 he hurt himself in the celebration process and wrought a post-game critique of his gymnastics prowess from Uncle Harry. To me, he represented the utmost appeal of the Premiership: that fans on the English Channel could revel in the goals and somersaults of a player from the Congo who learned to somersault on embedded truck wheels. No other league can claim such worldliness and to such degree.

Alas, he did not score, and I had not seen a somersault in person, and I did not know whether Fulham led 2–1 or the teams stood at 1–1. In fact, I still did not know as Portsmouth's frantic bids to score ended, as did the match itself. As the people turned to leave, I tried to glean from them whether their countenances suggested a draw mode or a loss mode. I could not tell, and figured a draw mode and a loss mode might mimic one another after a home match with Fulham. As my fellow Yank McBride and other Fulham players walked over to applaud their travelling fans, I still did not know. I thought of hollering to McBride, 'Did you just win or draw!?!?' but decided against. Portsmouth's point tally either had remained at 19 or had crept upward to 20, with either surpassing the dregs of late February 2006 when I'd first caught Portsmouth at Stamford Bridge. Gutless and clueless, I walked up the steps past the blank video screen and out of the ground. I went around the stadium and out past the KFC and the McDonald's across the street. I went down Goldsmith Avenue toward Fratton station and Smiffy's pub and beyond, still unaware whether I'd seen a loss or a draw. I tried to eavesdrop on people's conversations, hoping to ascertain some clue.

Finally, as I decided to walk into Southsea and trailed two Portsmouth fans along the sidewalk, I heard one say to the other that a draw hadn't been all that bad. So it had been a draw, and Portsmouth had 20 points, one fewer than Aston

Villa at that moment, and there had been no goal while I occupied the loo.

I kept hope, for I knew I could not get any dumber.

11

Knowing too much

From what I've noticed, English sportswriters seem to maintain their allegiances to teams much more than do American sportswriters. That's because it's less taboo, but I might submit another reason. It's also because they spend much less time in the company of the players.

Once you've interviewed the athletes and managers more than is generally recommended by health professionals, old fandom blurs considerably. Naturally, you begin to sense those you like and wish well, versus those you deem fraudulent and wish not illness or poverty or genital herpes, but own goals and red cards and fumbles and a general onslaught of humbling comeuppance. You begin to root – quietly, of course, in your own head – for a hodgepodge, the courteous manager over here, oh, but if he doesn't win, you can be happy for that pleasant quarterback with the long history of big-game failure over there on that opposing side. This tendency might've found its epitome in winter 2007, when a chronically decent man named Tony Dungy coached his Indianapolis NFL team to the Super Bowl title after years of flirtation, and all known media swooned, including those who loathed any road trip to Indianapolis. Had you ever conversed with or asked questions of Tony Dungy, you'd have swooned, too. That such a decent sort could win almost reaffirms faith that there's some sort of goodness in sports.

And then, opposite the Dungy effect, you may end up regarding a childhood favourite team as loathsome for the undeniable reason that, having talked to your childhood team at length, they're a batch of self-centred, ignorant, misogynistic ogres, complete with loathsome manager.

It happens.

But let's say you interviewed the Watford defender Jay DeMerit in late October 2006, for an assignment. You sat in the boxes above an empty Vicarage Road on a Monday for two hours, 15 minutes. Let's say this interview became more a conversation, and a sterling one at that. You re-heard his story about flying to London as an anonymous schlub/Chicago bartender with no contract and few contacts, and working his way from the ninth division to the seventh to the second to the first, even scoring a goal at Cardiff in the May 2006 play-off final. You heard him laud the English capacity to make light of most anything. You heard him speak of loving life in Camden, north London, where he might see somebody in an impeccable business suit chatting with somebody who's been pierced so many times he appears to have stuck his head into a fishing-tackle box. You heard how DeMerit describes the Premiership to American friends at home, how it's as if somebody took the entire NFL and shoehorned it into his home state of Wisconsin, pushing the clubs right up next to each other and galvanizing the passion. You heard him describe playing in the Premiership better than you'd ever heard it described. In the Championship, he said, you may see that a guy's coming toward you and then think to act, but in the Premiership, by the time you've had the thought, he's upon you.

So let's say this Jay DeMerit of Green Bay, Wisconsin, rocketed onto your ever-changing top five of favourite athletes interviewed, and that you decided he must've had wonderful parents, and that you even considered yourself a fan of his grandmother, who holds down a spot in the Wisconsin athletics hall of fame.

Now, weeks later, here comes Watford to Fratton Park, and you're supposed to wish this guy a potion of thumping defeat and profound embarrassment? You're supposed to see him and his mates as the bloodsucking enemy inveighing against the goodness of your side – you know, as you saw it during the pre-teen years? Of course not, and so you can end up hoping your team will collect the three points while also hoping this one defender on the other side will have himself a good day.

Fan-wise, this forms the very definition of lameness. I believe in retrospect they should've shredded my ticket rather than accepting it at the gulag.

On a mostly sunny day at Fratton Park, I pined away only somewhat for the colossal American-football game that day at Columbus, Ohio, the University of Michigan Wolverines versus the Ohio State University Buckeyes, an annual festival of mass mutual hatred drawing 100,000 spectators and known to result in people burning furniture in the streets. Meanwhile, over on the southern edge of England, my extraordinary lifelong friend Teresa, a fellow recovering Virginian who turned Parisian and is more fun than 10 of most people, joined me from Paris for Portsmouth vs Watford, a plus in every regard, including that she suddenly began talking later about the 'Blue Army' chant, which alerted me at last to what those people had been chanting. She could not sit with me, so I told her to pay close attention to No. 8 on the Watford side, because he seemed one of the more likeable human beings upon the planet. She later said she could not be sure about No. 8, but that No. 6 seemed to be American and seemed to have the surname DeMerit. We also noticed, as did everyone at Fratton Park, that No. 6 stuck out his head in the 32nd minute, connected with Ashley Young's corner and gave Watford a 1–0 lead.

It made me mildly happy and docked me Pompey points within my own cranium.

Portsmouth held down sixth in the Premiership, one point behind the three-way logjam of Arsenal, Aston Villa and Bolton, and it would really help to beat Watford, who held down 19th with nine points, ahead of only Charlton's eight, so I sought a 2–1 win. Again, I could not see any clock, but used my mobile phone clock to realize it had grown awfully late in the first half when Kanu equalized on a rebound from David Thompson's cross, jarring the roof of the goal above a horizontal keeper, Ben Foster. Teresa said Foster didn't impress her much, becoming yet another in the grand tradition of instant-expert Americans. The teams went into half-time drawing 1–1.

The second half seemed endless, as if played in a tub of goo, and I'd failed to calibrate my mobile phone, much as I failed to notice when two Portsmouth penalties apparently went unnoticed. Later, DeMerit would make himself available to reporters as per usual and say, 'I think in the box, referees tend to look at (famous) players a little bit more. You can't change those things. Darius' – Henderson, his team-mate – 'just needs to work on making himself a household name and becoming more familiar and recognized. He should go on *Strictly Come Dancing* – he is a good-looking guy, he might be able to get on there. I will suggest it to the manager.'

No sportswriter would pull against such a being, but then, I did cheer in the 89th minute even while unaware it was the 89th minute. I did sit – and stand – pretty close to where DeMerit dragged down the star Kanu in the box, which the referee deemed a penalty. I did feel bad that such a fine soul had such a thorny moment, but I did prove myself capable of standing and clapping nonetheless, just for the chance to break this draw against the gritty Watford squad and get the three points the morning had promised.

I had started on my way back to fandom, starving for the three points and drained of compassion, willing to steal the food of three points from a profoundly decent soul.

LuaLua took the penalty, and as Foster sprawled one way – can't remember which – LuaLua banged it right down the middle, securing a 2–1 victory when, moments later, the referee magically called a halt to proceedings. Aidy Boothroyd, the fine Watford manager who reads biographies of John F. Kennedy and Abraham Lincoln, among others, had upbraided the referee afterward, though I missed that spectacle. Soon, DeMerit would write on his website that not only had Kanu 'made a meal' of their intersection in the box, but that he had made an entire Denny's breakfast bar, Denny's being a chain restaurant where Americans observe our birthright of accruing a gargantuan amount of fat grams. Portsmouth had barged past Arsenal et al into a heady third place, even though my football guru, Tom, had told me not to pay attention to such things before the new year.

All seemed pretty routine, except that after LuaLua had scored his goal, he had run over to the corner right in front of myself and even closer to Teresa, and he had accepted hugs from team-mates but had done nothing spectacular in celebration – no somersaults, no forward roll, not even a headstand. I had to explain to Teresa how she'd missed a potential somersault. I felt disappointed as a know-nothing newcomer who needed a somersault to help me access the game, but I presumed LuaLua hadn't somersaulted because Uncle Harry might've admonished him for injuring himself that other time. I remembered Uncle Harry's classic quotation of 12 April 2006: 'LuaLua went off and did his treble back somersault with pike and twisted his ankle. It wasn't the cleverest thing he has ever done.' That must've caused the restraint, I thought, because I had not read any of the tabloids that morning, not until Teresa and I stopped off at a convenience store on Goldsmith Avenue and some head-lines screamed up at me.

In one tabloid, LuaLua had noted that he might not like to play for Portsmouth any more. He had noted that he might think about playing elsewhere because he had noticed certain fans posting messages about his late son, Jesus LuaLua. Jesus, aged six months, had died of pneumonia the previous 20 January, whereupon his coaches in the African Nations Cup didn't tell the father because they feared he'd return home. And some message-board geniuses, in criticizing LuaLua, suggested his son's death might've come as some sort of penance.

Now, ever since the Internet arrived and office productivity declined, we Americans have led the world in message-board sins. (We're so proud.) We know message boards for the frothing, roiling vats of lunacy (and worse) they can be on their best days. Very often, they're the best free entertainment still remaining in a money-grubbing society. I used to place a regular feature in a college football column: 'Deranged Message Board Posting of the Week'. I'd remember which teams had lost ingloriously the previous weekend, and I'd scroll through their sites, salivating. My all-time favourites include the Ohio State fan who greeted a young player's emergency surgery with, *What does this mean for the offensive line?*, but there's even an inarguable all-time champion American lunatic, spotted by David Whitley of the *Orlando Sentinel*. In early 2002, the venerable and cherished University of Alabama football programme had been cheating again. One of its moneyed fans had given $150,000 to a high school football coach so that the coach would steer a star player to Alabama. The NCAA, the governing body of intercollegiate athletics, slapped Alabama with major penalties, including a two-year ban from 'bowl games', the season-ending prizes for good seasons.

One Alabama fan responded: 'This is our 9/11.'

That's staggering beyond all human comprehension, but I'm still not sure it trumps for vileness the direct reference to a specific baby's death. So while I'm nobody's idea of a prude, for a moment at the convenience store on Goldsmith Avenue, I completely lost perspective. I felt just sick. I don't know why; it's naïve to assume another country lacks a maniac fringe just because you rate it more civilized in general just because its people tend to shoot each other less often than in your country. For a millisecond I thought I'd chosen the wrong club, but that's a rash American for you. We're always trying to view things in

81

stark, simple terms so we can flex our moralizing muscles, whereas English fans in their older culture probably just saw the story, shrugged with disapproval but not horror, and thought something along the lines of: *Life is absurd.*

Uncle Harry helped me with his post-match comments. He suggested an idea that hadn't dawned on me – and what a shock – that those did not count as Portsmouth fans. Then Jerry reminded me by email that some Chelsea fans had written death threats to Reading players that very week, after goalkeeper Petr Cech had suffered a skull fracture at Reading. You just try not to let it ruin a day at the ground.

After all, fandom's harder than it looks.

12

Away fan

It can take several away matches for a manifestly inefficient American to navigate the maze of buying away-match tickets in England. For one thing, there's the matter of figuring out that away clubs handle the away tickets until match day. This can be hard to learn and can require intricate research such as reading the club website. Before achieving that rocket-science knowledge, it's entirely possible to ride a train all the way to Newcastle knowing tickets remain available, walk around St James' Park for about 40 minutes, then find oneself in the home ticket office, which doesn't sell the away tickets. In some stadiums, they sell remaining away tickets at the away gates, but I don't know for sure about St James' Park because I never found the away gate.

I bought a home ticket, and as I took my choice seat in a lower section, I felt the Home Office might go ahead and deport me for my indiscretion. There sat my people, far, far away, a sliver in the upper deck, lined on both sides by the standard police protection, and barely could I hear the cheers or the trademark Portsmouth exuberance. I probably would've needed the Hubble telescope to spot even the electric-blue wig of Portsmouth fan extraordinaire John Westwood, the lavishly Pompey-tattooed partner in the Petersfield Bookshop who legally changed his middle name to 'Portsmouth Football Club'. I had betrayed my people, sitting with another tribe while my people sat so far from the action they couldn't even hear when that freckled woman from August 2005 called them 'f——ing w——ers'.

Maybe she didn't even call them w——ers.

I sat among a noticeably upscale crowd, in which lovely over-50 women wore lovely coats and hugged friends. About 15 rows below me, children and even a few adults watched in awe as the players warmed up, and I recognized this as one of the eternal signs of the end of time, for even as a sportswriter I hated to watch clubs practise, and believed that those who found this tedious drudgery fascinating must be sorely in need of some sort of hobby. In my backpack I had a brand-new Newcastle scarf, because everybody got one entering the stadium, and I decided to give it to a child as a present. The public address played the Killers' masterful 'Somebody Told Me', and I knew I still lacked my football chops when I got annoyed that they interrupted it to read the line-ups. The line-ups meant nothing to me as, through my eyes, Pompey still looked like an Impressionist painting of players, with any individual skills and tendencies pure Sanskrit to me. Week to week, Uncle Harry shuffled in the healthy and shuffled out the injured, but I just couldn't follow it expertly enough to know any significance.

When you fail to notice the absence of the leviathan Sol Campbell one week, you know you're in the forest *sans* flashlight.

I'd relished my first train ride as an away fan and American convert; it had seemed almost magical to behold. For one thing, we Americans tend to consider trains exotic. We don't ride them much because we inhabit a gigantic country and because train rides require us to be with other people when we'd much prefer to be alone in our cars stuck in traffic and gorging on oil products and getting infuriated at the uninformed rants of one of our vast collection of dim bulbs to whom we've given talk-radio shows. I felt energized as I boarded the train at King's Cross on a

Saturday night, only to discover that a great portion of London apparently had felt energized likewise, so that a lot of us stood in the corridors for the first two hours, swaying to and fro.

Then again, few Americans would regard a four-hour road trip as taxing. Until you remember the size of England and the astonishment that it ever built an empire from such limited land mass, it's bewildering to hear somebody refer to four hours as a long haul. To an American, English clubs always seem to play in the neighbourhood, or just down the driveway, much like the New York Giants going to Philadelphia or Washington, just down the pike. I think of the NFL's Seattle Seahawks, who play in Seattle, which rests gorgeously on the top left edge of the United States, its existence unknown or mysterious to many Americans. In the 2005–06 season, the Seahawks pulled off one of the great feats of American athletic history, in my lonely opinion. They went 13–3 and reached the Super Bowl despite their usual eight away trips howling with uncommon distance. They flew 2,456 miles to Jacksonville, Florida, 2,329 miles to Washington, DC, 1,723 miles to St Louis, Missouri, 2,380 miles to Philadelphia, 1,975 miles to Nashville, Tennessee, and 1,652 miles to Green Bay, Wisconsin. Their breather road trips included the 1,110 miles to Phoenix, Arizona, and the mere 679 miles to San Francisco. You know how, when you finish flying six hours, you usually feel dehydrated and slaughtered of brain cells? You wish to scream or undergo physical therapy or regurgitate? You certainly don't wish to ram into muscular humans any time within the next two days.

The Seahawks looked wretched in the Super Bowl, but then, they had to fly 1,935 miles to Detroit for that.

London to Newcastle: 249 miles.

I'd imagine that were I nine years old, I'd remember every-thing about my first Premiership away trip, so I tried to remember everything about my first one at the age of 44. After all, these Saturday trains in England, they're living, breathing animals of their own. They're tubes of passion, songs and information. You might learn scores of other matches in other divisions from people who hop on midway. You might hear people lamenting Coventry or, if you're lucky, extolling Brentford. You might sense that the locomotive itself has a blood-alcohol level three times the legal locomotive limit.

From London to Newcastle, I remember the nice woman in the concession area who had run out of many alcoholic products but placed my wine half-bottle into a bag of ice so that I could carry this bag of ice back to my seat and balance it on the tray like I'd just bought a new goldfish. I remember passing through Leeds and thinking I might've been a fan there had I popped in only seven years earlier when Leeds dwelled pretty close to the top of the world, and wouldn't that make quite a tale? And I remember, as ever, the skylines.

I'd come to recognize the true skylines of England, for they're built not by architects and Eastern European construction workers but by drinkers. The skylines of England appear on the tables of trains, and they're often impressive. There'll be a smattering of empty beer cans, forming the veritable Greenwich Village of the skyline, the smaller 'buildings'. There might be some taller beer bottles, say an overgrown green Carlsberg here or there, forming the less ostentatious part of midtown Manhattan. Then, the big honchos, the empty wine bottles, the Chrysler buildings, the Empire State buildings. All together, these cans and bottles will merge on a table, especially late in the ride, a Hong Kong of consumption. I have seen these configurations on many a train, but never so many as on that train north-east on a Saturday night. I listened to a whole gaggle of men solve the problems of English schools, and they did so loudly.

I'd never heard about Newcastle before that Rooney day in August 2005. Some Americans know that Newcastle sits in north-east England, on the River Tyne, not all that far from the North Sea, pretty close to the non-border with Scotland, but there aren't many. My football guru Tom told me that some people in Newcastle identify with Scotland and might root for Scotland against England in football. Centuries ago, England and Scotland conducted tragic wars, whose tragic residue spread across the centuries until they wound up enabling Mel Gibson to win a Best Director Oscar, thereby attaining their tragic zenith. Many Americans would be interested to note that Tony Blair may or may not hail from the Newcastle area, while many others might like to know that Tony Blair was the prime minister of the United Kingdom for 10 years, and that the United Kingdom is a nation across the Atlantic Ocean, and that the Atlantic is the ocean near New England and the Carolinas and Florida. Furthermore, some unfortunate Americans might've seen *Goal!*, the movie about an American who reaches the United States in the traditional way – running across from Mexico in the middle of the night so that his family can provide cheap labour to American businesses and lawn owners – then gets discovered in Los Angeles and winds up playing for Newcastle. This movie leads us to believe that a footballer's life of rampant sex and partying somehow represents an unwise tack. Our hero winds up scoring a goal on a free kick, but it's unclear whether he wins a trophy for Newcastle because the creators of the movie didn't want to stretch the truth any further than they already had.

They did make a sequel.

Newcastle, as it happens, is a beautiful town with a rowdy vibe. A taxi driver proudly told me it's one of the foremost party towns in Europe, and poppy for that. Like Boston Red Sox fans in the United States before the Red Sox quenched the 86-year drought in 2004, it's real love with Newcastle fans, I suspect. Their fans bargain with life for a pay-off that's larger than anything Manchester United supporters will ever feel. When the drought finally does cease, Newcastle will be the place to be upon the earth, greater than Miami Beach, Rio de Janeiro and Ibiza put together.

On a chilly, beautiful Sunday with cotton-ball clouds in north-east England, fourth-place Portsmouth played 17th-place Newcastle, but I knew better than to trust those positions. I don't remember much about the match except that I never got a feeling of an imminent three points. The home squad always seemed faster, fresher – perhaps a byproduct of the long, long trip our squad had made. I get a mental picture of David James sprawling to make superhuman saves. In the 69th minute, Newcastle's Charles N'Zogbia, on the left, directed a low cross to the centre, and Antoine Sibierski tapped it in. The replay showed that Sibierski should've been ruled offside, but I never noticed any need for an offside call and didn't hear any grumbling because I sat so far away from my new brethren, who no doubt could've detected the offside from there to Gosport. I sat only among people who stood and cheered lightly as Newcastle went ahead 1–0, and I stood with them but kept my mouth shut, but felt nonetheless like a dork.

Newcastle won, 1–0, and denied Pompey a shot at recapturing third place. In another 20 years, I'll remember probably only one thing from the day, a moment that would never happen in the United States. As I filed out among throngs of Newcastle fans, behind me there sang a single young-adult, male voice. He kept repeating the chorus in his own made-up tune:

> *He's big, he's French,*
> *He's often on the bench,*
> *Antoine, Antoine.*
> *He's big, he's French,*
> *He's often on the bench,*
> *Antoine, Antoine.*

This guy had thought up his own song about Antoine Sibierski, and he had decided to sing it to all the unsuspecting, exiting masses. He did not care who listened. He did not care to try out for *The X Factor*. He just sang. We don't have this too much in the United States. We should. Give us another 849 years of existence, and we just might.

13

The best goal in my admittedly limited lifetime

On Saturday, 9 December 2006, at Fratton Park, in the 14th minute, Kanu chased the ball nearing the halfway line with his back to the Everton goal. Simon Davies chased the ball from the other direction. Davies slid toward Kanu. They converged. As they headed toward opposite sides of each other from where they'd started, both touched the ball, and the ball popped upward, hard to tell just how. It floated lazily over to the right, and descended toward Matthew Taylor, 45 yards from the Everton goal. Before it could hit the ground, Taylor struck it with his left foot, sent it back upward. I thought he'd struck it casually, almost goofily. I thought he'd struck it in one of those see-what-happens modes. It flew high and flew toward me as I sat in the fifth row behind my fellow American Tim Howard in the Everton goal. It sailed to its pinnacle and then gravity summoned. Here it came, just beginning its descent toward Fratton Park soil, still two-thirds of the way up in the air, when there came an instant that would have to rate as one of the best instants you can know upon the earth.

Now, in the interim since I had made my inept away debut, Portsmouth had drawn with both Liverpool and Aston Villa. The goalless draw at Anfield on 29 November had seemed particularly impressive, coming only three nights after the trip to Newcastle. It became the first goalless draw I ever regretted missing because I, like thousands of other people, just about yearn to see a match at Anfield, and because I, like thousands of other people through the decades, hadn't got a ticket. So I still craved a Pompey moment, some game or chunk of game that 19,527 strangers and I could witness together and find unforgettable. A penalty in the 89th minute against a gritty Watford squad didn't count, no.

So as I still sort of fidgeted with this whole idea of adopting a club, and as I pretty much shrugged at Matt Taylor's ball even as it began its downward slope, the very next instant ranks among the best in a thousand stadiums. I refer not to any moment of landing, but to an instant when the ball remained airborne. The instant took maybe a hundredth of a second. Wonderful, delectable, available only in the flawed domain of sport, this instant qualified not only as a Pompey moment of a rare kind, but a Planet Earth moment of a rare kind.

No keen judge of trajectory, and in just my seventh game as an avowed Pompey fan, I had this sudden synapse zip across my brain. It went something like this: why, that thing's just about to dive down behind Howard's back and into the goal, and that's about to become the damnedest goal you're probably ever going to see in your whole damned misspent life.

The instant itself seemed elongated, marvellous, and, no surprise here, quiet. It might've been that moment of mass inhalation writ large. I'm fairly certain I threw a gasp in there, but I didn't hear it. It's as if time gave you an extra second there so that you could sense 19,528 people realizing something and maybe 17,000 of them relishing it. It just stands out among millions of fellow instants, that instant. Having lived it, I'd just like to wish everyone peace and happiness and one moment in which they see a football flying precisely from 45 yards, think little of it at first, lazily monitor its path through the air, notice its descent and then, somewhere while it's still airborne, become instantly certain it's about to land behind the keeper but in front of the crossbar and into the net.

Why bother with sport?

Oh, there's your answer.

Oh, and one other crucial element: it seems helpful if the team you're supporting strikes this ball.

Down it dived. By the end, it seemed to have transmogrified to develop eyes and maybe even a little smile, although I couldn't tell. It all but took Howard's legs and tied them into a square knot. He almost couldn't budge. He'd moved too far out to defend this comet, and he looked mildly like a baseball outfielder misjudging a fly ball that sails overhead because he lost it in the lights, and I suppose he looked mildly clumsy, but should we really vilify a goalkeeper for missing something this celestial? I mean, what's the goalkeeper protocol for defending bending 45-yard parabolas? I lacked the expertise to know, and I did not *want* the expertise to know.

I just know that as the ball came down behind Howard's body, I spotted the moment when it occurred to him that the gig was up, the play was over, the goal was scored. I saw his body twitch and then try to contort and then relax in concession. I saw him look fairly nonplussed, almost as if something like this happens every once in a while, all the way back to age seven in New Jersey. I'd seen something vaguely similar on TV with this Ronaldinho thing in Japan against David Seaman and England, but that happened when I was in New York at a wee hour in a SoHo bar, thus could've been a mirage. Howard seemed less wowed than myself, the neophyte, at how somebody could possibly, without even two seconds to take aim, direct a ball 45 yards so as to curl over a 6-foot-3 human being but still just in front of a crossbar. I didn't know for sure, but I thought these players might be even more talented than advertised.

I did know that in the instant that followed my favourite instant, when that thing indeed smacked down and rippled cords in the right side of the net – and to Taylor, the left – I got to participate in a mass ecstasy unparalleled on the planet that day. In one swoop, I closed my jaw and bolted upward along with a few thousand strangers in the Milton End and maybe 17,000 strangers in this old rodeo ground, and I got to hop up and down and up and down and up and down, a fine act I presumed bygone in my life, an act people simply don't practise enough. It felt uncontrollable. This had transcended the occasion. In video footage of the goal, I can't necessarily see myself back there, but I can see our entire row going mad. If I slowed down the video and looked carefully, I might well see my own mouth spew foam.

Meanwhile, Taylor rushed into the near corner like a mad fiend, having just had himself an experience that trumped even ours, that of *generating* such bedlam. And bedlam reigned. Bedlam reigned so much you could sense extra waves forming over on the Channel, and you could fall in love with the old sea town and the old British Navy and the chimes and the drums and the horn and all Pompey, all at once. Forgive me, but it's not overstating it to say that in that moment I loved England and the Queen and Churchill and The Clash – especially The Clash – all at once. I did not love meat pies, but time remained. Taylor's team-mates soon caught up to him for a pile-up, and it was all so wonderful that I wondered how the game could proceed.

It did, but we all adjusted to regular life, post-wonder. Well, some of us did. Others of us still felt giddy if not downright drunk or, in some cases, technically, both. The goal played repeatedly on the functioning video screen, and everybody pivoted and looked. At moments it seemed the players could've disrobed and nobody would've noticed. Portsmouth led Everton 1–0, and the segregated Everton section, just a notch over to my left, seemed peeved, as if they couldn't spot the majesty in Taylor's shot. I wondered if seasoned observers saw it as purely lucky. I wondered if, as an American, I relished the goal only because it had a certain bigness. Certainly, I'd rate Argentina's 26-pass goal against Serbia and Montenegro in the 2006 World Cup as more skilful and far more impressive, just to name one, but something about a howling 45-yard masterpiece right in front of you can put you in lucky-to-be-alive mode.

Just before the game, fans had heckled Howard, and he'd held an index finger up to his mouth as if to say, 'Shhhhhh,' and I found that appealing. Now, I saw him not only playing with that goal freshly in mind, but with a Portsmouth peppering coming at him. It could've been 4–0 by half-time, and as a signed-on fan, I suppose I should say it could've been 6–0 by half-time. It turned out 2–0 by half-time, and the weird thing was, the second goal also qualified as an outright beaut.

Merely 12 minutes after the first goal, Gary O'Neil sent a cross from Howard's left to Howard's right. It went in a line drive – apology for the baseball terminology – and it met with Kanu's left foot. Somehow, from the corner of the box, Kanu met this thing on the fly and sent it heading back to his right, where it hurried past a baffled – and hopeless – Howard. There could be no wondering about luck vs skill on this goal, for it was 100 per cent skill, 100 per cent superhuman familiarity with a ball at the foot – testimony, even, to the childhood football games of Nigeria. I felt awed by this goal, Kanu's ninth of the young season, without feeling the intoxicating rush of its predecessor.

The second half played along enjoyably, and David James had to make a few saves, and in a seminal moment, some Everton fans to my left somehow spilled out onto the pitch. I'd never thought of Everton fans as especially rowdy, so it surprised me at first, but I marvelled at the speed with which security people collected them and hauled them off to who-knows-where, maybe to some cell with a video screen repeatedly playing Taylor's goal.

Sport ranks among the few things in life that can give you the exhilaration I felt on the walk to the train and on the train ride home. The conductor even allowed some burbling Pompey fan to take the speaker and announce the final score: 'Portsmouth two, Everton nil.' Pompey stood third in the table, with 28 points. Here I'd signed on to a club partly because of my grandfather's mastery of tugboats and partly because of the dilapidated stadium but also partly because I thought it might be fun to ride the relegation tightrope, but this club had turned out somewhat, I don't know, but it struck me as good.

14

I hear my people

For Portsmouth's match at Arsenal on 16 December, I showed signs of unmistakable progress since the Newcastle match and sat closer to my people, the blue people. I did not sit *with* my people because my people snapped up all the away tickets either before they became my people or just after they became my people. In so doing, they clearly did not realize they were my people and did not care they were my people, and in general I worried they might not need any more people, or want any more people, especially people who before 2005 had no idea of their existence.

At least my people and I occupied the same tier of the stadium, the lower tier at the Emirates Stadium. At least I could hear my people, who sat in the corner a few sections over to my left, and I could try to decipher my people, such as when they booed that adorable little marvel Theo Walcott and for a millisecond I could not ascertain or even fathom why. Who on earth would boo Theo Walcott? Isn't he still 17? Hasn't he been 17 for about three years now? What'd he ever do? Did he keep an untidy bench at Germany 2006?

In the next millisecond, I remembered that my people seemed to dislike people who had played for some mysterious team called 'Southampton', such that it seemed that the Southampton team must resemble all Lucifer, seemingly treading in genocide, grand theft and chronically unseen handballs. We do have this sort of thing in the United States. I recall a basketball equipment manager for the University of Kentucky, an old teddy bear, who on the day before the rivalry game would not *occupy the same gymnasium* as one of the broadcasters from the University of Louisville. Apparently we Americans once boasted a *Santa Claus* in Florida – *Santa Claus!* – who tried to dissuade some helpless tyke from either Florida or Florida State. We have New York Yankees fans who, in an unscientific poll outside the Yankee Stadium one night, voted 8–2 they'd rather win zero of the next three World Series and have Boston win zero, than win two of the three with Boston winning the other.

As sportswriters who do get to see athletes and managers as human – even if, at times, members of the reptile-human hybrid subspecies – we tend to make fun of this roiling, frothing, irrational, puerile, bilious, fanatical hatred. This ignores the fact that without this roiling, frothing, irrational, puerile, bilious, fanatical hatred, we'd be unemployed, so I learned to console myself by noting that releasing the roiling, frothing hatred in a stadium might just beat all alternatives.

In the Emirates Stadium, down near the pitch, I said aloud that I didn't think I could ever bring myself to boo Theo Walcott.

'Give it time,' said my host.

I sat, of course, with Arsenal people, the other people. A benevolent editor invited me. In the splashy, shiny, brand-new Emirates Stadium, we occupied the front row, where we could look upward at the true gods of the age, the plasma TV screens inside the luxury suites, yet another crucial American contribution toward global decadence. The Arsenal people generally regard the entrenched Portsmouth people like myself as one regards a gnat, so they teased me and never did strike me with any blunt object. My host suggested I stand amid these foreign people and cheer my blue squad whenever appropriate, and I didn't and couldn't, because I'm from Virginia where we try to keep inconspicuous.

I found the match absolutely riveting, an entire new realm in football viewing, because the field-level view plus the presence of a big-four side equalled new understanding of the calibre of these athletes.

It's stratospheric.

Other, more seasoned spectators did not find the match quite so riveting, evidence of which I detected late in the first half when the older man next to me fell flat asleep. While marvelling at his capacity to sleep sitting up among 60,037 when I can't even sleep among 250 on an overnight 767 despite enough wine to deaden an unusually large moose, I also understood anew the multiple tiers of football spectators. There are those fumbling through the forest without a flashlight (hello), the mildly curious/somewhat knowledgeable, the knowledgeable, the very knowledgeable, the scarily knowledgeable, and then there's this level where you can behold your favourite 11, 11 of the best athletes in the world, and plainly deduce they're having a sub-par afternoon while some nitwit next to you sits enthralled.

The guy snored, but only once.

He woke in time to make a wisecrack as I returned from the loo commenting on its immaculate, state-of-the-art loo-ness. He said I thought so probably because we didn't have any loos at Fratton Park, and I even got the joke, which I counted as further progress in my seasonal education. It marked the first time I had been personally impugned as a member of my tribe.

I can't remember if he continued snoozing into added time of the first half, because that's when Matt Taylor launched a free kick from the outer-right portion of the pitch, and David Thompson's header bounced off the left post to the right, where it found Noé Pamarot, whose header from six yards went over Jens Lehmann and into the top right corner for a 1–0 lead to Pompey.

I could hear my people exulting even as I remained quiet and gave an infinitesimal fist pump, subtler than subtle, that moved my right five knuckles about one-one-hundredth of an inch. In the strange and inflexible terminology of football, Pamarot's goal happened at 45+2, especially weird given Taylor would score at 47. I'm not sure why 45+2 isn't 47, but I try not to ask such things because I yearn to avoid being a nuisance.

I did feel oddly gratified and oddly hopeful at 45+2.

Then, of course, I missed 47 for the aforementioned loo break, giving me my second ill-timed loo break in just two months of fandom. I heard some sort of roar from the corner, and I believe I heard the broadcast piping into the men's room and reporting doom. I emerged about to croak with curiosity and spotted a handy concourse video screen, which showed Uncle Harry standing on the touchline with an expression I shall never forget. Shy of a smile but north of a frown, almost concealed but not quite, the expression unwittingly communicated something like this: *Just last January, my squad lost 5–0 at Birmingham, and then just last March, we seemed to have permanent reservations in the relegation zone, but we clambered out of that and people called me Harry Houdini, as well they should, and here we're sitting fourth in the table, one point behind Arsenal, and 2–0 at Arsenal, the club I loved as a child.*

I'm not sure, but I think that's what he meant – and meant to hide.

He did lead 2–0 because of a sumptuous left-footed volley by Taylor on the left that sang an aria into the right top corner of the goal and no doubt stunned the home crowd into disappointment and quite possibly sleep. I returned to incur the bathroom joke and, not to say I felt any sort of mirth, but the fresh news of Taylor's goal pretty much did light up my soul like all Tokyo. It seemed I cared. It surprised me I cared. I wondered if caring this soon meant we're biologically set up to care and need only a place to plug it in, and I'd happened to plug it in on the south edge of England.

Of course, the problem with caring is that it leaves the door wide open for nervousness, and the problem with that is that when your plucky band of up-and-comers has gone 2–0 up at Arsenal, you're automatically, profoundly nervous. You're getting away with something, and you know it, but you can feel the authorities coming, sirens blaring.

People say the new Emirates Stadium suffers for lack of din, but I do not understand what they mean. It sounded incredible to me. The sound of the urgency and fear streaming from the innards and out of the mouths of 60,037 people (minus, of course, my people) tore into my front-row ears and even provided a glimpse of the real England. Maybe that's because I hail from a nation of relatively quiet stadiums, including one in Arizona where you can view a baseball game from a hot tub. I don't know.

It's just that in the 55th minute, Arsène Wenger, whom the referee had shipped into the stand, as I would learn when reading the Sunday newspaper, sent on a man named Emmanuel Adebayor. He wore No. 25. It grew clear during the ensuing few minutes that Mr Adebayor probably was the best athlete in the history of the world, with fresh legs to boot. He changed the match utterly and transfused his team's blood thoroughly. After he scored inevitably in the 58th minute, he retrieved the ball from the net and rushed it back to midfield, anxious to wreak further destruction into our backpedalling 11. That gesture had precedent, I'm sure, just not in my experience, and I found it appealing. What's more, I love the profundity that an American can sit in north London both cheering and fearing the super-human from Togo. It's the world Amelia Earhart envisioned when the aviator forecast, in the early 20th century, that eventually the entire globe would seem as if one neighbourhood.

Mr Adebayor scored because Theo Walcott went zipping down the right side while 60,037 people gradually rose section by section as he passed. As the noise built, I thought of the English capacity to see the goal before the goal, because they certainly knew before I did that this loathsome little bastard – sorry, this exemplary young man – figured to skitter that ball across to the danger zone, even if they're not dubiously neophyte enough to term it the danger zone. As if the ball itself had eyeballs that the cretin Walcott – sorry, that fine young man, Walcott – had installed with his foot, the ball dodged two defenders and found its way to Adebayor, who in baseball terminology bunted past a flailing David James.

The crowd began making the most formidable brand of crowd noise in all humanity, that of the home crowd sensing a comeback. Adebayor yanked out the ball and sprinted to midfield. Did we have to continue? Yes, we did, and some two minutes later, well, I may have this slightly mixed up, but I believe every single player in the Arsenal squad, including those on the bench, banged soccer balls in a furious anger at James, who did honourable work to save about 29 of them before Gilberto Silva's low, angled shot toward the left post demanded to go in. By my count, that made 2–2, and the din, even if tame to the seasoned, rattled my intestines large and small.

From ground level, the way Arsenal had attacked their deficit looked very much like science fiction. The Gunners seemed capable not only of outrunning and threatening my blue players but quite possibly of eating them. Impressionistically, Portsmouth began to appear as if they used only nine players, maybe eight. Maybe someone *had* eaten some of them. It seemed so very *28 Days Later.* If I hadn't known we'd reached the 21st century in terms of athletic evolution, speed, what-all, I'd have learned it that day. Certainly the score would go to 3–2, almost surely 4–2, quite possibly 5–2 and not-out-of-the-question 6–2. That it ended 2–2 suggested I'd inadvertently chosen a club with pluck.

To the Welsh anthem 'Bread of Heaven', all Arsenal began singing something I'd yet to hear:

> *You're not singing,*
> *You're not singing,*
> *You're not singing any more.*
> *You're not singing any more ...*

They sang it to that corner of the stadium to my left, and they sang it to me, but then, technically, I hadn't been singing. I'd been too agreeable during the first half, too nervous during the second, and such a neophyte anyway that I wouldn't burst into song until one more Saturday thence.

15

Europe

We're all going on a European tour,
A European tour,
A European tour.
We're all going on a European tour,
A European tour,
A European tour.
We're all going . . .

On a dismally dreary 23 December at Fratton Park came the first rewritten 'Yellow Submarine' in the challenged life of my eardrums. I thought somebody had just come up with it and had demonstrated a certain puckish cleverness. No, really. As it persisted, I also wondered whether a European tour for Portsmouth meant the UEFA Cup or perhaps the Champions League. No, really. We all go through different childhoods at different stages on different topics, and this would be Premiership childhood, imagining Portsmouth could hold down fourth place as of Sunday night, 13 May 2007.

Back then, who knew for sure? Well, everyone except myself, but on the plus side of my learning curve, I had taken notice of Manchester United and pretty much ruled out winning the league. This showed keen acumen. I'd also gazed at Chelsea and thought second place could prove rather far-fetched. This showed amazing acumen. Europe, however, and all of Europe, seemed freshly possible, even as I felt that old American bafflement from hearing English people saying they're going to Europe when we presume they're already there.

Sitting in the Fratton End for the first time, continuing my sporadic tour of the grand edifice, pressed on the far right side against some sort of faded white corrugated plastic wall, head next to a steel beam, I came under the impression that my beloved team had become, well, good. That's right: my team was good. I'd chosen a club for reasons that included half-hoping to follow the relegation tightrope, and within two months I'd ended up singing about some European tour. I'd planned to monitor the sludgy chase for 17th place and found myself tracking the white-hot run for seventh and fourth. I knew nothing about how or why Pompey had become good, and knew not the football significance of signing Sol Campbell from Arsenal or David James from Manchester City or Kanu from West Bromwich Albion. About Campbell, I knew with about 97 per cent certainty that he'd scored in the 2006 Champions League final against Barcelona; and about James, I knew only that he tried to learn a new word each week, which made me love him pronto; and about Kanu, I knew only that he'd scored a bag of goals in the early season, including a scintillating romp at Middlesbrough. I knew nothing of his status as the most decorated African player, nor of the brilliant old Arsenal song that went:

> *Chim-chiminy, chim-chiminy,*
> *Chim-chim chiroo,*
> *Who needs Anelka when we've got Kanu?*

I knew nothing except that whoever came up with that should be proud if not automatically knighted, and yet nine days shy of New Year's Day, and with head and shoulder pressed up against a steel beam, I'd used my whole throat to sing about a European tour. I did not join in singing to referee Graham Poll, 'You woke up/And then you f—— up,' because I did not yet know that song and the intricate lyrics simply would require more time. But I wanted this European tour thing. It sounded fun especially to an American, to whom a European tour often means jetting across the water, tearing through as many countries as possible, talking too loud on metros, complaining about a paucity of ice, making a general nuisance of oneself and then returning home to settle into a life of quiet desperation.

Under an awful sky so grey it made all other grey blush, through the winter-solstice gloom at this 51 North latitude, where the sun seems to stop by for a second before it whooshes off to somebody else, I sang, and when I sang, I thought Champions League, not UEFA Cup. I'm an American, and I'm conditioned to expect immediate dominance, not the UEFA Cup, which was so mysterious anyway.

English fans, hailing from an older culture, value fourth place or seventh place and know either can bring fabulous new life experiences in places such as Bucharest or Budapest. American sports differ, of course. In the NFL, by far the top American sport, fourth place is last place, although we do give play-off spots to the best four teams that do not finish in first place. We call those 'wild cards', and we used to give out only two of them back when men were real men and you pretty much had to finish first to reach the play-offs, before we started adding more play-offs because more play-offs could give us more money. We had to cope when the number of wild cards grew to four and then six, then we added two more divisions and returned to four wild cards, but we pretty much carried on. By now, because we like to keep things simple, we have eight divisions of four teams each, broken into two four-division conferences. The eight division winners reach the play-offs, as do the two best other teams in each conference. As an American, I sometimes wonder whether the Premiership wouldn't do well by splitting into four five-club divisions, then having four division winners play it off in May. I never suggest this in public, however, so as to avoid the appearance of idiocy.

Having retooled our NFL through the years with only mild angst, we reserved the full dollop of angst for the alterations of baseball during the mid-1990s. That game, of course, remains inscrutable to foreign people, such that an immigration agent at London Waterloo once said to me, 'I've been watching the baseball, late at night, and what is this thing, the RBI?' I explained the RBI (run batted in) as best I could and never felt more useful to my fellow humankind. That game gets credit – especially from itself – as our 'national pastime', so a nostalgic resistance movement cropped up when we introduced these wild cards during the mid-1990s, because they meant profound change. Baseball went from four divisions with four winners, period, everybody else go home and wait for next spring, to six divisions with six winners plus two wild cards. This fiddled with our innate sense of having to earn something by working hard or by dominating others through hard work, intimidation, corporate conglomeration, and intimidation from corporate conglomeration. It also meant excruciating change, for the post-season would contain eight teams rather than four. How would we go on if we allowed second-place people into our grand autumn pageant? Could we adjust? Would it mar our fine balance and turn us soft? We wrangled.

I read that Europeans conducted some of the same discussions when the Champions League inflated its number of clubs, but I missed those discussions in a fortuitous turn of luck, as two such discussions in one lifetime might leave a person either incapacitated or yearning for incapacitation.

We're all going on a European tour ...

We weren't in the first half, when even I could glean that our squad looked a mite comatose. Sheffield United served as the visitor, and I knew only four things about Sheffield United. They almost certainly hailed from Sheffield. They'd just won promotion last spring. They'd enjoyed a four-game upturn, claiming 10 points from a possible 12 to jazz up the match at Fratton. They had a manager, Neil Warnock, whose filter between brain and mouth either had eroded or had proved congenitally thin from the get-go. Impolitic thoughts went straight from the mind into the TV microphone and onto the page, and in the American sportswriting business, we have two words for managers like him: 'thank' and 'you'. These people enlighten us and spare us the strain of trying to interpret what coaches might really mean when they say something cryptic, and apparently Warnock had spared a lot of people the guessing game while exhibiting a mad-scientist strain. I don't know whether he embodied the words of Bill Parcells, the legendary NFL coach who famously said that big-time coaches are not healthy humans. I just know that he did not disappoint after Portsmouth vs Sheffield United, when he said he shouldn't comment on Poll and then said, 'A referee of Graham Poll's standard should be able to spot it when the ball goes out off a forward's ankle.'

His team had gone ahead 1–0 in only the fourth minute. Down below me and my steel beam and my corrugated heavy plastic and to my left, Derek Geary had made one of the best crosses I'd seen in all my days following football closely. Rob Hulse headed it in from the far post. Fratton Park seemed asleep. The sky seemed to contribute.

By half-time, I figured that if my team excelled in the least, it would deduce a way to solve this pugnacious Sheffield United threat. Uncle Harry would fire up the troops with something that makes managers 'geniuses' in American parlance. Well, 48th minute: goal. And 54th minute: goal. And 68th minute: goal. And 78th minute: almost goal. I read that Uncle Harry had calmly tweaked some things, which to me remained unrecognizable but very effective. I'd say we did what good teams do against upstart greenhorns, but I didn't feel qualified to use the word 'we'.

I enjoyed it all immensely. Benjani sent a low cross from the right in the 48th minute into that place often called 'the area', and Sheffield United's Phil Jagielka's attempt to clear it wound up directing it toward the goal, where Robert Kozluk's attempt to clear it from Jagielka's attempt to clear it proved futile and earned him a cruel 'og'.

Matt Taylor's corner in the 54th minute came from just beneath me, and I leapt up and dinged my right shoulder on the steel beam when I saw Campbell rise above the defence with that glorious big head primed to connect. The young males around me never did say a word to me, nor I to them, but some stray voice nearby said that would be Campbell's first Portsmouth goal.

The 2–1 lead made me nervous, which made me surprised, but a virtual replica of the previous goal came in the 68th minute, with Pedro Mendes directing the corner and Noé Pamarot supplying the header. I let out a guttural quasi-roar, proof that fandom can return after two decades of dormancy. Portsmouth had leapt to 32 points, six shy of their entire total from 2005–06 with still the possibility of matching that 38 before New Year's Day, and Parcells must be right.

I say that because here we stood, crooning about a European tour, the drum beating, the bugle gasping, just eight months after surviving by four points with the boost of a 90+3 goal by Pedro Mendes that Bradley Wright-Phillips almost cleared. It might be the one millionth example of sport's maddening narrow passageways. Yet as these capricious moments in games and seasons decide who wins, they also cement legacies that can grow downright eternal. Parcells himself won two Super Bowls, the first with a right mauling but the second when a difficult last-play field-goal attempt from Buffalo's Scott Norwood slid maybe 15 feet wide to the right. Flutter that ball 15 feet to the left, and we'd see Parcells as still excellent but less cemented. Would we label him great? Not as readily.

Well, here came Portsmouth, 17th in 2005–06, roaring toward the Champions League or as consolation the UEFA Cup.

Having shredded Blackburn and Middlesbrough, played well at Chelsea and Tottenham, drawn at Arsenal and shaken Everton like a rag doll, my team was good. In the recent absence of Lomana LuaLua due to injury, I'd even pinpointed a new 'favourite' player. I liked this defender Glen Johnson, even if I felt lost on the vagaries of somebody being 'on loan' from somebody else. I just found this Chelsea loan fast, strong, stalwart, intolerant of shenanigans from the uppity attacks who tried to wreck Fratton Park afternoons. As a grown person of well over 21, I didn't put his poster on my wall or wait for him at his car or anything, but I did rather like watching him play football.

16
Away fan extraordinaire

On a dismally dreary Boxing Day in east London, I managed to sit in the away section and applaud the away team. The process of locating the proper gate at West Ham, presenting the ticket and occupying the away section would fall under the category of mundane for those who emerged from English birth canals. For an American, it's downright nouveau. It laps at the shores of thrilling.

First, I took the Tube. The idea of taking a subway or metro system to the stadium can feel special to an American, even one who has lived in New York. New Yorkers can take the 4, B or D subways to see the baseball New York Yankees or the 7 to see the baseball New York Mets, and those trains lend to the experience a gritty charm and a charming grit. When the left window of the uptown 4 reveals Yankee Stadium shining in the Bronx night, or the outbound 7 turns and pulls up beside Shea in Queens so the whole lit-up construction attacks your eyes, you've grabbed yourself a chunk of magic there. You haven't lived until you've ridden the second car of the 7 subway returning from Shea Stadium toward Manhattan after the Mets have played the Yankees, treating yourself to the ludicrous barbs that ricochet back and forth between the two sets of fans.

Oh, no, wait, never mind, that part's not all that great.

It's better than driving, though, and other than New York, Boston, Chicago or Washington, we just lack stadiums embedded in cities with trains that materialize near the gates. The size of the country prevents such gems, as does our desire to shower money upon automobile and oil companies. If we travel to Boston in the summer and take the T subway to Fenway Park for baseball, we might return home and rave about it for several days and beam over our T ride as if we've authored the Pythagorean theorem.

To hop on a Tube, then, and to ride a bunch of stops to West Ham, then to proceed down Green Street to Upton Park, feels both phenomenally convenient and borderline Captain Cook. Heading down the street, seeing the many signs in Arabic and marvelling at how London became the capital of the world despite its chronic hosting of a cloud convention, I found the sign 'Away Fans' maybe one block shy of the stadium. This diverted me from the clear and direct route to the stadium and sent me down a street of trademark English terraced houses. It felt almost like going into quarantine, as though I could not be with those other people over there lest I cough on them and give them a bug that makes them develop a man crush on Matt Taylor or start chanting, 'Linvoy for England'. I thought about the people living in those houses, how if I lived in one of those houses, I might get a cup of tea and wave at Aston Villa fans going by, or perhaps invite in some people from Sunderland who would've made an exhausting journey and might be tired, or perhaps buy a tape of a large dog and play it and fling open the door just as Arsenal fans happened by.

I figured I'd see much of England there from my window, but I saw nobody on Boxing Day observing the Portsmouth fans, maybe because they realized Uncle Harry once coached West Ham, but probably because they flat did not care.

Down the street, around the bend to the right and up an alley, beside some warehouses and in a concrete, industrial setting that reminded me of northern New Jersey, there stood the away entry gate to Upton Park, amid police officers plus a few police horses. I approached somewhat nervously, slightly wondering if any

West Ham fans might stand by and heckle us or perhaps attempt to slug us. That preposterous inkling stemmed, of course, from the old image of English fans still flickering in the brain, a human organ not very adept at banishing old reputations. Way over in the United States, at parties, at dinners or in casual conversations, it's still very possible to hear Americans label English football fans as truculent pugilists, even after 20 years of initiatives that have made England the model for curbing violence. This misconception is not so surprising, because Americans don't keep much track of other countries, partly because we're self-centred but largely because we're too busy working, which, in our defence, did help us invent such boons as the television, as well as such horrors as the television. Besides, regarding English fans as truculent pugilists enables us to indulge in our national pastime of thinking everybody else is so much more frigging crazy than we are.

Nobody spoke to me at the Upton Park away gate – not even a horse – and on I went into the segregated area, surprised to realize we had our own segregated concession stand and our own segregated toilets. I sat among my people, and felt like thanking them for letting an interloper sit with them at the cost of merely £26. In gloom that seemed to put a 10-pound dumb-bell on the eyelids, we watched as football revealed again its vagaries.

Just seven months prior, Portsmouth had celebrated locating the escape hatch, a discovery that happened barely in time. West Ham, meanwhile, celebrated in Cardiff, where its Hammers played Liverpool in the FA Cup final. West Ham fans, in some cases, probably also celebrated the winning of that FA Cup, what with a 3–2 lead in the 90th minute before Steven Gerrard sent a heat-seeking device from central Swansea into the left side of the goal. They'd also finished ninth in the Premiership, eight places ahead of Portsmouth. They liked their squad and their manager. Some Portsmouth fans still regarded Uncle Harry as Judas.

When we found them on 26 December, they sat 18th in the table, their manager had gone already, they had the stress of new foreign ownership and they seemed rather subdued. Our newly mighty squad further subdued them by pretty much dominating the first 70 minutes and getting two corner-kick-header goals from one Linvoy Primus. I applauded alongside my people, and pretended to comprehend the rarity of a Linvoy Primus brace. The goals came from Pedro Mendes corners at 16 and 38 and became Primus's first and second goals since December 2004, a fact I learned the next day. A 2–0 lead at half-time seemed mostly safe, even after a Teddy Sheringham goal in the 81st minute left the result at 2–1, and even after the referee announced four minutes added time and the woman next to me spoke to me for the first time in the match to say the referee had a serious bias against Portsmouth.

Thereafter, I joined my people in a chant of 'Linvoy! Linvoy! Linvoy!' For this curious new holiday, Boxing Day, I got to watch my blue protagonists win while cheering for an admirable and dreadlocked defender from Forest Gate, London, who had toiled his way up after 127 appearances for Barnet. I rode home just a bit giddy, and figured this must be how English people withstand the gloomy winter at the 51 North latitude. Football. It's really the heart of England.

With three points making a whopping 35, and with zero losses in five matches, Harry Redknapp's Blue Army rolled up north only four days later. On a dismally dreary 30 December 2006 at Bolton, I began jumping up and down uncontrollably in the quarantined upper deck, in just the second minute, when Andy Cole fed a through ball to Taylor, and goalkeeper Jussi Jaaskelainen headed out, and Taylor sidestepped Jaaskelainen and scored for a sudden 1–0 lead after only 72 seconds against a good side that hadn't allowed in a goal in four matches. I found my reaction strangely involuntary. It was official: I had become somewhat the person I had belittled for years, the fan for whom the caprices of games could prompt helpless hopping. Bolton sat fourth in the table, tied in points with third-place Arsenal. Three points would catapult fifth-place Portsmouth over Bolton and, with Arsenal losing at Sheffield United, into third place. As we sang about the European tour within the first five minutes, I began to think of my team as not only good but very good. I began tabulating the points and envisioning the 38, all but adorning my head with a flashing red light of naïvety.

I had ridden the train from the city centre with a Pompey couple from Scotland. Using that surely tiresome refrain 'Now, in the United States . . .', I'd noted that, now, in the United States, we'd never had a situation in which a coach left heaven for hell but then came back to heaven. The woman said England had never had such a situation, either. There in the distance sat the Reebok Stadium, which dates all the way back to 1997 and feels American. It's shiny and with shiny ads. It's suburban and sits next to a giant strip mall with a McDonald's in the middle of the parking lot. The strip mall floods with cars on a Saturday – or at least the last Saturday of the year. Like all strip malls, it's ugly, and it made me wish some other country had invented the strip mall.

Rain fell wrathfully.

Inside, in the spiffy new stadium, the visitors at Bolton occupy an upper deck, completely warded off from the Bolton supporters across a divide and down lower. A visiting fan could venture into the home section only by flying trapeze. I had a beer and my first ever sausage roll, which did not kill me immediately. I chatted with a Pompey fan who'd stayed in the hotel inside the stadium and found it pleasant. In the stadium, a roof protected us from the monsoon that turned parts of the pitch to slop and turned the sky at one point into a sickly shade of green. Some 22,447 of a possible 28,723 showed up, and I had a whole row to my right on which to hop up and down if necessary. One–nil up, Pompey began a thoroughly enjoyable sequence of the best passing I'd yet seen, keeping the ball away from Bolton in skilful midfield sequences. Maybe my squad qualified not only as very good but as excellent.

Then David James whiffed on a Gary Speed corner at 30 minutes, resulting in Abdoulaye Faye's equalizing header, and James made a marvellous save from Kevin Davies at 40 minutes, resulting in Ivan Campo's header for 2–1, and Sol Campbell inadvertently deflected a Davies cross toward the goal at 62 minutes, whereupon James parried and Nicolas Anelka followed up for 3–1. Campo garnished his goal with a festive slide.

Two songs I'd never heard summarized my trip back to Pompey earth.

The Bolton fans serenaded us to the tune of the Village People's 'Go West' with:

> *One-nil, and you f— it up,*
> *One-nil, and you f— it up ...*

And in return, we sang, to 'Guantanamera':

> *Sing when you're winning,*
> *You only sing when you're winning ...*

I loved that song, but I loved especially the sights I beheld after Cole scored beautifully in the 89th minute, but Bolton stayed in front and won 3–2. First, recognizing James's rare error but reminding him he was ours, we chanted him a rendition of 'England's, number one, England's England's number one'. This beat to shards the American habit of booing the home team, with booing long the official civic dialect of Philadelphia, just to name one city.

Then, after a visit to the remarkably plush men's room of the Reebok, I heard noise still going outside, so I walked back out through the tunnel. There, at the top of the visitors' section, with the home section already emptied, a row of young Portsmouth fans remained at the top of the stadium, entertaining themselves and the stewards. Somehow, in the gloom of a latitude above 50, on a day of a deluge that really could've marked the end of time, next to a strip mall, after a defeat, they continued chanting and singing and dancing. A young man of maybe 22, shirtless in the cold, played the drum. It looked like a mix of defiance and buoyancy and maybe even, if I may, celebration that we're alive and we get to watch football on a Saturday in a good country.

From fans who'd allegedly just lost, it trumped anything I'd ever seen.

17

The distinct horror of rail replacement

An inherent guilt bit me occasionally early on, for I had not suffered for my club. I did not cringe as it fell to the third division in 1961, although I did have the ready excuse of not having been alive at the time. I did not wail as it tumbled again to the third division in 1976, and I'd completely missed out on the oblivion that followed, between 1976 and 1980, years that included a dip into the fourth division. Most Americans don't even realize there's a fourth division and many would probably believe that Satan resides there, even if Satan doesn't but Milton Keynes Dons do.

That dreadful sequence in the late 1970s when the club had to raise £25,000 from fans to avert bankruptcy? I missed that.

I'd missed Portsmouth's astonishing ascent from the fourth division all the way to the first within nine years, its qualification for the top flight under manager Alan Ball in 1987. And then, resolutely failing to suffer when the 1987–88 team went smack back down, I missed that year even though that team featured the first American to play in the Premiership, John Kerr.

One season up bled into 15 seasons down, a time I spent not cursing or suffering or yelling at inept referees who couldn't spot handballs, but gallivanting through life watching sports with forced *objectivity*, unaware of either Portsmouth or

Southampton or that Portsmouth functioned eternally below Southampton.

I knew neither the significance of 27 nor the significance of 45. While that kindly man at West Bromwich Albion had explained about that remarkable Sunday in 2005, the one on which West Brom fans cheered for West Brom, but Portsmouth fans also cheered for West Brom so as to relegate Southampton, only lately had I picked up on the fact that the day had curtailed a 27-year top-division residency for Southampton. Only even more lately had I read the fact that these events had placed Portsmouth in a division above Southampton for the first time in 45 years.

No Southampton fan had ever behaved obnoxiously to me during those 45 years, mostly because I had never met any Southampton fan nor even come across any Southampton fan, at least not knowingly. No, I simply hummed along and showed up just in time to inhabit the top 10, sing about a European tour, and think I'm singing about the Champions League while seeing the UEFA Cup as a consolation. Where many a Pompey fan had mastered the art of seething, I had seethed almost too minimally to mention – really, only when the Bolton fans informed me and others that we'd had one-nil and we'd f— it up. I couldn't be sure the Pompey throng should let me wear the sprightly yellow crescent given my wholly unused seethe-o-meter.

Well, on a pristine 1 January 2007 in southern England that soon developed clouds and then rain that turned rapidly biblical, I decided that I had suffered for my squad, for I had endured rail replacement. Rail replacement occurs when there's engineering or construction work on a certain segment of track, and the rail companies provide buses to carry passengers to the stations the train cannot access. There's no discount for rail replacement, and while I'm not qualified to call for a discount given my non-citizen status, I do believe it wouldn't be too much to ask that the bus service provide free cocktails.

Because my ride to and from Fratton Park for the New Year's Day bout with Tottenham Hotspur proved particularly harrowing.

I'd ridden rail replacement before, but for some reason, this would be a more extensive rail replacement, fanning out into the Hampshire countryside, or the real England to American eyes. I saw the greenest green, the adorable villages, the movie-set pubs. I saw a horse in a pasture wearing a nice blanket, the charming houses that looked like Kate Winslet's in a wretched movie I'd just seen. On the sidewalks I noticed a decided lack of vomit as compared with London, which had just wrapped up its annual New Year's Eve bacchanal, an evening somewhat distinguishable from the bacchanal of its other 364 annual nights. The rail replacement reached Haslemere. It made it to Liphook. It accessed Liss. I believe we did see Midhurst. Since I began riding trains from London to Fratton, I'd always wanted to see both Liphook and Liss, just preferably not with the clock going tick-tock, tick-tock, tick-tock at 2.08 p.m. before a 3 p.m. kick-off. The bus, in fact, seemed to stop everywhere, and it seemed to discharge passengers who all seemed to have a clue of their whereabouts, so that soon, on New Year's Day in the countryside heading supposedly for the grit of Fratton Park, I became the only passenger. That's right, I had my very own rail replacement service, just myself in the next-to-last row on the left, staring out of the window of a huge bus, and the driver, way, way up ahead. I thought about asking him if perhaps we'd reached the end of the line and he had not seen me back there and he was in the process of driving the bus to park it maybe up in, say, Woking. But I'm male and from Virginia so I could not bear to ask this question and risk the 'you're an idiot' look on his face when he'd tell me I might be able to make it to Fratton by injury time. Besides, this driver, in his clear and ongoing tryout for Formula One, took the roundabouts with such dispatch that I did not wish to distract him. I merely read my newspapers and learned that we had entered the transfer window and that Sol Campbell might just leave. I felt puzzled and thought, *You mean, he can just leave if he wants? Just up and leave?* Now, in the United States, if he's still under contract, he can leave but only if he asks for a trade and then the club provides the trade.

In a trade, his club would send him to another club in exchange for something from that other club. That might be one player of similar quality. It might be two players of lesser quality. It might be five players who pretty much suck at the professional level. Or it might be one pretty good player plus one hoard of cash. Or it might be one really good player plus 20 free plane tickets to Maui with a venal congressman from the club's district.

(All right, that one's a bit of a stretch.)

Or, commonly, it might be for future 'draft picks', as once each year, each major sport conducts a 'draft' in which clubs choose from the best university and sub-professional players, in reverse order of the previous year's finish, the process going multiple rounds. If the Premiership had held a draft in summer 2007, Watford would've selected first, Manchester United last, whereupon Watford would've had first selection in the 'second round', restarting the whole process. Drafts in the NFL, for instance, last seven rounds and require two days in New York, a highly questionable use of time in New York. One day in October 1989, the NFL's Dallas Cowboys and Minnesota Vikings exchanged a record 18 players and draft picks, with five players and eight future draft picks going to Dallas, and one tremendous player (Herschel Walker) and four draft picks going to Minnesota, and Dallas getting the better of it. The concept of trades gives people a chance to sit in bars and think up prospective trades, or call radio shows and suggest trades so preposterously unrealistic that you believe these people should not have the right to vote. When one day they examine the rubble from the crumbled American empire, they might well note the presence of these prospective-trade suggestions, and they might study what happens when star athletes who request trades do not get them, whereupon they often stay around and speak of the unfairness of life and make the entire city miserable and make us wonder why we bother with this puerile tripe.

Finally, we merged onto the M3, which seemed pointed to Portsmouth, and I felt relieved.

Next, we exited from the M3, and went to Havant, and I felt stressed.

My mobile phone clock showed 2.20 by now, and I saw a little sign indicating Havant Town Football Club, and I wondered if perhaps Havant Town Football Club might have a match beginning at 3, so I could simply go and see that. I saw a card shop called Havant Forgotten, and I just hoped the driver Havant forgotten to go to Fratton Park at some point during the afternoon.

A young woman joined the bus at Havant, which encouraged me that the bus line hadn't ended and the driver hadn't headed off for some bus-storage facility without noticing his lone passenger. I thought of my friend and fellow sportswriter Pat Forde, and how we each often would utilize the phrase 'my ineptitude', and how it's a good feeling in life to embrace this ineptitude, luxuriate in the ineptitude, stop fighting the ineptitude and accept one's own ineptitude for its inevitability. Example: in 1995, the Cleveland Indians made the baseball World Series for the first time in 47 years, so that all the Cleveland fans with tickets and all the Cleveland fans without tickets and all the people pretending to be long-suffering Cleveland fans had converged upon Cleveland and rented hotel rooms. As we'd often collaborate on travel plans, Pat asked me on the day before we left for Cleveland if I'd made a hotel reservation, and I said no, and I asked him, and he said no, and so we spent the Cleveland part of the World Series not in Cleveland but in eastern Ohio way over near Pennsylvania, in a fine and clean hotel we wound up dubbing the 'Squirrel Inn' for its forested rusticity and its threat that on the walk from the car to the building we actually risked being gnawed to death by ravenous squirrels.

Finally, as the bus driver continued on his determined path toward a spot on the McLaren racing team, I could spot the swamps of Fratton, the marooned boats in the mud off to the left. I could see that large white thing on the Portsmouth skyline, and I wondered for the first time as to the identity of that large white thing. There stood the majesty of Fratton Park, its lights shining even in the gathering afternoon darkness and menacing cloud assembly of 2.52 p.m., with some bulbs, as usual, refusing to participate.

That rail-replacement ride, almost interminable, only pre-ceded another rail-replacement ride, the one from the stadium all the way back to Guildford. I began to ponder that if the first, nervous rail-replacement ride might constitute a suffering that would equal, say, one-half of one season in the second division between 1988 and 2003, the rail-replacement ride back to Guild-ford might just entitle me to claim I'd suffered the equivalent of an entire season in the fourth division between 1978 and 1980. This particular rail-replacement bus roared through the side roads of southern England on some sort of different trek from before, and in the dark. It doubled as a refrigerated van in which somebody could've successfully stored raw seafood. I realized my new year had begun riding a moving meat locker, and I thanked lucky stars I don't believe in omens. From my perch on the upper deck, I could see my exhalations. No, really. When an American sports-lover can see his exhalations, he immediately thinks of glorious old NFL films from the 1960s and 1970s, of games in, say, Minneapolis, where players exhaled out through their helmets in big and wonderful bursts of smoke, before we really grew obsessed with comfort and installed in Minneapolis a climate-controlled dome.

This thought of the old NFL often charms us, unless we're on a rail-replacement bus.

Worse, every once in a while, some tree would reach out from the side of the road and smack this bus, causing me brief and damaging heart palpitations for which I'll pay later in life. After about three of those, I started to think maybe I qualified to claim one season of fourth division suffering plus another half-season of third division, perhaps from the early 1980s. The bus seemed to move on for hours, too speedy to be safe but still somehow well south of London. I began to think that for fairness given the exorbitance of train fares, it should drop off each of us at our homes. Finally, we made it to a train, where I overheard some aged Tottenham fans discuss the insouciance of Americans, one even having heard an American mispronounce the 'Petula' in 'Petula Clark', emphasizing the first syllable ('PET-ula') rather than the second (the proper 'pet-U-la'). I quietly had to agree that anyone mispronouncing a concept as great as Petula Clark would seem lost in the world, but mostly I felt relieved that my hands had thawed.

In between those two rail-replacement penances for past sins, Portsmouth did draw 1–1 with Tottenham to reach 36 points. Benjani Mwaruwari had scored with somewhat of a fluke at 29 minutes, the ball ricocheting off Tottenham's Calum Davenport, and one of the greatest names in sports history, Steed Malbranque, had equalized off a pretty Danny Murphy cross at 50. Mr David James himself had preserved the one point with Superman saves from Jermain Defoe and Tom Huddlestone. But mostly, attention hovered on a play when Noé Pamarot inadvertently kicked midfielder Hossam Ghaly and some of Ghaly's teeth flew out. Television replays treated us to slow-motion views of the teeth flying out, and it heartened me to know my country did not stand alone in obsession with violent images.

That idea that you can occupy the southern edge of England during a monsoon while a Zimbabwean athlete scores for the home side, a Belgian-born French athlete scores for the away side, and a French athlete accidentally kicks an Egyptian athlete to cause the ejection of several teeth, astonishes me no end. It almost makes rail replacement joyous but somehow does not, quite.

18

An FA Cup debutant

If you're an American waking for your first FA Cup third round, there's always the chance your new club might play some wee club with the kind of magical name that renders us Americans simply aflutter with romantic thoughts. It could be something like 'Crewe Alexandra', who upset Chelsea in the third round in 1961, or maybe 'Grimsby Town', who beat Middlesbrough in the third round in 1989, or the phenomenal 'Kidderminster Harriers', who beat Birmingham City in the third round in 1994, or 'Shrewsbury Town', over Everton in 2003, third round. Just one January before my debut, Fulham had lost to 'Leyton Orient', and I'd been agog upon arrival reading the tables and finding a team called 'Leyton Orient', a name that suggested some sort of far-flung wonderland and does exist in some far-flung wonderland, called London.

For my first FA Cup third-round viewing experience, I got Wigan.

This did give me a chance to semi-reunite with my fellow Wiganites from the Sunderland match of 2005, and as I saw them in the distance, I noticed they numbered about 99, or maybe 101, or maybe 103 – when I counted I kept getting confused as some people seemed to be returning from the loo.

On a dismally dreary 6 January 2007 on the southern edge of England, Portsmouth played Wigan. Fratton Park filled only to about two-thirds capacity, at 14,336. The Milton End remained so empty that for the first time I could see that its seats spelled out blue letters 'P' and 'F' and 'C'. Huh. I chose a ticket in the North Stand so that I could claim the full dinner set of stands. We got under way in drizzle. Fratton Park seemed beset with a large helping of ennui. The match felt sloppy, whether it was or wasn't. It seemed to occur in a lower gear. There seemed no urgency from the players, really. I couldn't blame the players for fatigue after that Christmastime schedule which had worn out even myself and forced me into questionable eating habits that led to the predestined sausage roll.

Now, if I grasped this correctly, it seemed that the FA Cup third round had engendered romanticizing through the years, but that the romance had then begun to ebb due to the growing presence of, well, money, which has been known to ebb some romanticizing on this planet. Indeed, the four Goliath clubs had won every single FA Cup since 1995, such that it seems downright misprinted when you look at the list and see that Wimbledon won in 1988. Money changes everything, as sang the Brains and, in remake, Cyndi Lauper. Why, just look at New Year's Day in the United States. We used to spend it wondrously inert and watching university football teams play in 'bowl games', neutral-site prizes for good and great regular seasons. The day brimmed with wonder, and the games had storybook names like the Cotton Bowl, the Rose Bowl, the Orange Bowl, the Sugar Bowl, each of which would invite two excellent teams to their games. I know this all sounds weird and maybe even hallucinogen-induced, but we think it normal and even downright poetic. Sometimes one of these bowls would boast the top game featuring the unbeaten teams, sometimes another. Then they learned they could make a lot of money by taking the top game and moving it to another date, say, 3 January or 4 January or even 8 January, where it could stand alone free of viewing competition. (Have you ever heard of a country, say, shifting the time-honoured starting times of a pastime?) New Year's Day went – sigh – from plum to precursor. It has just about flatlined.

Yet on 4 January 2006, for example, 35 million Americans, more than one-ninth of the national population, tuned in to watch the University of Southern California play the University of Texas.

It's a given and a cliché and often a sigh that money keeps blurring the traditions on us, but for me, I'd missed the FA Cup past, so the FA Cup present felt fresh. Enthralled as this day began, I took a sheet of paper like a child again and made myself a chart of the 32 matches slated for the weekend, and I found the concepts pretty darned romantic, what with Chelsea playing Macclesfield Town and so on. But there's something else about sporting romance: once you start labelling something romantic and considering it romantic and talking about how romantic it can be, you're automatically straining, and in that it loses its romance.

There's a country I can think of which stages the NFL draft each April, the process going on for two days, with anyone still keeping track by the seventh round probably in need of some sort of electric-shock therapy. This draft long had a certain faraway mystical quality as a peek at the future, often instilling hope in the hopeless. I adored it as a child. It stoked a curiosity. Then the curiosity became a marketable concept and soon we drowned this draft in discussion. By now we spend weeks in springtime projecting the potential picks in the draft. Then, on a Saturday in April, we hold the draft, and it's televised nationally, replete with analysis about every single player drafted or not drafted or drafted too late. We learn of his speed, his power, his desire – just about everything but his pharmaceutical cycles. We learn how much money he'll expect, yawn, and how much of that might be in signing bonuses, double-yawn. Certain high-profile prospective picks attend the draft, and that gives us the spectre of a player pegged as a high-profile prospective pick but then not chosen for an hour or two in the draft, thereby sitting idly for hours on national TV being not picked. As live TV goes, it's ... well, it's live TV. Fans attend this draft and sit in the draft audience. Fans, especially from Oakland, dress up elaborately, with face paint and costumes. Yes, they're voting age – double, even. And in a case so well known in the United States that it's common cultural literacy by now, the fans from Philadelphia once booed Philadelphia's selection, a quarterback named Donovan McNabb, because they wanted somebody else.

No, really.

As the draft drones on all Saturday, its steep analyses begin to sound roughly like science – or, help us, business. Speaking of business, Chelsea defeated Macclesfield Town 6–1.

At Fratton Park, things proved much more taut, as the teams slogged away to a 0–0 half-time, and sometime early in that second half, I began to have my first ever conversation at a Portsmouth game with a person next to me, an affable middle-aged woman named Mary. We began with the weather, which had brightened somewhat. Within moments, I feared I had begun to disrupt Mary's viewing experience as I repeatedly asked questions about Pompey while her husband watched from her other side. Even though I'd half-figured this already, she kindly explained to me that the term 'scummers' applied to Southampton players, Southampton managers and Southampton fans, and she did not say this but I reckoned also Southampton trainers, masseurs, water personnel, residents and the distant family members of Southampton residents. She spoke of this term 'scummers' with such a detached bemusement that I felt sure she never used it in daily life even as she loved her Pompey and felt gratified to have taken the £2,000 gamble on season tickets way back in Championship days. She sounded almost like an excellent tour guide, explaining that many people in this area use the term 'scummers' while I imagined listening with a set of earphones to be returned at the exit.

As an American, it seemed to me rather dour that Portsmouth did not play Southampton every year, so I asked Mary if it weren't a shame that Portsmouth and Southampton don't play each other unless they're in the same league, which has seldom happened, or unless they're drawn together in the FA Cup or League Cup. I'm raised on knowing that the NFL New York Giants will play the Philadelphia Eagles twice per year (once in each stadium), and that the baseball New York Yankees will play the Boston Red Sox 18 times per year (which is too many for the national health), and that, in bygone days, the NFL San Francisco 49ers would play the Los Angeles Rams twice per year, which had great meaning until the Rams picked up and moved to St Louis. With the universities, we can know which month we occupy simply by which rivalries appear. I know it's the second Saturday in October without looking if the University of Texas plays the University of Oklahoma in football, and that it's early December when the University of Southern California (USC) plays the University of California at Los Angeles (UCLA) in football, and that winter solstice is coming in a minute or just now arrived when the University of Kentucky plays the University of Louisville in basketball. There'll come a few Saturdays in late November when all across the football land, fans will flock to college stadiums to indulge in intra-state or neighbouring-state contempt in a gorgeous national symphony of hatred. There'll be Alabama vs Auburn, Michigan vs Ohio State, Florida vs Florida State, Louisiana State vs Arkansas, Clemson vs South Carolina, Georgia vs Georgia Tech, Texas vs Texas A&M, Nebraska vs Colorado, Oregon vs Oregon State, Harvard vs Yale. The best of all of them would be the December confluence of Army (United States Military Academy) vs Navy (United States Naval Academy), a rivalry so meaningful that Navy players have 'Beat Army' chiselled into the barbells in their weights room, yet so touching that it concludes every year with both teams massing as one on the field and singing each other's school song, together.

Standing on that field and seeing this as a sportswriter in 2004, I couldn't help it, and I grew teary-eyed, which just goes to show how moved we can become when we briefly overcome the other side's unmistakable vileness.

Mary answered that, no, it would be a terrible idea to have Portsmouth play Southampton every year, and that she hoped Southampton would remain in the Championship, even as it had climbed to fourth at the time, flirting with promotion. I could hear in her words and her voice that this had nothing to do with wishing ill and damnation and cholera upon Southampton. To understand this, she said, I'd have to have seen the last time Portsmouth played Southampton, which would've been April of 2005, a day that found the South Coast Derby at a pitched pitch because Uncle Harry returned to Fratton Park as the manager of the ninth concentric circle of Hell. I said I'd like to have seen such a thing, and she cautioned me in a motherly way that I would not have liked to have seen such a thing. She told tales of riot police and bad vibes and traffic hassles due to the riot police and the bad vibes. I hadn't even known that Portsmouth had played Southampton in the FA Cup itself in 2004, or that Southampton had won with a Peter Crouch penalty, or that Peter Crouch once had played for Portsmouth. I knew Peter Crouch only as the Liverpool player who scored a World Cup goal by yanking himself upward using the dreadlocks of Trinidad & Tobago's Brent Sancho just as I had begun to wonder how England might respond the next day should its national team draw 0–0 with Trinidad & Tobago in a World Cup. Thank goodness Brent Sancho wears dreadlocks.

Mary, by now a gem in my book, also told of another FA Cup match, a quarter-final at Fratton Park in 2004 won 5–1 by Arsenal. She edified me with the common knowledge that Thierry Henry had become a Fratton Park favourite that day because he admired the home support and concluded by donning a Portsmouth shirt. She said he'd missed two goal chances and that the Fratton End had responded with a rendition of 'Henry is a Pompey Fan'. She said Portsmouth fans had remained raucous to the end, and while I'd been amazed at Bolton when that row of devotees played drums and danced after the gloomy fact of 3–2 against, it floored me that a group could sustain support at 5–0 against, dreaming of 5–1, singing about winning 6–5.

I felt actually proud.

As we engaged in the taboo of chatter, Portsmouth seemed bound for a 1–0 win and a place in the fourth round. Andy Cole had gathered a cross from Sean Davis and scored in the 64th minute. Then, shockingly, in the 83rd minute, Wigan's Lee McCulloch scored to equalize, and Wigan players exulted before the scarcely populated section of some of the hardiest fans extant, Wiganites who'd travel clear to Fratton for an FA Cup third-rounder.

I briefly wondered what happens when teams draw in the FA Cup, and then I remembered, but just as I mulled a grand return to Wigan, walking past the strip malls near the stadium and feeling proud of such ambitious American architecture, Pompey utterly willed itself a goal. My man Glen Johnson – warrior! – sent a seeing-eye cross from the far right to Kanu, and Kanu headed in the winner. In injury time. To raucous cheers. And a whistle. And the fourth round.

19

Cheering for a toilet-seat thief

On a globally warmed Al Gore January Saturday, the 20th, with blue skies and cotton-ball clouds, on the 1 p.m. train 88 minutes from London Waterloo to Fratton, as men outside the window struck golf balls in shaggy fields or on actual courses, I relished the day. Then I dug into my usual pile of newspapers and came upon seven dreadful paragraphs.

They heckled me in unsparing succession from page 7 of the sports section of the *Guardian*. No, the writer hadn't done a dreadful job; he simply had dreadful realities to report.

Keeping score, I'd rate paragraphs No. 1 through 5 of Jeremy Wilson's dispatch as run-of-the-mill dreadful, with paragraph No. 6 very dreadful and paragraph No. 7 dreadful in its preposterousness.

Paragraphs No. 1 through 5:

> Fratton Park might be the Premiership's most outdated ground but it is also among the most intimidating, and no one at Portsmouth is pretending that Ben Thatcher can expect anything other than a torrid 90 minutes when he faces Pedro Mendes this afternoon for the first time since knocking him unconscious while playing for Manchester City last August.
>
> 'He's going to get stick, he's going to get grief – it's obvious,' said the Portsmouth manager, Harry Redknapp.

Photographed in his natural habitat, the bright-red ecosystem of South West train service, here's one of the most awesome creatures in the entire animal kingdom, capable of unusual keenness, rarefied astuteness and impromptu haiku.

▲ It's difficult to believe that any human being could make saves like this and also write lucid columns in the *Observer*. (Topfoto/ProSport)

As referee Graham Poll attempts to explain to three Pompey players how on earth he disallowed Niko Kranjcar's goal that would've beaten Arsenal and sent Portsmouth into Europe, he appears to point to one ear, perhaps to say, 'I sort of just play it by ear'. (Getty)

Yeah, us too. (Getty)

▼ Note the palatial grandeur of Fratton Park in this view towards the Fratton End, which even when empty bears the echoes of lyrical din and poetic profanity. (Getty)

Matt Taylor celebrates after a left-foot strike that flew 45 yards and descended into the goal on 9 December 2006, when anyone sitting only five rows behind the goal became lucky to be alive. (Getty)

▼ Upon the handsome head of Tim Howard, the American who keeps goal for Everton, note the hairlessness that allows a bit of extra room for astonishing 45-yard goals to dive down just behind him. (Getty)

▲ At the moment of this unassuming little scene, Rio Ferdinand's own goal has just rolled in and become the best own goal in the lifetime of one fan. (Getty)

Dignity, nobility and honest effort or, in other words, Linvoy Primus, not that fans fall in love or anything. (Getty)

Lomana LuaLua performs the trademark goal celebration that first endeared him to an American, as well as proving again that it's very easy to impress an American. (Rex)

▶ Uncle Harry, benevolent soul, tries to sort out a way to continue bringing us the victory we so desperately crave. (Getty)

▼ Ben Thatcher, newly of Charlton, nears the side-line at Fratton Park on the lousy day of 20 January 2007, and receives the kind of much-deserved reception that makes managers go all gushy over what their players must endure. (Getty)

Uncle Harry joins those gathering round the unconscious Pedro Mendes after a 'tackle' that earned a suspension but inarguably warranted deportation to a reopened Alcatraz. (Getty)

▶ For a tourist watching English football for the first time, six months before relocating, Wayne Rooney was ever so kind enough to score at Newcastle, then charge over into the corner and yell, 'F**ing beauty,' thereby giving a newcomer a most hospitable indoctrination. (Getty)

The view from the Fratton End gives an indication of an intimacy ideal for spotting, say, the severity of a blown call by Graham Poll. (Rex)

▼ Here stands Sol Campbell, mighty defender, capable of single-handedly assuaging public fears and thwarting uppity offences as they attempt to sour the Fratton mood, thus earning the fickle love of the new fanatic. (Rex)

▲ By the end of the season, I had demonstrated my dazzling newfound aptitude by recognizing that Portsmouth's newfound success had much to do with these two particular players. (Rex)

Evoking the Taj Mahal, the Egyptian Pyramids or the Eiffel Tower, the JJB Stadium can draw in a tourist for a Premiership debut. (Rex)

Uncle Harry and Paul Jewell, manager of Wigan, shown here beneath the fitting fog and deathless gloom of JJB Stadium in February. Wigan found a way to defeat Portsmouth 1–0. (Getty)

Riot police work a Portsmouth–Southampton match, back when they used to have Portsmouth–Southampton matches, a scene I never beheld in my Johnny Come Lately season of top-10 merriment. (Getty)

'It doesn't matter what I say or anybody else says, it's not going to make any difference. The fans will be on him.'

Thatcher's date with Mendes has arrived three weeks earlier than he might have expected because of his move to Charlton, although he has tried to soften the likely backlash by admitting he is ashamed. He wrote to Mendes at the time to apologise for his forearm smash and, with a 15-match suspended ban still hanging over him, hopes his £500,000 move to The Valley can provide a fresh start.

'This has happened but things have moved on and there is no bad feeling towards the player,' Mendes said. 'If he comes to shake my hand then I will do so.'

Redknapp is of a similar mind and says his squad do not want revenge. 'I've never spoken to the players about what happened,' he said. 'It's history. We haven't got the type of players who will think about getting him back for what he did.'

Well, great.

In my daily study of my new league, I'd somehow missed Thatcher's relocation from Manchester City to Charlton, even while I had hoped for his relocation to Vladivostok. Thus I had boarded the train at Waterloo unaware I'd be paying to see somebody who ought not to be in the league for at least another year after battering Pedro Mendes. How depressing. What a chore, being a fan. You're just trying to get away and have a good day, and you have to pay money to see somebody who did something depressingly creepy. Many times, you have to cheer him, as would Charlton fans that day.

Oh, yes, the old cheering-the-indefensible routine. It's rife in sport and probably always has been. My thoughts turned to University of Nebraska fans, who hail from the middle of the United States, from the heartland, anointed the American breadbasket of law and order and decency. They fill an American-football stadium that seats 85,000 people, and they have treated it to a record 297 consecutive sell-outs, dating to 1962. Their 1995 team ranks absolutely among the best in our history of grafting glorious big-business sleaze onto our beloved university system. Nebraska won all 12 of its games and annihilated previously unbeaten Florida 62–24 in the Fiesta Bowl for the national championship.

It also saw six of its 100-odd players receive special attention from the police, including a gifted running back who got mad at his girlfriend and dragged her down a stairwell by her hair. It remains the textbook case of fan bewilderment because of its stark contrasts. In one vein, you had a fan base stockpiled with citizens who preach toughness on crime, a no-nonsense, conservative group that often enters voting booths with law and order among its thoughts. In another vein, you had a typical fan base that adores, well, winning, and will espouse a benevolent liberalism on one condition. It will believe deeply in its heart in the rehabilitation potential of misguided young men so long as these men can gain 100 yards on a Saturday and help us beat those bastards from Oklahoma or Colorado or Missouri.

So when the university first dismissed the player, then reinstated him in the subsequent month, many Nebraska fans felt uncomfortable, but others applauded in the stadium. Then the applause increased as the victory total increased. It reached din level at the championship game, in which the player excelled. Nebraska's conservative, widely admired coach handled things abominably, making bizarre comments about the players such as, 'It's not as though Lawrence is an angry young man all the time or a threat to society. But there are occasions every four to five months when he becomes a little bit explosive.' Yet the citizens still adored the coach because he'd hooked them up to the methadone of victory, so after he retired two years later, his district elected him to Congress in a landslide. There's a chance they elected him because they noticed his impropriety and deemed Congress the best place for him, but that chance is probably remote.

As Charlton hobbled into Fratton sitting 19th in the Premiership with 16 points, with Portsmouth sixth at 37 points, we'd have to see Ben Thatcher play football, but I knew full well the aftermath might bring an added wretchedness. If England were anything like the United States, the aftermath might subject us to a manager moaning on about what his player had 'been through', or if not moaning, then expressing some sort of quasimanly respect for how the player had 'handled' his adverse situation.

There's a word for that: ugh.

Now, if you ask a reasonable human, which means not a coach or manager, most would agree there's some justice in a player getting stick or grief for having, just for example, gratuitously attacked a player on the opposing team. Most would agree the stick and grief rate doubly justified if the offender happened to receive, say, a paltry penalty. Further, a great many would agree that fans put up with enough crud without having to listen to some craven manager moan about the player enduring 'adversity' when the 'adversity' would fall under the heading of 'self-created'.

I should've known it'd be an accursed day when I forgot to consider the predictable Saturday Tube delays, and the electronic Tube board that showed the 'Sorry Not In Service' line coming in eight minutes, then seven minutes, then three minutes (as apparently it had speeded up).

Still, Mr Wilson, the reporter, had not finished his work, bless him.

Paragraph No. 6 went like this:

> Portsmouth's Lomana LuaLua was arrested in the early hours yesterday on suspicion of causing actual bodily harm. Police were called to an address at the Port Solent residential development at 1.50 a.m. and the 26-year-old

forward was detained. He spent the night at the city's central police station, where he remained yesterday. It is the second time he has been arrested after incidents at Port Solent – he was held in October after a dispute involving his fiancée but was released without charge after 17 hours, the delay caused by difficulties in finding a translator for her. He has not played for six weeks because of a thigh injury but attended training on Thursday. Portsmouth have refused to comment.

Yes, the road from objectivity back to fandom lies pockmarked with many a garish sight. You might adopt a favourite player. You might like his biography, his will, his gymnastic capability, his recovery from malaria even if the malaria resulted from forgetting medication. Then you might see that the police detained him once, but you might invoke the old saw 'innocent until proven guilty'. Then you might see that the police have detained him for a second time, whereupon it becomes possible to grow squeamish and feel conflicted, when feeling conflicted is not fun and fun would seem high among the reasons to follow this stuff, even if we'd have no idea what else to do with our time otherwise.

That's a lot to digest on a Saturday at 1.30 in the afternoon.

Yet Mr Wilson, perhaps suffering from autocratic editors, had more to do, still. Paragraph No. 7 would be one of those that come along only occasionally and force the reader to look upward from the publication and stare out of the window in an attempt at comprehension.

Paragraph No. 7:

It also has emerged that Pompey's Glen Johnson was fined £80 for trying to steal bathroom fittings from a B&Q store on Wednesday. The full-back, on loan from Chelsea, and Millwall's striker Ben May were seen putting a toilet

seat into a box with a cheaper price tag and then hiding
a set of taps beneath a sink unit they were paying for.
Both players were issued fixed-penalty notices.

Most people would agree as to the extraordinariness of that
paragraph.

Even after seven lousy paragraphs, that sort of seventh paragraph can leave one begging for an eighth, but Mr Wilson ran
out of room, so I went flinging into my other newspapers. I
wondered as to Johnson's weekly salary. Reports had it at
£30,000. I wondered whether the Dartford B&Q possessed
CCTV equipment, which could deepen the profundity of the
stupidity. It did possess CCTV equipment. I wondered how the
store discovered this toilet-seat thievery by a guy making
£30,000 per week. An employee told reporters, 'We all recog-
nised Johnson. No one could quite believe that a bloke like him,
with all that money, would be moronic enough to nick a toilet
seat. They were spotted by one of our security guards, a chap of
74, and cops arrived as they were trying to leave.' The employee
indicated that the two nitwits grinned and giggled when questioned by authorities.

In one swoop, I'd read that my first favourite player might've
endangered his partner, and I'd read that my second favourite
player had attempted to steal a toilet seat by placing it in the
box of a cheaper toilet seat. The last residue of my old anti-fan
snobbery turned to dust and yielded to a fresh respect for this
durable subspecies the fanatic, who persists despite being put
upon and overcharged and aware that often he has placed his
fervent and heartfelt hopes in the hands of a bunch of lunkheads
(or worse).

It's not an easy plight, and it doesn't seem to get any easier
across time. I figure you must try to recover from these things. I
decided it could prove mildly fascinating to watch somebody
play after getting caught trying to steal a toilet seat. Not knowing
much, I inaccurately considered him too marginal to incur

heckling at away matches, but I thought it might affect his play just to know that people knew he had been caught trying to steal a toilet seat.

That, and I had to fumble around for a new favourite Portsmouth player. I thought straight away about David James, who opined with amazing thoughtfulness in his *Observer* columns, and how even though we have our share of keen athletes who know about more than themselves, I doubt we have his equal. Still, I sort of wanted a non-goalkeeper even while having nothing against the goalkeeping profession which does beat, for example, congressman. I settled quickly upon Sol Campbell. I decided that this fearsome giant provides an important public service. When some opposing attack tries to depress the Pompey public with some sort of bid at a goal, Campbell often cleans it up by himself. His public role entails warding off misery or defusing worry. It's important in the life of a village.

The only potential caveat I knew about Sol Campbell was that as an Arsenal player he once, flustered, drove away from the stadium at half-time after a sub-par performance. I decided that qualified as one of those things a fan could strain to forgive, especially if there's a smidgen of honour in his disgust with himself, or if by leaving early he beat heavy traffic and left a smaller carbon footprint upon the earth.

20

'Have we just . . .'

Mildly woozy, I turned up in the Fratton End at about 2.58 p.m., ready to cheer my squad against Charlton but feeling embryonic as a fanatic. Having spent decades in objective and moralistic press boxes, I had not cultivated the hard shell of rationalization that adorns many fanatics and helps them through such fanatic crises.

Many fans could rationalize that of the Portsmouth players on the pitch that day, almost all had refrained from acts vile or base during the preceding week, with fully ten neither striking a fiancée (vile, if true) nor attempting to stash a more expensive toilet seat in the box of a less expensive toilet seat (base, and true). Other fans would react otherwise. The wise, grizzled, weather-worn fans of the ancient nation of England, long since inured to the lunacy of the world, might read about LuaLua and Johnson and roll their eyes or sigh. The green, hopeful, starry-eyed sorts from the young nation of the United States, trailing by centuries in the development of a clue, might disbelieve the LuaLua part – he's an avowed Christian, he'd never do that – while writing off the Johnson bit using the oily PR sentence 'He made a mistake.'

Still other fans, like many I'd seen in my homeland, might think Johnson entitled to the odd toilet seat. They might say that so long as he stifles the attack of the foul, horrendous opposition with regularity and ferocity, B&Q would be wrong to halt him

139

on his way out of the store. They would think that if, in fact, his house counted among those rare mansions that require maybe 10 or 15 toilet seats, B&Q ought to allow him to nick an expensive toilet seat each week for the entire winter, or at least until he had enough toilet seats to suffice. These fans believe that B&Q should stage a weekly Glen Johnson Larceny Day, in which Johnson would be allowed to steal at least one bathroom accessory while the security guard went out for tea or set up the table at which Johnson could sign post-purloin autographs, holding a pen in his writing hand and an exquisite spigot in the other. In fact, these very thought patterns might well include the following: *B&Q is at fault here. Its draconian insistence that people not steal its goods without paying for them has disrupted the player's concentration and thus impinged upon our squad's preparation for Saturday. Let's boycott f——ing B&Q.*

Still other fans would reserve a dose of resentment for Mr Wilson, the reporter, or for other reporters. They might accuse them of 'stirring up' stuff which has impinged upon the squad's preparation for Saturday. I have seen such people. I have known such people. I have *dined with* such people. These people raise children and hold down jobs and reserve the right to vote, and we continue to let them. Still others would wonder why the police didn't just ring up Uncle Harry and let him come over and take care of it. A subgroup within that group would delineate morally: the police definitely should ring up Uncle Harry if the team's going well, but definitely should continue to do their jobs as prescribed by law if relegation seems imminent or if Uncle Harry's substitution pattern has seemed especially inept in recent months, because in that case, police integrity might hasten the sacking of Uncle Harry.

There's still another crowd that tacitly assigns LuaLua's fiancée some blame, but those macabre people probably con-stitute too wee a minority to let ruin your day, with many of them seeking lowbrow professions like American-football coach or United States congressman.

I, meanwhile, still took the time to cringe, my inexperience a naïve and glaring deterrent to my enjoyment.

I winced a bit through the Portsmouth–Charlton first half, listening for creative stick directed at Thatcher while watching for scientific evidence: does a failed attempt to pilfer a high-end toilet seat on a Wednesday detract from the capacity to play high-end defence on the following Saturday?

The Thatcher stick proved durable yet insufficient. It included both eloquence and beautiful ineloquence. The eloquence came from a sole burly man about five rows down from myself, who kept yelling, 'You're a disgrace, Thatcher!' This, I found oddly civilized and inarguable of content. The ineloquence came from all around and specialized in the kind of language you might call modern-day Tony Soprano. Yes, I occupied the rowdy Fratton End, the stand I'd chosen after months of sampling, but I occupied the less-rowdy edge of the rowdy Fratton End, on the left, halfway up, behind the goal but off to the left of the goalkeeper's left shoulder, rather than the middle, all the way up and directly behind the goal, which teemed with hard-boots who had endured a second-tier year or 20 and who thought up all the best stuff. I could decipher their words only seldom. I did make out 'bastard' one time. Around myself, the 'f——'s-sake'-o-meter reached seven, unprecedented in my lifetime. I often heard that word almost unused in American dialect: 'rubbish'.

At one point midway through the first half, Thatcher himself suddenly alighted in the corner of the pitch 20 rows down from myself, and I do know I felt a hot flash of contempt I did not know I had in me. Otherwise, I wished him no ill save for a ceremonial removal from the premises plus a suspension of roughly two seasons.

In between the hot flashes and the vain attempts to understand the dialect of the hard-boots, I monitored the essential scientific question of the afternoon. I had to surmise that attempted toilet-seat larceny does detract from performance, for I detected an unusual assortment of botched possessions, useless passes and feckless defence from shirt No. 4 on the Pompey side. Whether Johnson actually committed more botches and uselessness and fecklessness than usual, or whether I simply noticed all of the above out of micro-studying or perhaps even mild resentment, would remain the last, lingering scientific question of the misspent afternoon.

The first half transpired without a scintilla of intrigue, with sixth-place Portsmouth (37 points) and troubled 19th-place Charlton (16 points) combining for zero goals and seemingly half-empty effort. Just then, the public-address announcer reminded us that if we all looked down the pitch at the giant video screen, we could re-watch the 'highlights' of the first half, and even as a know-nothing, I wondered whether some wise guy had infiltrated the public-address area, perhaps holding hostages, in order to make wisecracks such as 'highlights'. They showed the highlights, which contained no highlights. Still, with Charlton already having suffered through 15 losses and one managerial change and this only January, and with Charlton sitting 0–1–10 away or, in American parlance, 0–10–1 away – zero wins, 10 losses, one draw – I still reckoned three points imminent.

Then the second half insisted on occurring and that proved a merciless insistence, as the match droned on goalless and I began to think the sure three points might morph into the dreaded one point. Eventually we all reached the 79th minute, when suddenly, at the other end, far from my view, a ball seemed to loop into the net that James had fought gamely to defend. Charlton players seemed to run over into the corner and carry on some rare exultance together. Charlton fans, just behind the Charlton players, seemed to jump up and down. A boy two rows in front of me, listening on the radio, turned around and smirked and explained to his father that Amdy Faye had scored the goal for Charlton. I wondered what the boy might have against Faye, and learned later that the boy meant only disappointment in that Faye once had played for Portsmouth, plus bewilderment in that Faye didn't tend to score goals and that in fact Faye had *never* scored a goal in England. This goal sort of caromed off his shin, and Uncle Harry would sneer, 'They fluked a goal through Faye.'

And what enabled this fluky shin goal? The answer would be a misdirected defensive header from one Glen Johnson, who after this mistake would have to go home to some second-rate toilet seat.

The final 14 minutes of the match, then, featured one excellent Portsmouth chance in front of our end – Charlton goalkeeper Scott Carson hauled himself to the left to save Andy Cole's promising strike – and the sight of Charlton, stalling. At any chance, any stoppage in play, Charlton's players would stall for, by my estimation, stints of five minutes or 10 minutes. Before one throw-in, I felt certain that 20 minutes had passed. I began to develop completely irrational contempt for the hapless bald linesman. Thatcher remained on the pitch, offending all known human sensibilities, and the agony waned into added time and then clunked with the final whistle, whereupon Charlton's red patch of away fans jumped up and down with delight.

In just that moment, I felt a middling envy of those people over there on that other side. Because I had fallen for my club the previous spring as it sailed the wacky seas of relegation avoidance, I knew ever so slightly the seafaring thrill of relegation avoidance. My club had turned out to be this titanic Champions League powerhouse – slight cough – for which losing to the likes of Charlton felt particularly stinging and unwelcome, while these Charlton fans had gone along, ridden trains or buses or cars, and kept track of their team just hoping to squeeze a modicum of glee out of the process. They had come to Portsmouth expecting little, and they had come out of it with a 1–0 win that instilled hope. I had gone to Portsmouth expecting three points, and I had come out of it with a chilling loss, the wretched memory of watching Ben Lucifer for a day, plus the realization that my favourite two players included an alleged fiancée-abuser and a bona fide toilet-seat thief who even lacked the essential toilet-seat-thief skills, such as common sense.

'Have we just lost to Charlton?' said the man who sat three seats to my left for that day and for the rest of the season.

It seemed that 'we' had, and it seemed the 19,567 of us had witnessed Charlton's first away win in 14 months and 25 days, the previous one also at Fratton Park.

Uncle Harry chimed in with, 'This was our worst performance of the season.'

This, all told, would be one of the things you forget when you're a sportswriter: that the people in the seats around you, or outside the press-box windows, have paid money, and they have cared, if even lightly, and they have used up one of only 52 Saturdays granted per year, and for all that risk, they still might undergo a visual abomination. At least when a sportswriter witnesses an abomination, he or she has received a salary, however insufficient to our towering societal importance that places us in the same stratum with heart surgeons and Nelson Mandela.

The thing you never forget as a sportswriter, however, would be the capacity of managers to utter inanities they actually deem earnest. So here it came, later that night, in my ill-advised light reading on the match, an assortment of comments from the popular and nice Alan Pardew, new manager, Charlton.

'We all do silly things in our lives that we regret and Ben wants to forget that one.'

(Yes, from time to time we all knock other people unconscious during sporting events.)

'He has apologized for it and today he was brilliant.'

(Oh, when does the Ben Thatcher honorary parade start?)

'I just whispered in his ear . . .'

(Anyone have an airsickness bag?)

144

'. . . that with what he had to endure he gave a thoroughly professional performance.'

(Yeah, let's drag out the violins for the woeful duress one must face after one causes somebody a seizure and oxygen treatment and a night in hospital.)

As lame manager pronouncements of faux valour go, these, I guess, count among the moderately lame. They're lame, but I've heard lamer. Managers, in the end, must unify their clubs, so they can't go around saying such truisms as, 'Well, of course he got stick, deservedly, after he damaged a player from the home squad.' Further, managers often must uphold some sort of male credo, wherein we all reserve the right to attempt to crash stupidly into somebody, and then to turn around and cry victim, having our bravery extolled after those really mean people yelled at us for attempting to maul the pure living hell out of somebody else just five months prior. In a sociological sense, all of this might even help to explain why, of the two known genders, one has caused the world immeasurably greater destruction.

21

New Trafford

On a dismally dreary and cold January Saturday in Manchester, 71,137 people swept from the city train line toward a gigantic stadium. We passed the 'Love United Hate Glazer' decals on the lamp posts. We crossed over a bridge. We passed various vendors selling either clothing items or the kind of food that heightens the earnings potential of cardiologists.

These multitudes felt, of course, American. This could've been Giants Stadium in New Jersey, walking en masse with 80,242 to see the NFL New York Giants or the New York Jets. It could've been Invesco Field in Denver, home to 76,125 of the NFL's most ardent fans, except that I couldn't spot any snow-capped Rocky Mountains. Or it might've been Cleveland Stadium, which seats 73,200, except that Manchester United had won at least one title during the most recent 43 years.

More so, this Premiership walk resembled American college football. The American South alone includes American-football stadiums at the Auburn University in Alabama (87,451), the University of Alabama (92,138), Louisiana State University (92,400), the University of Florida (90,716), the University of Georgia (82,122), the hugest of them all the University of Tennessee (104,079), and the home of the country's best fans, those of the University of South Carolina (80,250), where losses couldn't quell enthusiasm even during the entire, futile 20th century. Many of these places absolutely hate many of these other places, which makes for a gorgeous symphony of hatred we call the 'Southeastern Conference', where the need to keep up with those bastards across the state – or in the next state – has spawned a lavish legacy of the most colourful cheating, most of it by regular churchgoers.

We're a really weird country.

These and other American stadiums share a stark similarity with the Old Trafford types who graced the FA Cup fourth-rounder between Manchester United and Portsmouth: on many occasions, these people go to the stadiums 99-per-cent certain of the outcomes. This holds true in college football, where early in the season big universities invite a few opponents they know they can defeat, whereupon the smaller university gets a nice pay cheque in appreciation for its contribution to the public flogging for, without an opponent, the bigger university will have opposed only air, usually a minuscule distinction from what actually transpired. Among professional sports, the imbalance between big clubs such as Manchester United and smaller clubs such as Portsmouth holds truest in baseball, where certain clubs (like the New York Yankees) play in metropolitan areas with a lot of TV sets, thus enabling astronomical cable deals for the broadcast of their games, while certain clubs (Kansas City) play in the proximity of fewer TV sets. We begin each season knowing certain poorer clubs simply cannot reach the play-offs; meanwhile, the bigger clubs somehow treat their titles as serious accomplishments. The NFL, by miles our best league, has a salary cap for each club, and shares gargantuan TV money equally, and basks in parity, in which any club can bolt from the ashes any year, except for the Detroit Lions or the Arizona Cardinals, which theoretically could win but have exercised their free will under the United States Constitution to serve as portraits of chronic ineptitude.

Then, during periods of NFL parity, we sometimes decide that parity is formless and boring, so that imbalance is boring and parity is boring and life is absurd.

Like several thousand Portsmouth brethren, I travelled to Manchester knowing Portsmouth would not defeat Manchester United. I walked up to the stadium wearing my spiffy new Pompey ski cap knowing Portsmouth would not defeat Manchester United, and I entered the quarantined away zone like a lab rat and walked up the quarantined stairs knowing Portsmouth would not defeat Manchester United. As I noted that the Old Trafford away zone seemed plusher and cleaner than other away zones, and as I yecched that the away concession area sold Budweiser, which I don't mind but did not move all the way to England to rediscover, I never once thought Portsmouth would defeat Manchester United.

Still, I went, we all went, we all support the systems that uphold the tedium, possibly because we prefer the tedium at the stadium to the tedium at home. Besides, I could always check off life's list that I'd been to a match at Old Trafford and cease having to tell people I'd been there only for a Friday-morning tour with a Hungarian father and son incensing the tour guide by trying to walk out onto the pitch.

Out we went into the seating area in the upper deck of Old Trafford, where the seats proved comfortable and the surroundings roofed and so protected from any elements that I actually felt as if indoors. Then again, each seat lacked the one feature each seat probably needed, that being a telescope. The match began, the fourth round of the FA Cup, everybody and Gary Lineker and Steve McClaren in the building for this 5.15 p.m. kick-off, and our Pompey ants began trying to fend off the advances from their Manchester United ants. The people supporting their ants didn't seem so loud, possibly because we sat so far away from them but also possibly because they'd experienced roughly eight Premiership titles in the last 14 seasons and waited to be impressed rather than trying to inspire their players into achieving the impressive. A chant began from the Portsmouth section, the one up near the moon:

You're supposed to,
You're supposed to,
You're supposed to be at home,
You're supposed to be at home ...

I sang along with this chant even while figuring that they could not hear us from our post in the outskirts of Bolton. I learned later that they chanted 'Town Full of Seamen' at us, and I wished I'd been able to hear them to accept the honour.

Even from yonder up there, I could see that Portsmouth played gamely and admirably, perhaps even yanking an actual goal right out of the mouth before the referee could see it had been a goal. At 12 minutes, United's Nemanja Vidic sent a header trickling just over the line, but the glorious Pedro Miguel da Silva Mendes rooted it out of there and back to safety, while Sir Alex Ferguson raised a ruckus – as opposed to his non-ruckus in January 2005, when Mendes himself scored for Tottenham into that very same goal, only for goalkeeper Roy Carroll to clear it out similarly, unbeknownst to the referee.

If in the NFL, Sir Alex would've possessed – in a pocket, maybe – a pretty blood-red flag, which he could've thrown down dramatically to the ground in that situation, whereupon a referee would have halted the game and gone over to a video player inside a TV camera and stuck his head inside a bizarre little draping that covered only his head and neck, so as to avoid glare while he checked the accuracy of the earlier judgement. While he had his head stuck in there, the whole stadium would've waited, giving some fans a chance to go to the loo and others a chance to order another beer at their seat. In the event of long and careful looks at the videotape, which do occur on occasion, other fans would've had the chance both to order a beer and go to the loo, although these delays aren't so long that the trip to the loo would result from that particular beer, but instead a previous beer. In certain cases, the referee looking at the porn movie, I mean, football play, would come back and reveal that the video evidence had not proved sufficient for the overturning of the previous call on the field.

Not that we're weird or anything.

On this young evening at Old Trafford, the referee certainly would've emerged, announced that a goal had been scored and become the most popular guy in the stadium for about two minutes.

We reached half-time goalless, but I had not kidded myself. I knew Sir Alex had not fielded his best possible squad, in the hopes of resting some guys for future contests like the upcoming tilt with mighty Watford, or maybe to recover from the 2–1 loss in an Arsenal thriller down in London the previous Sunday. I had been around long enough to know there existed these advanced nations of humanity that had long since proved capable of playing for more than one trophy at a time. I saw no Cristiano Ronaldo on the pitch, and no Wayne Rooney. Of course, the thought that Sir Alex could simply bring on Ronaldo or Rooney hovered in goblin mode over the entire match, much as lines of Rudy Giuliani's police cars glowered outside New York night-clubs during the 1990s.

The silent majority below in fact did seem to receive a blood transfusion from the appearance of a single 21-year-old not all that far removed from a childhood of Everton support. When Ferguson beckoned Rooney at 60 minutes, the Manchester United attack went from threatening to doubtless, and all of James's excellence through the match – big saves against Michael Carrick, Paul Scholes – would amount to a loss. Rooney tapped in a Ryan Giggs cross at 77, and the masses below chanted 'Rooney! Rooney!' so that even we could hear them.

Those chants mushroomed utterly six minutes later when Rooney treated everyone to the game's lasting memory, a 20-yard chip that drew gasps of awe even from the Portsmouth supporters, many seeming glad they'd witnessed such a treat. As if imbued with five senses, this ball left Rooney's foot and fluttered up over James and then down into the gap between his tall head and the crossbar, freezing the goalkeeper and doubling the lead. This ball sang, it did, and it quelled whatever doubt or ennui still lingered in the home supporters. Manchester United would advance to the fifth round of the FA Cup, and Portsmouth would call it a good FA Cup at four rounds and resume concentration on that UEFA Cup spot.

We all knew that, but at 87 minutes, the lad next to me suddenly decided we shared a bond or perhaps even a family tree. Throughout the match, I'd sat on the end of the row by the stairs, while this guy and his two friends, all about 25 years old, hopped and roared next to me. The stewards kept telling them to sit down so the people behind them could see, and I kept feeling sorry for the stewards, having to do such things, and I marvelled that the 20-year rehabilitation of the English football image had evolved to where the fans we Americans deem fearsome had to sit down so other people could see. These lads never looked my way nor spoke to me.

Yet when Mendes managed to bounce a shot off Kanu's leg at 87 minutes, and when that thing fooled goalkeeper Tomasz Kuszczak and rolled into the net, just below us, close enough that we could see it like you see the Grand Canyon out of an aeroplane window, this guy grabbed me and squeezed me and began lifting me up and down. Again, there went the stunning resiliency of the English football fan, 2–1 down, hopeless, witness to a Rooney masterpiece only four minutes prior, yet exultant because we had just scored a goal at Old Trafford.

He hugged me again on the way out, after the 2–1 loss, just as James came over our way, down on the pitch, and looked up while we chanted 'England's number one!' at him, as if to say, *Don't worry, we understand, we know you just got frozen solid in front of 71,000 people, but it literally could've happened to anyone, and besides, those other great saves ...* I actually found this about as enlightened as anything I'd ever seen in the grand annals of fandom.

On my way out, in my Pompey ski cap, as I peeled through

the masses in the cold, one Manchester United fan hissed at me, and another grunted. The old image of English football fans may linger in uninformed circles, but all I ever got was one hiss and one grunt.

22

Eavesdropping on trains

At the outset of my Premiership wandering, I viewed trains as metallic vessels; by January 2007, I saw them as integral in the football experience, almost as important as strikers or referees who cannot detect obvious handballs. On trains, you can hear people giving scores from other matches, discussing what happened in other matches, stating their relegation fears and maybe even arguing. I began to make it a habit to eavesdrop on trains. I began to love eavesdropping on trains. I began to completely forget any etiquette training about eavesdropping on trains that I had received in my small Virginia hometown. Actually, we never rode any trains, so I never got any such training.

Sometimes, eavesdropping on trains can be unavoidable. If you're coming back to London from, say, Manchester United vs Portsmouth in an FA Cup match on 27 January 2007, and you're seated in the row behind two women and one man, all Manchester United fans, and those three happen to be talking at a volume higher than, say, commuter-train volume, you cannot *not* hear them. They might discuss their evaluations of everything Manchester United, they might even discuss past players of Manchester United, whereupon they might discuss David Beckham, and wonder why *he* married *her*. You might decide you've almost never heard people eaten up with something so much as these people seem eaten up with Manchester United. If an Arsenal fan were to board the train at, say, Milton Keynes, and briefly taunt these Manchester United fans over Arsenal's 2–1 win the previous Sunday, you might hear them retort to the Arsenal fan, 'Twelve points adrift!' and you might marvel at the English vocabulary, because you'd never, ever hear anyone in the United States boast of a lead in the 'standings' – our word for 'table' – by using the word 'adrift'. Most of us would say 'behind', although one sports columnist in my hometown used to use 'in arrears', for which people accused him of being all uppity.

Sometimes, on a train, you're not so much eavesdropping as cringing or even thinking inappropriate thoughts, because a fellow passenger, a child, apparently has come across some sort of message from Planet Annoyance that mandates he must begin singing loudly. This might happen to you, say, on the way home from Manchester United vs Portsmouth in the FA Cup fourth round, and it might be a boy of maybe 10, all the way from the back row. It's possible you'll ride the train with a boy who, yes, does have a father travelling along, but whose father not only doesn't seem to mind the boy singing, but seems to find it somehow cute, the way people do with their own children even while they'd want to throttle somebody else's. So over and over and over again, you might have to listen to an unsolicited version of this classic to 'London Bridge is Falling Down':

> Gary Neville, he's a Red,
> He's a Red,
> He's a Red,
> Gary Neville, he's a Red,
> He hates Scousers.

One oddity about children singing that I've noticed from being extremely observant is that if they happen to be singing lousy songs at grating decibels, and if one or more of their parents either ignores them or even approves, they don't seem to mind singing the same lousy song at the same grating decibel over and over and over again until you want to eject them from the moving train which, of course, wouldn't be right. But during the course of the 20 or so renditions of that song along that galling ride, I started to wonder whether we Americans had any equivalent.

Certainly we have rivalries, and certainly we have rivalries wherein the rival – say, Liverpool – occupies the frontal lobe of the fan's brain more than, say, the team Manchester United just played that day – in this case, Portsmouth. But I've experienced only one rivalry in which fans routinely sing loathingly about another team even when that other team is not present.

In the spring of 1985, a friend and I plunked down in the rafters of Madison Square Garden in New York to see the ice hockey Rangers play somebody else. As interlopers to the forbidding New York ice hockey demi-monde, we felt startled to hear song after song about the New York Islanders, who were not the team playing the New York Rangers that night. The New York Islanders, born in 1972, do business out on Long Island, about 27 miles away from the Rangers or, if you're driving, about three hours. The New York Rangers, born in 1926, sit right there on 33rd Street and 7th Avenue in Manhattan. The Islanders, despite that late birth, won the championship, for which they got the Stanley Cup, the best trophy in North America, four times in a row from 1979–80 through 1982–83. The Rangers, despite that early birth, did not win the Stanley Cup in any year between 1939–40 and 1993–94, the drought finally ceasing on a magical June 1994 night in New York as a sole fan held up the greatest banner in the history of American sports: NOW I CAN DIE IN PEACE. Unsurprisingly, the Rangers fans of 1985 brought to the game a beautiful resentment of Islanders that, I'm told, lingers today, and still results in the songs that made our youthful jaws drop that night, such as, to the *Mickey Mouse Club* tune, an homage to Islanders great Denis Potvin:

P-o-t-v-i-n
S-u-c-k-s.

Somebody told me recently they still sing that ditty, extra-ordinary given Potvin retired in 1988, after earning at least as much hatred as Gary Neville may or may not have for Scousers.

Eavesdropping on regular human conversations on crowded commuter trains rates less socially acceptable, but I did it on the clear and tolerable winter night of Tuesday, 30 January. What with people going home from work on the southbound from Waterloo whilst only some of us headed for a football match at Fratton Park, I happened to sit in one of those six-seat configurations eating my turkey-on-wholewheat-bagel and listening to two guys clearly Fratton-bound. They talked about football a little and about how they'd managed to leave work early – one said he'd fled while his boss talked on the phone – but I began the art of eavesdropping-in-earnest once I heard one of them say the magical English word 'Sydney'. He'd move to paradise come July. He'd follow his (English) girlfriend as she relocated for a job. He'd have to get the visas in order.

Alone, I craved conversation but shied away because I'm from Virginia. I wanted to talk to them about Sydney and bore them to smithereens with my stories of the 2000 Olympics and 100,000 people crooning 'Waltzing Matilda' and so on, but didn't because I'm from Virginia. These guys seemed maybe 27, 28. At Woking, they spotted their friend through the window, and laughed because he'd have to clamber through about three or four cars to reach them. He soon arrived and brought along a wit so dry as to be glorious, obvious in the reactions of the guy moving to Sydney.

Now, we've all heard a hundred thousand individual laughs on this mortal coil, but this laugh just about vibrated the train carriage. This laugh, loud and disarming and natural at the same time, didn't so much cuddle up to the eardrums as go blasting into the inner ear threatening to dislodge the hammer, the anvil and the stirrup. It startled me at first in this crowded, confined space, but I kept thinking of my friend Janet Graham back in the United States, and how she has this great and ready laugh, and how a great laugh so often comes from a great soul, and so on. And a thought came to me: *I'll bet that in a pub at, say, 2 a.m., that's one of the greatest laughs in world history.*

Sure enough, once the train pulled into Fratton and revealed the majestic light stanchions of the old stadium through the window to the left, shining in the night like, well, like an old rodeo ground, I bounded out of the station, scooted to the left down the street, crossed another street in the stadium traffic, walked down another sidewalk and suddenly, again, heard that laugh across the street as these three guys ambled down the opposing sidewalk.

Evidently the Woking guy had achieved wryness again.

Portsmouth had not won in the Premiership since Boxing Day at West Ham, and did not win against Middlesbrough even though they had managed to win at Middlesbrough by 4–0 only five months earlier. The 0–0 draw on 30 January denied Portsmouth both a leap to fifth place and the chance to establish some distance between them and the howling, trailing pests just below, such as Everton and Reading. It vaulted improving Middlesbrough to 10th. It kept Portsmouth below 40 points at 38, and as a person who had not endured the 1990s, I grimaced at the 38, ignorant of its exceptionality. I'd imagined nine points from January fixtures against Sheffield United, Charlton and Middlesbrough, and I'd received two. I wanted more, see, more! And more! And more!

The game reports said Sol Campbell had played wonderfully, and I saw nothing to discredit that, even though I cannot judge defenders or, for that matter, strikers, midfielders, goalkeepers, physios or water personnel. After the match, Uncle Harry said, 'It's amazing when you get up there in the table and expectations rise,' and likewise, it's amazing when you drop into a new country with no knowledge of legacies and find it irksome that your club has drawn 0–0 with Middlesbrough five months after blasting same by 4–0. That happened to be the first night I spotted the wall of honours for deceased fans, appealing in its simplicity, with just an arrangement of plaques, including the one about Thelma York and how if you listen in the wind, you can still hear her singing 'Play Up Pompey'. She withstood decades of slumps, and here I'd lamented one. She'd been to the fourth division and back, while I'd spent the entirety of my fandom with Pompey in single-digit Premiership positions, as if some spoiled American or something.

One game moment did count as memorable, though, that being Uncle Harry's insertion of one Lomana Tresor LuaLua for the first time since November, at 73 minutes. Crowd reaction seemed tepid, maybe even confused like myself. LuaLua infused some energy but also took a ball in midfield and declined for some time that seemed like about 45 minutes to pass it to anyone else, soon losing possession to some ravenous residents of Boro. Muddled as ever in new-found fandom, I didn't cheer LuaLua, but I didn't boo him and I also didn't complain at his gaffe, which placed me in the statistical minority for our section. I merely and quietly wished for his good health plus his immediate removal from the match. I also wondered how I'd have responded had he scored a goal, whether I'd have cheered or frowned or both.

About five or six seasoned fans chatting on the train ride home, though, said not a word about whether LuaLua may or may not have endangered his fiancée. Yet this crew did go on for some time about how LuaLua did screw up that possession in midfield near the end. They also held a long political discussion about the propriety of capital punishment, but I should stress that this conversation existed in entire separateness from the conversation about LuaLua screwing up that possession in midfield near the end.

I know all this because I eavesdropped.

23

'We were mental'

On a dismally dreary afternoon in north-west England, I alighted at Wigan for a second time in a single lifetime, setting an American record. No one greeted me at the train station with a plaque or a cup on Saturday, 3 February 2007, but I let it slide and marched around the appealing downtown, then out to the strip malls and the stadium. Eighteen months prior, I'd turned up in Wigan in a black sweater hunting the first clue, and now I turned up in Wigan in a dark-blue Pompey jacket hunting three points and heartened by the line describing Wigan's recent form: LLLLLL. Had that form line run to the last eight matches rather than the customary six, it would've looked like this: LLLLLLLL. It had been hard for Pompey to score lately – two fluky goals in four league matches in 2007 – but it had been harder for anybody in the Premiership to lose to Wigan.

Clearly, losing to Wigan would take some doing.

With 22 points, Wigan sat two points above the drop zone that at that moment included Watford, Charlton and West Ham. Wigan fans responded in kind, filling the JJB Stadium to only 15,093 out of a possible 25,138. Gloom ruled. Clouds menaced. I sat in the away upper deck among Pompey faithful near some Pompey children who'd turned up with their Pompey parents, and it felt warm to join everyone at a place so far away from Fratton Park. Weirdly, I experienced that feeling one gets when one travels to a foreign place but sees someone one knows, the caveat being that I didn't know any of these people.

Wigan's attack awakened and began bombarding the Pompey goal with serial threats. Campbell and James and the ever-honourable Primus cleared out trouble here and there and over there, but the whole Pompey exercise felt unmistakably uphill, and against Wigan. The match remained goalless at half-time. We did croon the greatest hits of Pompey cheers, including one that had become my favourite for its poetic simplicity and its sheer unlikelihood among football brutes:

> *We love you, Portsmouth, we do,*
> *We love you, Portsmouth, we do,*
> *We love you, Portsmouth, we do,*
> *Yahhhhh, Portsmouth, we love you.*

Still, our crowd was somewhat sparse, and our songs steadily waned. Somebody tried to dredge up the European tour song, but it just sagged, because even though Portsmouth held down a radiant sixth place in the Premiership, they could not score any more, and couldn't even pretend to threaten to hint at a score against the newly impenetrable Wigan defence. I wondered if the lyrics could change to, say, 'We might be going on a European tour,' and I began to resent hearing the other version for its prematurity, never mind that people should always sing about a European tour whenever you can sing about a European tour. For years I'd witnessed teams in slumps from press boxes, and even cringed trying to think up questions to ask the players when the answers would seem so obvious. So here was a slump from a fan's view, all piddling little three weeks of it, exasperating because you can't do anything about it and because the team just can't score and because there's that fear of plummeting through the table into somewhere like 13th place, which I absurdly found unacceptable.

Then, just after half-time, I swear somebody began piping

161

fog into the stadium through the gap in the stands to our left. It seemed to stream in with such abandon that I briefly wondered if the Wigan club had bought some sort of fog machine and produced the fog in hopes it would help muster a draw, even as it played a club that had forged its own offensive fog. The fog accrued and called to mind January in the NFL.

January in the NFL would be the greatest annual month in American sports, even if some would argue for October in baseball or March for college basketball. January brings the NFL play-offs, four weekends of them if you count the early-February Super Bowl, and while the play-offs aren't always storybook, they have enough storybook history to make the days shine just anticipating them. Play-off season in the NFL through the years has wrought vivid meteorological tales, such as a championship game at minus-59 degrees Fahrenheit one day in Cincinnati, a championship 'Ice Bowl' in minus-13 one famous day in Green Bay, and the exhalations visible like smoke from players' mouths in Minneapolis. A rampant snowfall helped define a landmark play-off game near Boston in 2002, and one day in Chicago in 1988, actually on 31 December back when play-offs began before January, the Bears and Philadelphia Eagles played in the so-dubbed 'Fog Bowl' next to Lake Michigan. Fog descended – or whatever fog does – and then thickened. After half-time, the teams simply could not pass the ball, and the broadcasters strained to call a game they could not see, and used puckish lines like, 'Gain of five, I think,' although not enough of them.

After half-time at Wigan, as Wigan came to resemble Chicago, I thought of the Fog Bowl, then learned fog can be a blessing. Fog can prevent you from having any inkling of how, at the other end of the pitch, David Unsworth crossed, and Lee McCulloch turned up on the edge of the box, and the ball broke to McCulloch, and McCulloch struck for a 1–0 lead, a reward for Wigan's match-long superiority. I could see their celebration, but murkily.

Now, here was one dreary day. That 1–0 lead would prove every bit as insurmountable as it looked, and Wigan's new form line would read LLLLLW. Woo boy, a loss to Wigan, to garnish the loss to Charlton. As we began to file out, the Pompey drum played and about 14 Pompey supporters danced, and I found these people rather Herculean. As I ambled back toward town in the fog and the gathering darkness, I passed through one of several adjacent ugly-American strip malls, and off in the distance I could see yet another of our contributions to global health, Burger King. Only the lights had gone out on some of its letters, so in the mist it read only RGER NG. So English football days can go like this: you're in the gloom, you're walking through a strip mall, you've just witnessed Wigan's first victory in nine matches, it came at the expense of the club you came to see, and you're looking at a sign marked RGER NG.

I did feel depressed, doubtless from light deprivation, then tried to count it as an important component in the suffering aspect of my Pompey development. I had a pint in one of Wigan's handsome downtown pubs, then boarded the train.

As the train rolled, I began to eavesdrop upon a remarkable conversation between two 18-year-olds just across the aisle. It grew clear that they supported Brentford, and that they had spent the day way, way up at Blackpool, at a stadium called Bloomfield Road. I guessed Brentford occupied either the Championship or League One, and as for Blackpool, I'd visited only during the 2001 Open golf at Lytham, and had found it extraordinary, mostly because my own country lacks the ripeness to boast a resort in which everyday tourists guffaw at drag-queen shows.

Well, here came another episode of the England football Saturday funnelled into the Saturday football train.

Chris and Jak – I'd soon learn their names – went on about Blackpool vs Brentford with such exuberance and with such endurance that I began to believe they deserved their own *Match of the Day* show. They analysed every single

163

aspect of the match their minds could recollect. They dredged detailed memories for discussion. Had that train continued on through London under the Channel, they'd have reached Paris without exhausting their topics. They epitomized the appeal of the post-match rehash.

Why?

Well, you want a slump? Now, *they* knew a slump. I didn't know any frigging slump. I knew three matches in which Portsmouth couldn't score and seemed to have left the knowledge of how in a dresser drawer somewhere. I knew a lull that threatened to swell into a slump. They'd gone 24 league matches with one win. They'd gone four months without an away win.

They had gone 11 away league matches without an away *goal*.

As Chris and Jak effused over there, I opened a newspaper and checked all three lower tables, just to see where this Brentford club would turn up. I found it 24th out of the 24 clubs in League One, with 23 points, five behind Bournemouth and six behind Cheltenham. I did not see, but soon would look up, that Brentford's season had begun with three wins and four draws in the first seven matches. Then it had plummeted. A goal in a 1–1 draw at Millwall on 26 September would serve as the last away goal until – well, until 3 February. In league play on the road, Brentford had lost by 2–0 at Rotherham, 3–0 at Oldham, 2–0 at Nottingham Forest, 2–0 at Cheltenham, 1–0 at Port Vale, 2–0 at Carlisle, 2–0 at Swansea City, 1–0 at Bournemouth, and 1–0 at Yeovil Town. Home losses included 4–0 to Crewe, 4–0 to Doncaster and 4–1 to Millwall.

Yet Chris and Jak had gone to all the home games and most of the away, and here they'd gone on 3 February, all the way up to Blackpool, four hours on the train, to stand among the attendance that day, as listed adorably in the Brentford match report, as '6,086 (202 Bees fans)'.

Suddenly, in all their travels and travails, they'd come upon a jewel, with a Brentford goal just 12 minutes in from Andrew Frampton, but wait, with another Brentford goal at 29 minutes from Jo Kuffour, but hold on here just a minute, another Brentford goal at 30 minutes, again from Kuffour, only 90 seconds after the previous goal. *Three!*

'We were mental,' they said, a line I shan't forget.

Indeed, they described themselves jumping literally all over the stand, feverish in their unforeseen mirth. Against a Blackpool club with hopes of promotion to the Championship, last-place Brentford won the match 3–1, and the Brentford match report would read, 'Brentford finally broke their away hoodoo,' reminding me of the glorious word 'hoodoo'. But first there would come what was, in my opinion, the best *Match of the Day* in the whole land, that of Jak and Chris on the Virgin train from Preston to London.

'You support Portsmouth?' one of them said to me suddenly, having noticed my jacket.

'Yeah,' I said with my American accent, providing my short-version explanation of how I'd come to do so.

They'd heard the Wigan score, but I noticed they just didn't consider it all that arresting. Unlike myself, they had lived repeatedly through the long slog of the English football season, and they knew the vagaries, especially in a sport more capricious than most. Besides, they hadn't seen an away goal since September, and, really, what's a loss at Wigan with an RGER NG in the fog?

For hours we talked. We disembarked at London Euston and walked down Tottenham Court Road to a pub and talked more. I asked their opinions of all things football, and from them I gained another layer of understanding of how English football fans fancy their clubs no matter the circumstance. After all, Jak said something that would attach itself to my brain for the remainder of the year. He said that if Brentford did suffer relegation from League One to League Two after the season – as, ultimately, it would – he would feel sorry, yes, but as a consolation, he would also look forward to the League Two season.

It would give him a chance to experience some of the League Two grounds.

That statement gave me my latest epitome of fandom, plus a glorious mental picture of two devotees, come September, turning up in the away stand at, say, Bury.

24

Chimes and mammals

On a pleasant February Saturday in London with patches of blue visible in the sky, I crossed Waterloo Bridge toward the station employing one of my favourite little tricks of life. When walking through a metropolis that has become old-hat to myself, I often attempt to picture it as I saw it for the first time, back when it seemed so mysterious and rife with possibility, long before I returned and brought along all my credit-card bills and middling worries. In London's case, that would be 1986, when two friends and I danced like rubes at the Hippodrome and absurdly saw Sarah Ferguson go by in a bridal gown and horse-drawn carriage. Just as I'd transported myself back to how vast and haunting London had seemed back then, Big Ben played its chimes and whooshed me to the present.

That's because when I heard those chimes, my brain immediately and without provocation heard, 'Play up Pompey, Pompey play up!'

Once, I had seen Big Ben in one of those surreal there-it-is moments when you realize something you've seen in a thousand photographs actually does exist and, in fact, towers over there before your eyes. Now, 20-years-and-change later, the chimes of Big Ben forged a cranial chemical reaction which immediately transported my mind to the Fratton End of a stadium near the English Channel. Hearing 'Play up Pompey' about eight or 10 times per match had imprinted the lyrics somewhere within my skull.

I counted this either as progress or dementia and headed for the southbound train. That day, slumping Portsmouth would welcome to Fratton Park the same opponent that had backlit the phoenix routine 11 months prior. That would be Manchester City, mercifully *sans* Ben Thatcher and languishing 15th in the table, albeit with only eight points fewer (30) than seventh-place Portsmouth (38). To Americans who follow this stuff, Manchester City has a distinct parallel, the Los Angeles Clippers of the National Basketball Association. The Clippers, like Manchester City, share a town with a cultural icon (Manchester United, the Los Angeles Lakers). The Clippers, like Manchester City, remain anonymous to foreigners who follow the game only casually, such that said foreigners can hear there's another club in the same city and respond with outright bewilderment. The Clippers, like Manchester City, plod along without titles while the in-town titan hoards them (in the Lakers' case, eight).

The Clippers, unlike Manchester City, share an actual building with their in-town giant, so that instead of a 'derby' pronounced 'darby', they play a 'hallway rivalry', their locker rooms only a hallway apart. The Clippers, unlike Manchester City, have never actually won anything, what with Manchester City winning a League Cup as lately as 1976 and an FA Cup as lately as 1969. The Clippers, unlike Manchester City, have never been relegated, but they have deserved it on many, many occasions.

The Clippers, in fact, have done worse than Manchester City, for years and years and years, forging a favourite joke from the one-time talk-show host, Arsenio Hall, who said Los Angeles has everything because, 'If you like basketball, we've got the Lakers, and if you don't, we've got the Clippers.' The Clippers, in fact, have been so woeful that there's a coach named Larry Brown who twice – *twice!* – got them to the play-offs during the early 1990s, and even though Brown remains the only American coach to win both the NBA (Detroit, 2004) and the huge college basketball title (Kansas, 1988), I consider his Clippers feat towering enough to rank him maybe even alongside Galileo, Aristotle or Bill Gates among all-time sages.

That's how woeful the Clippers have been, and so I thought of the Clippers as I rode toward the match with Manchester City, when suddenly, on the train, no kidding, I heard that laugh. You know, *that* laugh. From about eight rows away. I could not believe it. *Could ... not ... believe ... it.* My ears did the ear double-take. Craning my neck, I recognized also the guy with the Saharan wit, who kept instigating the laugh. I marvelled again at the laugh, but also thought of this bizarre case in the United States in which a woman's body had detrimental physical reactions to hearing the voice of *Entertainment Tonight* presenter Mary Hart through her television. The afflicted woman's ears could not go anywhere near that voice or, if we're to believe the reports, her body would crumple with some sort of seizure. I wondered whether this remarkable laugh from the Middlesbrough and Manchester City trains might produce such reactions in some people, when suddenly the guy with the laugh stood up and walked out of the carriage toward the loo, but carrying his backpack, which briefly got stuck in the sliding doors before he yanked it on through. I figured he planned to move to another carriage, meet up with someone.

The conductor happened by, and I asked him how many carriages comprised the train that day, and he said five, and I couldn't believe that with a 20 per cent chance, I once again had turned up on the same train, in the same car, as this laugh.

We rode on a bit.

Just then, that sliding glass door at the end of the carriage reopened, and ...

Well ...

Oh ...

You have to be kidding ...

The guy with the laugh came back through into the carriage dressed as a 5-foot-11, furry, electric-blue bear, but with a yellow-crescent Pompey insignia on the front. I looked over and saw two teenaged lads chatting and saw them stop and saw them grin and heard one say to the other, 'That's brilliant.' I was in such a state of disbelief that only as the day wore on did I notice that the bear had blue paws, that the bear had a bear head but with a hole open for the human face, and that the bear had blue-bear ears.

This type of situation, of course, immediately raises a whole phalanx of questions.

Is it not possible to wear the bear suit right from home without enduring jeers from neighbours or glares from scared old ladies or capture by an overzealous zookeeper? (I guessed not.) Must this guy plot to don the bear suit only when safely within the greater Portsmouth fan zone area? (Perhaps.) Doesn't that thing get hot during games in, say, May? (Surely.) What kind of soul does it take to go to football matches dressed as a blue bear? (A singular one, I reckoned.)

As the train rolled on toward the inevitable rail replacement, I could see that bear head bobbing and tilting during conversation, eight rows away. I could not hear the laugh very often, which made me wonder whether the blue bear fur actually muffled the sound of a laugh. Four guys nearby blithely ignored the blue bear and played cards loudly on a table and seemed to believe that everybody on the train held a vital interest in the outcomes of their hands.

Then came rail replacement, and we all disembarked at Havant. Rather than 60 or so humans lining up to board a double-decker bus, we were 59 or so humans and one blue bear. The blue bear lined up with his friend and the rest of us, and by the time we boarded, the lower deck proved full, so we hiked up the stairs to the equally crowded upper deck. The gaudy mammal sat on the right side by a window, while I sat on the left by a window. I did not hear the laugh, and reckoned the blue bear might've been just as miffed as myself once the bus became stalled in stadium traffic and once it seemed we might not make the kick-off.

In light of such duress, I believe it's a moral imperative that rail replacement should include an open bar.

During the anxiety, though, I did notice that as the bus windows repeatedly fogged up, I had to use the left sleeve of my new blue Pompey jacket to clear the glass, so that I could see outside when we passed such sights as the muddy sound with the moored boats near the stadium, or the cemetery with the Pompey flag sticking up from one of the gravesites. Meanwhile, the blue bear, I noticed, would clear the glass with his right blue paw, and so for one moment, I wished that I, too, had a blue paw, preferably a left one.

We disembarked just in time in front of Fratton Park, and I walked close behind the blue bear and his friend, essentially following them into No Sumo Wrestler Alley where, of course, we had to walk single file. A fat bear couldn't have made it through. I listened as the blue bear absolutely guffawed at something the friend had said. Oh, what the heck. I'd decided to be a fan and not a sportswriter for this season, but I simply could not quash the 20-year habit of asking people for interviews when a blue bear stood right before me. I introduced myself, and we shook hand and paw, and he gave his name, 'Charlie.' I said that I was sort of a Charlie too, and asked him if I could interview him sometime, and gave him a (yuck) business card, whereupon he handed the card to his friend because of course – of course – he had no pockets.

How stupid to hand a business card to a mammal I knew had no pockets, a mammal I knew full well to be not a kangaroo.

Within five minutes of kick-off, off a Matt Taylor corner, Pedro Miguel da Silva Mendes sent a heat-seeking blast from 20 yards, and that thing literally jolted the roof of the goal, and the goal drought had ended, and I hopped up and down alone amongst my people, and Fratton Park felt a twinge of a searing, gorgeous memory from 11 March 2006. The game proceeded apace, Portsmouth looking fresh and sparkly, until late in the first half when suddenly Mendes went down in a heap. Manchester City had struck again.

This time, the ruffian Joey Barton had got miffed at something and wound up trying to crush Mendes's heel. Mendes left the pitch on a stretcher. The Fratton End had its justified topic *du jour*, and the 'stick' once directed at Thatcher went full-on at Barton. I heard mighty and majestic songs I never knew existed.

Loosely to the tune of 'She'll Be Coming Round the Mountain', there came:

> *If Barton plays for England, so can I,*
> *If Barton plays for England, so can I,*
> *If Barton plays for England,*
> *Barton plays for England,*
> *Barton plays for England,*
> *So can I.*

I figured that song old, but I figured it brilliant.

There came a chant about 'dirty northern bastards', the kind of thing that still, after all these months, startled me, because in the United States we frown upon unvarnished profanity in the presence of children. Then I remembered that Jak and Chris had told me about that man they knew who set unyielding rules for his own children about language appropriate for football grounds versus language appropriate for the house. Then I thought about the philosopher Bertrand Russell's line, 'Sin is geographical.'

Then I heard a mysterious song, crooned to Barton, to the 'Guantanamera' tune:

Down with your brother,
You're going down with your brother,
Down with your brohhhh-ther,
You're going down with your brohhhh-ther ...

I didn't ask anyone because I'm from Virginia, but I jotted down the lyrics and wondered about Barton's brother. Did he play in the Championship, or more likely, League One or League Two? And for whom?

Songs continued to flow from the heart of the Fratton End, a heart that did include, I noticed for the first time, a blue bear, as it's easy to spot a blue bear in the distance. Suddenly Manchester City equalized at 62 minutes. Bernardo Corradi headed in a Darius Vassell cross, one of only three goals he'd score all season, and once more, Portsmouth vs Man City seemed trammelled at 1–1. The minutes wore on. Uncle Harry brought on Kanu up front.

Just then, at 81 minutes, a certain soul named Glen Johnson made a defiant run and supplied a clever reverse ball just below me in the corner to the left of the Man City goal. He got the ball to Kanu, and Kanu toe-poked an eight-yard goal into the right side of the net, and the team hugged in a blob below me, and I actually felt welling tears of a dubious nature. Oh, I'd weathered most of the long, hard, goalless January, and had come upon a moment when the attack flowered again, a mere hour of gloom next to the Brentford brand.

My tears came viscerally, because the goal and the group hug seemed so frenetically emotional. They did not come on behalf of Glen Johnson, although I did get my answer as to the recovery time from failed toilet-seat larceny to public rehabilitation, and that time frame would be 21 days. And they certainly did not come for Barton, who received jeers all the way off the pitch after Portsmouth's quenching 2–1 win.

I did, however, do some Internet research on Barton's brother, and learned that he played neither in League One nor League

Two nor even the Conference, but sat in prison for murder. Such a song would seldom fly in the United States where we're more cautious with humour, but then, sin is geographical.

25

Lonely walks he who walks to Plainmoor

If granted three guesses, most Americans can surmise that the French Riviera must be somewhere in France. Some of us have heard of the Italian Riviera, and a percentage can link the Italian Riviera to Italy. Almost none of us know about the English Riviera, so it gave me a huh to read that I would watch some football there on 17 February.

While the FA Cup moved on with its fifth round, and Portsmouth spent the Saturday idle, and while some kid somewhere went to see Manchester United while singing on a train that Gary Neville hates Scousers, I sated a long-held curiosity. Ever since alighting in England, I'd cast my eye now and then at the bottom of the League Two table, and I'd wonder how it must be on a Saturday at the ground of the club standing 92nd in the 92-team, four-division Football League. As a lifelong fan of extremes, as somebody who once revelled in writing about a Kentucky high school that had lost 46 American-football games in a row – I lauded them for not quitting – I scanned down the mid-February tables until I found it, there at the bottom . . .

Torquay.

Technically, that'd be Torquay United, reposing down there with 25 points, five points adrift of Wrexham and Macclesfield Town, and 91 spots and three leagues adrift of Manchester United. Once an American has identified the word 'Torquay',

175

the second act is to learn the location of this mystical Torquay, and that's when I began to do some studious studying, and that's when I learned Torquay graces the English Riviera portion of Devon, south-west England, and that's when I learned there's such a thing in the world as the English Riviera.

The English Riviera turns out to be utterly lovely, even if February does not necessarily count among the prime times to visit the English Riviera. When you walk through central Torquay down to the mall and behold Tor Bay, you have come upon one of the lovelier sights in England, in my opinion.

When you walk up an elongated hill from town toward Plainmoor to see Torquay United play football, though, well, lonely walks he who walks through Torquay, in the rain, on a dismally dreary February afternoon, straining to see 24th-place Torquay United (25 points) play third-place Hartlepool (61 points) in a League Two tussle.

Lonely walks he while the rain starts angling in sideways and he begins to soak and to question just where he went so awry in life.

Normally, you can find a stadium you've never seen by following the traffic line, but no apparent traffic pattern materialized for Plainmoor, so I just continued upward, into the little village there, then turned right as per directions, looped around a curve, and *voilà*.

Plainmoor, as it happens, has an outdated edifice and outdated old light stanchions and looks like a slightly more beleaguered Fratton Park and so, at once, I felt charmed. More was the charm, then, when happening into the club lobby to the apparent ticket window, and inquiring about a ticket, only to find that you don't necessarily buy tickets per se, you just pay £15 at the gate as you would to enter a county fair or such. For still more charm, note the wall of honours in the Torquay lobby there, which include a framed certificate that reads as follows:

'This is to certify that Torquay United won the Barclays League Fourth Division play-offs 1990–91.' Other frames include notice of the club's monetary donations for an air ambulance, a lifeboat group and a hospice (£510.62).

I had hoped that the bottom of League Two would look something like this.

If there's an American likeness to Plainmoor, it's probably one of any number of high school American-football grounds. That's not a slight. High school football engulfs American towns, especially in Tennessee or Florida or Georgia or Alabama or most especially Texas, where stadiums can expand once one community decides it wants to keep up with that snooty community over there. Just a few Texas high school capacity figures: Pizza Hut Park in Frisco, 21,000, Mesquite High School in Mesquite, 20,000, Ratliff Stadium in Odessa, 19,300. I love the Friday-night lights of stadiums in Tennessee mountains or in Alabama hills or California boulevards, because those lights make me wonder what vivid lore lurks below. In Gold Beach, Oregon, there's a high school football ground right up next to the Pacific Ocean where, no kidding, osprey have dropped eels on the team's training, and deer have taken the field during games and run so fast that coaches have tried to get their parents to relocate into the school district. Torquay itself has animal lore, I learned, in the form of the famed police dog named Bryn, who during the last match of the season in 1987, while the whole place trembled over potential relegation, suddenly jumped out and bit the thigh of one of the players, Jim McNichol. Seeing as how McNichol had scored earlier to halve visiting Crewe Alexandra's lead to 2–1, it seemed that Bryn must've been a dog with secret away leanings. Paul Dobson scored famously in the bulging four minutes of injury time for the draw, and Torquay United stayed up, as they had entirely since joining the Football League in 1927, always in lower divisions, until spring 2007, when they plummeted.

As the crowd of 2,194 filed in – far shorter men's-room lines in League Two – I remained unaware (as usual) that referee Andy Penn twice had emerged to check the condition of the pitch, and might have come close to ruling it unsuitable. This would've been quite a downer after two changes of trains, four hours of train rides, and one train malfunction that led to the boarding of another bus, and without even a single blue bear to lighten the ride. Luckily, Mr Penn decided the match could carry on, so that I not only got to see Torquay United play, but I could behold a match in the wondrously muddy conditions suggestive of the NFL play-offs.

I took the kind of folding yellow wooden seat that proves that people had tougher glutei maximi back in the day when men were men and they built stadiums like Plainmoor. I sat near the press area, observing eight beleaguered reporters hunched together outdoors – outdoors! – and suspiciously devoid of a free buffet. Ludicrously, I sat near a man wearing a cap with an insignia of the Anaheim Ducks, a National Hockey League club that plays ice hockey near the California Disneyland. I saw a church jutting up from behind the corner of the stadium in the grey greyness. I heard the public address announce that Kevin Hill, presumably the Torquay player, had proposed to his girlfriend Laura on Valentine's Day, and that Laura had accepted, and I yearned for a day when I might hear a similar announcement noting that the woman actually declined, just for variety.

Other than shivering, I relished the day at Torquay.

As the match with Hartlepool began, the Torquay players took the pitch and I stood and applauded with the Torquay supporters mostly because I'll always applaud someone who'll play for our entertainment in a downpour. One player, the aforementioned Kevin Hill, turned around and applauded the fans. I noticed that Torquay United wore the appealing colours yellow and blue, again suggestive of Portsmouth. The 100 or so Hartlepool away fans began singing that Hartlepool was the greatest city 'the world has ever seen', and I made the inane realization that many people sing that claim, not just Pompey supporters plus scattered others in the Premiership. They also chanted to their own 'Blue Army', and I got a greater sense of the universality of blueness. They also cheered a goal at six minutes, when their Eifion Williams, who once played for Torquay United, found himself alone in front of goal and supplied a 1–0 lead.

I saw and heard some excellent things at Plainmoor. Not only does the stadium remain so small that you often can hear the thud of a foot striking the ball, but many of the players' passes simply had no chance of reaching their targets. You'd hear the thud, and then the ball would roll along, and then it would hit a little puddle of water or a pit of mud, and it would just stop there, all bogged down and ornery, while players had to turn around and give chase. This added another dimension to the sport. Torquay had one player who looked just a little bit like some California biker dude, and I loved that. Torquay's goalkeeper looked a little chunkier than David James or any Premiership goalkeeper, and I loved that, too. Hartlepool's manager wore a suit, which I found noble on a day I felt an urge lingering from childhood to wear only a pair of shorts and go out sliding around in the mud. The mud began to cake and then cover the kits of some of the players, which I adored thoroughly out of an innate American affinity for those memorable sporting events that complicate the laundry.

The match slogged on, mildly eventful in the mud, and highlighted when one Torquay player who shall remain nameless sent a long, looping back pass toward his goalkeeper and almost scored the most incredible own goal I'd ever seen. Torquay peppered the Hartlepool goal without scoring, the 1–0 Hartlepool victory seemed somehow imminent, and come 4.35 p.m., maybe 15 minutes from time, I heard the fans of the 92nd-best of the 92 Football League teams begin to sing:

Torquay till I die,
I'm Torquay till I die,
I know I am, I'm sure I am,
I'm Torquay till I die.

Thereby did I hear the most touching 'till I die' I'd heard yet. Hartlepool finished off its victory and pointed toward eventual promotion to League One, while Torquay's players got an ovation from their crowd – from us – for their game effort in the muck. I decided to have a beer in the pub that's *attached* onto Plainmoor at one end – nice touch – and I received a flyer about some sort of action the fans' group might undertake. Before I did that, though, I decided to make a circular tour, and as I did, about 10 or 15 of those 'Torquay till I die' supporters marched out through the exits into the street, chanting. I couldn't quite translate their chants, but they seemed to be peeved at some guy named Roberts, and indeed, when I checked later, a guy named Roberts ran the club and would cease running the club on the ensuing Wednesday.

With a couple of police officers looking on to forestall any shenanigans, the Torquay-till-I-die-ers continued their chants in the street until the chants died off and everybody went home or into the pub affixed to the stadium. I thought about the world, and how even when you go to the 92nd-place club in England, or the college in Montana, or the high school in Kentucky, or the cricket ground in India or Pakistan, there's almost always somebody who's mad at the chairman or the coach or the general manager or the athletic director. I thought about this as I found my way to the waterfront of the English Riviera, and I thought about this on the long train ride home, where I didn't have to eavesdrop on some guy's serial mobile-phone calls, because his voice blared throughout the carriage. His beloved Derby County had lost 2–0 to Plymouth Argyle in the FA Cup, and had incurred two – two! – penalties in the match, whereupon the match ended and some police officer misconstrued something this guy's father said, so they had to go to the police station, where the father probably would have to spend the night.

I heard this story roughly five times.

By contrast, Torquay had been a dream.

26

A Blackburn fiasco

It can baffle a greenhorn American to hear away fans lauded as the 'truest' of fans. Sure, away fans have got up and got out of the house and refrained from sedentary afternoons spent bitching through a TV screen because the referee just missed a handball obvious from here to Inverness. Sure, away fans make the effort so that they can ruin their afternoons bitching in person about the obvious handball. Away fans make the drive or ride the train or ride a coach that has no bar or no loo. Away fans risk urinary tract infections.

It's just that it can take time to appreciate the grit of away fans when you hail from a gigantic country wherein college kids make 10-hour drives to American-football games, then drive home all through the night taking turns napping while risking their grade-point averages, their lives and the lives of others. In the United States, some people make three-hour round trips just to meet somebody else for breakfast, even if such people always reside in the Los Angeles area. In England, no trip would exceed about five hours.

The sacrifice can pale.

I have learned, however, that careful study hones the appreciation for these people, the away fans.

Let's say that, just for example, you have an imbecile from the United States. Now, let's say the imbecile books a £40 pair of single train tickets three weeks ahead of time in order to travel to Blackburn and back. Let's say the imbecile manages to coordinate that feat with the booking of a £25 away ticket for Ewood Park, with Blackburn having famously shaved ticket prices during the 2006–07 season. Let's say the imbecile congratulates himself on his excellent preparation skills and how he's really learning this game of fanhood.

OK.

Let's say, then, that the imbecile has failed to consider that Blackburn still breathes in the UEFA Cup, so that might nudge the schedule of Blackburn vs Portsmouth on Saturday, 24 February. So the Premiership might just eyeball an upcoming Blackburn UEFA Cup date on 21 February and, out of common decency, shift Blackburn's match to Sunday, 25 February. Then the imbecile will have to telephone the train company and seek to change the ticket.

Now, it would take some kind of frigging imbecile to call up a train company seeking to change two single tickets, when anyone with remote seasoning in England would know that after some time on hold to hear that the call may be recorded, the answer would come back that it would be wiser for the imbecile to go ahead and buy a whole new return ticket, using the original tickets as coffee coasters or as fireplace kindling.

Even then, the forfeiture of another £63.90 would not ensure that the imbecile wouldn't just go and step on the wrong train, the 10.05 to Wolverhampton, rather than the 10.01 to Lancaster across the platform, if trying to reach Blackburn. If the average American can't find Texas on a map without two hints, even somebody who has been to all 50 states can have trouble getting to Blackburn from London. That's even given the knowledge that Blackburn lies somewhere up there above Manchester, which at least rules out accidentally going to Torquay. So it's still possible to buy two different tickets to get to Blackburn and wind up sitting for an hour and six minutes in the station at Rugby, waiting for the train one should've boarded an hour ago. And after that, it's still possible to ride that train experiencing one of the wretched turns of 21st-century life, the overhearing of others' mobile-phone conversations. That alone exalts away fans. And then, that train – or any train – always reserves the right to stop just shy of any given station for 10 precious minutes – it's 1.45, 1.46, tick-tock, tick-tock, kick-off at 3 – because some dunderhead up ahead apparently kept his local train on that track for too long.

So the away fan, especially if an imbecile, might wind up in Preston at 2.34, with the next train for Blackburn not actually a train but a bus, arriving at 3.45, so another £30 might go into a taxi for the 12 miles to Blackburn, and more than £30 if you count the possible overdraft fee from extracting the £30 with only £9.79 lingering in the account. The American away fan deals with absurd costs, yes, but the English away fan often deals with two costs so widely lamented as to become national issues – the cost of football tickets and the cost of trains – plus the occasional cost of taxis in the event of runaway stupidity.

Either that, or he/she rides a coach for eight aggregate hours.

And still, after all this strain the away fan, if imbecilic enough, runs the risk of arriving in the 23rd minute, feeling excitement because three points would make Portsmouth leapfrog from eighth to sixth in the table, plopping down at Ewood Park, checking the big video screen over to the right and finding his club 1–0 down already (that secured in the very first minute via a rare Sol Campbell blunder I could muster relief at having missed). Whereupon the imbecile might proceed to absorb the most abominably pulse-less performance humanly possible from the away club – a 3–0 loss that resembled 6–0. The home club might've played miserably just four days prior, drawing 0–0 with Germany's eighth-place Bayer Leverkusen to exit the UEFA Cup meekly, whilst the away club might've played nada for 14 days, yet the away fan still risks that those two factors will appear reversed during a turgid display of feckless football from the away fan's club.

That, and, lest we forget, the away fan takes a chance his

father might end up spending the night in jail in Plymouth.

If after 90 minutes on Sunday, 25 February, the public address had announced there would be a minimum 24 hours of added time, Portsmouth still would not have scored or much threatened Brad Friedel, that swine who'd ignored a respectful interview request from myself two months prior. A good chance in the 74th minute found Andy Cole in front of goal fashioning a promising header, which he promptly headed into about the third row of the stands, some feat itself. At some point a Pompey fan near me angrily reminded our squad, 'You've got to shoot to score!' – and if only they had heard him, they might've caught on. It grew so bad that possession seemed a *disadvantage* to the visiting squad. Possession seemed to entail an automatic transfer to Blackburn possession.

Watching this rubble of Pompey, the bubble of thought floating above my head suddenly contained that fan at Birmingham. That brilliant, brilliant fan. OK, so it's a tired old trick in England, but to an American, that fan who ran onto the pitch during the 2006 FA Cup quarter-final 7–0 loss to Liverpool and tore up his season ticket in front of manager Steve Bruce – that non-violent trespasser qualifies as novel. He became the first guy of my experience to shred a ticket before a manager, and long shall he turn up in my accounts of the Premiership to curious fellow Americans, even if I later learned he only mimicked a Middlesbrough fan from February 2006. Long shall he occupy a beacon's spot in my cranium, even while I could never do such a thing to Uncle Harry.

Blackburn, meanwhile, having managed to refrain from scoring for an hour and a half against mighty Bayer Leverkusen, somehow deluged our net with three goals and repeated threats while generally resembling Arsenal. They crafted sublime crosses. They grimaced at their point-blank misses. They didn't even care when they flubbed a 58th-minute penalty granted them by our wacky, tackling *goalkeeper*, so nattily coiffed for such a mindless ruffian. By that point, they inhabited the happy realm of toying. And they did all this despite the thick, dispiriting swatches of empty blue home seats that exhibited how Premiership prices might've reached their realistic crux.

Yet through this afternoon desolation, something floored me again. Through several minutes in the 60s, the drums and throats in the top visitors' rows carried on an impressively durable and upbeat chant of 'Blue Army'.

In the 79th minute:

> We love you, Portsmouth, we do,
> We love you, Portsmouth, we do,
> We love you, Portsmouth, we do,
> Yeahhhh, Portsmouth, we love you.

We do?

Yes, we do, because in the 84th minute, there again went that hapless horn, that respiratory rogue of a bugle, that same Pompey fan playing on again, giving the distinct aura of encroaching death yet playing on, hitting every third note or so, skipping entire notes in a way that gave a mental picture of punctured lungs. Resilience of the fan species had found new definition – in my book, anyway – in this soul gasping air into an obstinate instrument in the 84th minute of a débâcle.

Then, suddenly, in the late-80s minutes:

> We are staying up,
> We are staying up!

And when the match did end – an occurrence some might interpret as proof of the existence of a higher power – which group of fans would forge the last human noise of the day at Ewood Park?

Their club had just played hopelessly. The European tour of which they'd sung for months had slid firmly into doubt. They had travelled afar and risked, in certain circumstances, the prospect of spending an hour in Rugby despising themselves. They had paid outrageous ticket prices. They had paid outrageous train prices or outrageous fuel prices – or ridden a coach for four hours. The smattering of home fans had mocked them and then filed out. Their goalkeeper had committed a penalty in the box, then lorded his ensuing save of the penalty kick over the home fans even though his team trailed by a score organically close to 10–0. The home fans had mocked this visiting goal-keeper. With justification.

Yet there they lined the upper rows, my heroes, roughly 25 in number. One held a stuffed Portsmouth elephant. One held a stuffed Portsmouth bear (brown, not blue). Two guys who couldn't have been older than 23 had gone shirtless even though they'd yet to age enough to develop the fat that helps fend off the cold. One twirled his shirt, round and round, as if in the 62nd minute of some wrenching melodrama of a match. All chanted and sang. Drums played. Moments later, out in the streets, amid the quietly sated Blackburn fans, about six Portsmouth types marched along singing about a European tour.

If you can take a dismal 3–0 day and transform it into an early evening spent marching down the street and singing that you're going to Europe, you have an indomitableness simply lacking in the 99-per-cent majority of the 300 million Americans. You do. You simply do. That's what I learned about myself at that moment: having emerged from a US birth canal, I'm simply not conditioned to celebrate eighth place, especially after a chance to vault to sixth fails to lend my side even the slightest apparent inspiration. What's that old poll result about American children, who'd finish, say, 10th in the world on a maths test but, when asked where they suspected their country would finish, always answered first? I had come along in that. We emerge from the womb with a pancreas, a spleen and a built-in arrogance. We simply don't handle eighth all that well, which might help explain why we don't live as long as do Britons.

For us, it can take a blue bear to supply perspective. For

seasons, a blue bear emailed to me soon after the Blackburn match, Pompey fans have wished and strained and added up potential points just aching to conjure the 40 that guarantee clearance of relegation. This season, 40 came ludicrously early, on 10 February, when Pompey hit 41 and the slots literally gushed coins. Maybe nobody knows quite what to do, the wise creature explained.

Nobody – save for 25 crooners, two drummers and a breathless bugler.

27

Never miss a chance to hang out in a pub with a blue bear

Those emails from a blue bear had become the first ursine emails I'd ever received. I confessed that I'd stalked him inadvertently, and that I knew already that he'd follow his girlfriend to Australia in the summer of 2007, and that he'd cleared his bus window with his removable right blue paw, and that at that moment I'd wished that I, too, possessed a removable blue paw. He somehow refrained from freaking out and invited me to the Shepherd's Crook pub, just a David James punt from Fratton Park, before the match with Chelsea. The match with Chelsea would begin at 5.15 p.m. rather than 3 p.m., a source of frustration to long-term fans but perfectly ordinary to a Premiership interloper like myself.

My football guru Tom, who can tell you the Liverpool score from most any important juncture in his life, has lamented that in preferable days of yore, a Saturday in England would've brought 10 games, all starting at 3, simple as that, none of this 12.45 or this 5.15 or this Sunday at 12.45 or Sunday at 4 or whatnot. This lament reminded me that the NFL games once started at only 1 and 4 on Sundays save for one game on Monday night at 9, and how that brought routine and familiarity to my childhood, and how I never could wait for my parents to drive us home from the drudgery of church so I could shed the wretched 40-pound church shoes and strangling tie, plop down for the pre-game show at 12.30 and watch until 7. Now, with games strewn all over the clock, even two on Sunday nights, a child conceivably could miss church altogether, start watching the NFL pre-game shows at 11, then watch games from 1 p.m. until 12 midnight, leaving even less time for homework and further contributing to the decline of a superpower.

England's rescheduling for the real god of TV, meanwhile, has posed challenges even more fundamental. It has tested the awe-inspiring English digestive tract and forced it to prove again its uncommon sturdiness. Where once, pub-goers could schedule their beer reasonably from, say, 12.30 to 2.45, now they have these 12.45s and these 5.15s which distort everything. For the 12.45, the drinker must shove down the amount of beer requisite for viewing pleasure by about 12.30, thereby interfering with a recent breakfast or threatening the organism as a whole if there has been no breakfast. The 5.15 might be even more perilous, for that subjects the consumer to beer's cunning sneak attack over extended periods lasting several hours. As life on earth has shown, judgement about whether to have a fourth pint can blur after a third, and judgement about whether to have a fifth pint can vanish altogether after a fourth.

And then, if you have a 5.15 on the same day you have a Liverpool–Manchester United enticement at 12.45, so that everybody wants to get to the pub by soon after 12.45 to watch that match, let me just tell you that I have experienced this on 3 March 2007 and that your vision can get sort of furry.

By about 4.51, you might be having the fourth pint while conversing in the Shepherd's Crook with a blue bear and his friend dressed as a regular human, Dan, whom you recognized straight away from the Middlesbrough train. At some point between 2 and 4.30, their other friend from the Middlesbrough train and the No Sumo Wrestler Alley might've walked in, and they might call him Hopkins, one name only, like Madonna or Ronaldinho. The bear might've rushed across the pub to actually bear-hug Hopkins, the bartenders might've poured more beers, one of the world's better laughs might've rattled off about 20 times, and you might've chatted with two or three other Pompey fans. You might see the blue bear sweat in his suit and wonder new things, such as whether the dry-cleaner handles such outfits and whether there's even a place for them on the little dry-cleaning form somewhere near 'shirts' and 'trousers' and 'jackets'. You might not ask, though, if you're from Virginia.

Pretty soon, everybody might end up having to scurry over to Fratton Park at the last minute to see José Mourinho, Didier Drogba, Frank Lampard and the like, as if just remembering why we all came to town in the first place. Breathless at your seat, play already under way, you might find in your pocket two wallets, the second belonging to Charlie, because you had to hold it hours ago, because one of the problems with being a bear is having no place to put a wallet. Then you might watch Chelsea's 2–0 win over Portsmouth, and you might think it perfunctory, with the amazing Drogba's 29th goal of the season at 33 minutes plus Salomon Kalou's at 82. You might not recollect too many of the details.

True, Andy Cole's header at 77 minutes almost tied the match, and that can ring sort of memorable, and Petr Cech's save rose to the level of world-class according to Uncle Harry, and, true, Cech contorted himself so improbably for that save that I could've sworn there were two of him.

Yet my vision of Chelsea's gritty win seemed unclear even by my clueless standards. I did not join in the early-game rendition of 'Where's Your Title Gone' (to the tune of 'Where's Your Momma Gone'). I did not notice anything particularly notice-able. All blame, of course, goes to the 5.15 kick-off, which also explains why I crib here from Glenn Moore's eloquent report in the *Independent*.

The report, like all that day, had little to do with Portsmouth, and not because the Blackburn eyesore had dropped Pompey to eighth behind the big four plus Bolton, Everton and Reading. This match figured in the title race between Manchester United and Chelsea. When the day began, the twice-defending champions Chelsea trailed by nine points, but then Manchester United scored a shock goal in added time to win 1–0 at Liverpool, and Sir Alex Ferguson bounced in joy as if he'd suddenly lost half his age, even as I tried to explain to a blue bear how I hadn't understood that Joey Barton song. Manchester United led the table by 12 as Chelsea took the pitch under pressure to get it back to nine in the rugged Pompey den. As Moore wrote of Fratton Park after the match, 'The location of Mourinho's press conference, by the gentlemen's toilets in a draughty concourse under the ancient main stand, illustrates its uniqueness in the sanitised modern game.'

As added backdrop, Mourinho and Sir Alex Ferguson had some little back-and-forth snit-fit going, a reminder that at the helm of great teams stand unmitigated divas, their diva-ness contributing inescapably to their success. I tune out this stuff very rapidly these days, but Mourinho evidently had complained about the refereeing in Manchester United matches, possibly because of the fact that Cristiano Ronaldo had spent the year bolstering Portugal's hopes in the Olympic diving competition for both Beijing 2008 and London 2012, in both platform and springboard. In turn, Ferguson had responded to reporters that Mourinho should 'button his lip'. In Fratton Park after the win, Mourinho had responded to Moore and other reporters, 'Why should I shut up? He was allowed to talk about referees for the last 20 years of his career. What's the difference between me and him?' In life, high school actually never ends, even though they hand you a paper and tell you farewell. The prom kings and prom queens continue to snipe at each other for the duration.

So much meaning and undercurrent in the match, but to myself it seemed just to ooze on by. Much like the 2–0 Chelsea win in 2006 when first I saw Portsmouth, this seemed the depressing foregone conclusion against one of the big four. I might've even wondered why I bothered, had I bothered to wonder. Even the only bear named Charlie I'd ever met said he'd spent a good portion of the early evening obsessed with the moon, which looked downright red. He removed his paws and rang me frantically after the match, wondering if I had his wallet. We met up again at the Shepherd's Crook because we definitely needed another beer. Dan and I discussed the eternally strange story of the ineffectualness of England's national team, and he theorized that the English media freights the whole operation with spiteful pressure. I chimed in with my American tales of teams that adore media doubters so that they can 'prove the experts wrong' and then say, 'Nobody respected us.' The United States literally crawls with such athletes who have made a cliché of alleged disrespect. They can find the one denigration amid 1,000 compliments, even if it came from a fishing columnist in Nome, Alaska. They're desperate for somebody to say they're hopeless so they can locate some motivation.

It long since grew tiresome.

Sometime after I finished subjecting these unsuspecting souls to my diatribe on that particular cultural difference, we began to make our halting way home. We stopped at the little Tesco near the stadium to amass supplies, which included some abominable snack sausages and some heavenly little éclairs. This seemed a ritual for the three. Dan and Hopkins had met at university in Portsmouth, and in the Fratton End, Hopkins met Charlie, who hails from a lineage of Pompey allegiance. All three were 27, i.e. newborn. They became the first Portsmouth fans I knew personally, and this would mark an upgrade in my development as a fan. Once you know some Other People who follow the club, your fanhood intensifies. You begin to watch the club while wondering what they might be thinking while they watch the club, even if they're just thinking about a red moon.

If knowing Other People means walking the streets and train platforms with a blue bear, then I heartily endorse it, for a blue bear just makes life better in ways you don't expect. For one thing, people tend to greet you in pubs, and children might wave at you out of car windows.

On the glum side, our ride home somehow included a rail-replacement bus. We all sat on a back row, one row behind the only other apparent passenger. We offered him some sort of food which he accepted, and he continued existing somehow. The blue bear fell asleep during that ride, then woke and asked for an éclair only to hear Hopkins utter a deathless line, 'Eclairs are dead to you now.' Eventually, we did get to ride a train, on which a young male-female couple boarded with the male dressed as a Southampton fan. He immediately saw the blue Pompey bear and, proving that it's fearsome to see a blue bear on a train, immediately disclaimed any Southampton fandom. He said he'd dressed for a costume party.

As we rolled toward Waterloo, a singular blue bear repeatedly stated his loyalty to Portsmouth with what I came to regard as a haiku:

> *Any manager,*
> *Any players,*
> *Training on the moon,*
> *Fratton Park as it is,*
> *Pompey till I die.*

Over and over he said it, and I must tell you that you haven't really lived until you've ridden home on a train with a blue bear vowing support for his club given any manager, any players, and with Fratton Park as it is, no renovations or new stadiums necessary. Just the same, none of us could discern the meaning of the passage 'training on the moon'. Hopkins asked for an explanation of this peculiar 'training on the moon', and none came. But somehow, I felt giddy to have heard this haiku from a mammal on the South West Trains service back to Waterloo.

At Woking, Hopkins would disembark, but as a blue bear wished the party to continue, he tried to prevent Hopkins's departure. Hopkins managed to escape and exit and then, with the train waiting for five minutes and the doors still open, turned around and taunted the blue bear as if to say, *Come and get me.* Repeatedly the blue bear sprinted off the train toward Hopkins, only to hurry back for fear the doors would close. Repeatedly Hopkins tried to lure the blue bear once more. Repeatedly Dan and I doubled over on the train, and while it doesn't sound funny in the least, everyone really should see a blue bear chase somebody on a train platform late on a Saturday night at least once.

We said our goodbyes at Waterloo, and they headed for Kilburn to continue a session that would run until 9 a.m. (That rowdy Kilburn.) I thanked them for letting me interlope, figured I might not see them again and walked home through the vibrant London night glad I'd seen them for at least one red moon.

28

Betraying a kind Reading fan

Even when an American has lived three-quarters of a full Premiership season, some part of his underdeveloped brain retains a vague big-bad-wolf fear of the English football fan. It's irrational, but then, I'm from Virginia, and I come by irrational fear honestly. My mother once became the only person in global history to buy that flight insurance in the airport, and my beloved maternal grandmother, of course, envisioned the concept of carjacking way back in the 1970s before it ever became fashionable in Miami.

That's the only way I can explain my ludicrous behaviour of 17 March, when I spent a whole game declining to come out of the closet as a Portsmouth fan to a Reading fan, despite the Reading fan being clearly one of the most decent people extant – so decent, in fact, that he had relinquished a corporate job to work at the Royal Society for the Protection of Animals. People who work for less money to protect animals generally tend to refrain from berating or slugging other people, even opposing fans, but you never know.

I came to sit beside Mark in the Reading section via my usual ineptitude. To begin, Reading vs Portsmouth did not shout from the schedule when the Premier League drew up the 2006–07 fixtures, but it had sprouted as a little March colossus plump with European implications. Reading, having never graced the top flight previously in its 118-year history, had debuted with aplomb and picturesque football. Portsmouth, having just poked its head from the abyss of relegation 11 months prior, was flirting with its best top-flight season in 50 years.

By the sun-splashed morning of Saturday, 17 March, a chunk of the table looked thusly:

6. Everton – 43
7. Reading – 43
8. Tottenham Hotspur – 42
9. Portsmouth – 41
10. Blackburn – 40

Understandably, all the home tickets had sold for No. 7 Reading vs No. 9 Portsmouth, and with Reading only 44 miles from Portsmouth, we away sorts had to enter an away-ticket lottery. I had no idea how to enter an away-ticket lottery, because being a sportswriter for 20 years thoroughly debilitates the portion of the brain that deduces how to enter away-ticket lotteries. That's how I wound up standing on the sidewalk near the away entrance of Madejski Stadium, watching my people pass by, hoping someone might commit a crime and sell me an unused ticket.

Well, tick-tock, tick-tock, tick-tock, and I began to wonder where I'd spend the match. Madejski Stadium sits outside of town, suburban and all, very much like many an American stadium. It's next door to a B&Q, which must've made it either haunting or enticing for Glen Johnson. It's a lovely, spiffy stadium, but its alleged neighbourhood doesn't exactly teem with pubs in which I could watch a little colossus of a match. Maybe one day they'll put pubs in that field on the other side of the parking lot, but on 17 March there was no way they could complete them by kick-off.

Finally, before conceding and boarding a bus back into town, I decided to circumnavigate the stadium. At the door of the home ticket office, I played ditzy American tourist – one might call it typecasting – and I asked a guy if this match happened to be a sell-out when already I knew the answer. He replied that he thought so but that his father had not been able to attend and that he sought somebody to buy that ticket for £30. I volunteered eagerly, but I thought it might worry him if he knew he would be bringing in a Portsmouth fan who, for all he knew, might start taunting Reading fans, creating a gigantic brawl replete with hurled projectiles, and getting him banned from Madejski for life.

Note: Virginian-Americans often possess nimble imaginations capable of envisioning astonishing layers of potential doom.

So with kick-off nigh, Mark and I hurried toward the gate together, and we marched right on up the steps to his family's seats in the top row, which in cosy, 24,200-seat Madejski Stadium actually affords a grand view. We sat almost straight up behind the goal David James defended during the first half, all the way across the stadium from my people, so as to render my people inaudible. I dug into my pocket and excavated the £30. The match had begun. I figured Reading would win by probably 2–0, and I could not dislike Reading, as I'd visited training on assignment one day, found it a jovial place and interviewed goalkeeper Marcus Hahnemann, who said his two sons chide him about his unacceptable American pronunciation of the crucial English words 'Harry Potter'.

That's appealing and all, but I wanted Portsmouth to win some kind of badly, especially because I'd begun to fear Blackburn getting bumptious down there in 10th, as I'm that rare Pompey fan who'd spent my entire fan experience exclusively at single-digit Premiership positions, fearing the spiralling darkness of double digits. In a testament to my lucky timing, I'd only just learned that until 2005–06, Portsmouth had not played in a division higher than Southampton since 1960. Here I worried about Blackburn and Reading, not to mention Everton and Tottenham, while for 45 years – forty-five years – Pompey fans often seethed about a rival 17 miles away. I'd never even really seen a Southampton kit except on a train, and that one evidently was bound for a costume party.

In my scant experience, Southampton seemed dead as éclairs.

Well, Reading menaced our David James fortress early on, and I started to feel both nervousness and the wish to contain it, which I typically achieve by practising perspective and thinking about calamities such as typhoons, poverty or Tom Cruise. For the match's early stages, Reading kept making game bids, and Sol Campbell and the ever-admirable Linvoy Primus kept thwarting them, and I kept suppressing the urge to stand up and salute quietly, and I kept feeling guilty I had not told Mark the truth.

Moreover, Mark and I began to chat.

One of the first things I had noticed about English football was that people don't chat during matches. You never hear anybody talking about how they've bought a new sport utility vehicle, or how they're having trouble with the middle son who recently egged somebody's house in the adjacent neighbourhood, or how the workmen adding the deck to the back of the house have taken far too long so it might've been better to have hired Mexican illegals. In general, we Americans chat more during games. We might not chat so much at the NFL because many NFL fans only grunt, but we chat a bit at basketball during routs and timeouts, and many of us chat profusely at baseball, where the slowness lends itself to chatting. On the right side of the ocean, I've never heard English fans speak much more than brief comments to an adjacent person about a certain incident or the subterranean IQ of the referee or linesman. It's never about, say, their wife's annoying new poodle.

That's why I felt self-conscious just sitting there chatting even with a profoundly kind individual. Mark talked about how his job change has left him driving home from work feeling his workday has boosted the world ever so slightly. He talked about how British politicians all espouse pretty much the same ideas, and that American politics seem to display more contrasts. He talked about Hillary Clinton. He talked about how he's never been to the United States but saw England win the rugby World Cup in Australia. I talked, too. I talked about how I still couldn't believe rugby's the game played by gentlemen while football's supposedly the one played by ruffians. I talked about how David Beckham exudes a certain decency, as I'd just seen him on the previous Wednesday at Old Trafford thanking Manchester United fans at half-time of an exhibition. I talked about Iraq. I talked about how Senator John McCain refused to appease the religious right wing when it had clout during the 2000 presidential campaign, thus costing him, and how now he plans to appease the religious right wing for the 2008 presidential campaign just as its clout has diminished, thus costing him. I talked about the United States' huge college football stadiums and its plush dressing rooms vis-à-vis Manchester United. I talked about Reading's unpretentious training facility and how players have to walk outside from their showers back to their dressing area wearing nothing but a towel, and along the way they sometimes kid the 40-ish female locker-room attendant, who rolls her eyes.

Mercy, did we talk, and of course, I talked more than he did, and even though I tried to keep the tone relatively hushed, I felt certain I saw this blumpy guy in front of us tire of overhearing the chatting and glare at me through the corner of his left eye.

On the pitch, Reading's first goal seemed ever more inevitable, and I still did not tell Mark of my dread. A Steve Sidwell header darted somehow wide, and I still did not tell Mark of my relief. Campbell the giant defused a Dave Kitson chance, and I still did not tell Mark of my ga-ga pleasure at that defusion. Some fans around me sang the Pompey chimes only with 'F—up, Pompey', and I still did not tell Mark that his brethren lacked creativity.

No, I just sat there gabbing but not telling, and I learned that the longer you wait to tell somebody you're posing as neutral while feeling very partial, the harder it gets to tell somebody you're posing as neutral while feeling very partial. I let on that I'd been to Fratton Park many times, but also that I'd been to Madejski Stadium twice, and to Villa Park and St James' Park and the Reebok Stadium and the JJB Stadium (twice!). I felt lamer than lame, unable to divulge my true self to this gentle soul while the match played on and I definitely wanted my club to rip the pure living stuffing out of his club.

Then the energy reversed after half-time, and Portsmouth began conducting the show, and Benjani Mwaruwari thumped a great shot that Hahnemann saved. As time dragged by, I began to think Pompey might get out of there with a point, even if the melodramatically troubled West Ham couldn't possibly win at Blackburn. I also began rationalizing that my secrecy made perfect sense. Any rational person would wait until the end of the game to tell this Reading fan he'd harboured an infiltrator.

Suddenly, boom, at 81 minutes, a Portsmouth player I'd seldom noticed, Richard Hughes, struck one from 30 yards out just below us. It beat everybody, including Hahnemann, and for a fleeting second I thought about sixth place. Then it banged off the right upright and straight back out of danger, and I smothered an intensely guttural groan. I could not express to anyone how desperately I wanted that shot to glance off that upright and into the goal, or to miss the upright altogether and depress my fellow American in goal down there. I don't know why. I certainly felt no disdain for Reading. Something had bitten me, and after a lifetime of viewing 'standings' – tables – bookishly, objectively, I wanted sixth place so much more than, say, 10th.

When the match ended, nobody had scored, whereupon we walked out, still talking, and I decided I'd loathe myself even more than usual if I did not tell Mark that all along I had been supporting Pompey with undetectable twitches and phantom fist pumps. Before he made off I thanked him for everything and I confessed, even telling him how that Hughes post-banger had left me in a mild state of anguish. 'I am sorry for betraying you,' I said.

Well, he seemed so very nonplussed as to make my game-long misgivings seem toweringly ludicrous. He even told me that either the best man in his wedding had been a Portsmouth fan or that he had served as the best man in the wedding of a Portsmouth fan, I can't remember which, because I felt too consumed with my own absurdity. But at least Portsmouth got a point to reach 42, and somehow, apparently with a referee's help, West Ham won 2–1 at Blackburn. It had been a lucky, if preposterous, day.

29

Just disgusting

The March portion of the Premiership season contains these gaping breaks so that the national team can flourish on certain weekends without distraction. On Saturday, 24 March, England played Israel in a Euro 2008 qualifier, and I walked all over central London seeking a pub with enough room to stand and watch. 'Twas a challenge. I finally found one near the British Museum, where I could only squeeze inside the door and watch from a crummy angle in the foyer. This qualifies as irony, for the dismalness we watched – on a big screen, so we could observe it more closely – gained its best summation from Rod Liddle in the *Sunday Times*. Having suggested that the TV rights for England's national games should go for '£8.50, a used Oyster card and maybe a couple of bags of Walkers crisps', he then wrote, 'By pure chance I was in Tel Aviv last Saturday and could have gone to the game. My options were: watch England play Israel, or go to the West Bank and get bricked or maybe beheaded by angry and oppressed Palestinians. No question: "Shalom! Take me to Hebron!" I shouted to the nearest taxi driver.'

This ceaseless national melodrama counts as choice entertainment for Americans, seeing as how we're probably too spacious to have our own similar bonding-and-griping experience. When we lose at a game we invented – example: basketball, 2004 Athens Olympics, semi-final, to Argentina – we often just opt for some excuse (didn't bring our best players) and get on

203

with it. Or if we lose at a game of privilege we ought to dominate – example: Ryder Cup, repeatedly – we just turn our attention to something else, usually the NFL, where we'll never lose, mostly because almost nobody else actually plays the game.

We're sunnier sorts, in general. It's probably the weather or the newness as a nation.

But after marvelling at another cycle of English national team angst – at least, media angst – it can seem the Premiership season was discontinued long ago and that, oh, it's time for that again, and good. I'd never been to Craven Cottage, never heard much about Craven Cottage, never knew if Craven Cottage really had any lore. I had to dig into my London A–Z to find the location of Craven Cottage, and I made my way on the Tube on 31 March, a luminous Saturday. Amazingly, the Pompey troika had continued to email me, and we'd made loose plans to convene so I could even meet 'Ms Pompeybear' before she led her mammal off to Sydney. In our third and fourth cases of running across each other by accident, I found myself standing next to Dan on the platform at Notting Hill Gate, and after we boarded, we found ourselves in the same Tube carriage with Charlie, furless in civilian clothing, and with Ms Caroline Pompeybear, an outright gem from the get-go.

At some point in that ride on the District Line to Putney Bridge, or out of the station through Bishop's Park along the Thames, we discussed one of my favourite new subjects of my Premiership tutelage. As Dan had explained on Chelsea day at the Shepherd's Crook, there's a sign in Craven Cottage, just as you enter the away end. This sign has an arrow. It gives directions to the uninitiated.

It reads: 'away and neutral fans'.

That 'neutral fans' bit just really galled Dan, to my great amusement as a native of a country of stadiums rich in neutral fans such as business travellers, weary parents or those people who drive around on clichéd baseball pilgrimages, collecting stadiums and wasting petroleum. Where I would've never given it a thought, Dan found 'neutral fans' borderline-appalling. How could a person even be a 'neutral fan', and why would a 'neutral fan' even bother? That, in turn, made me eager to witness this sign for myself, here in this country of devout football partisanship and partisan football din. I mentioned my excitement that we'd see the 'neutral fans' sign – he rolled his eyes – and my theory that perhaps the neutral-fans zone of the stadium could serve as some sort of temporary holding place. Maybe somebody would arrive as a neutral fan, but then during a given match might take a shine to a player or a club or a club's colours, whereupon that person could proceed to another section or go to a newly formed subsection of the neutral-fan zone. (The post-neutral zone, possibly.) Or maybe a home or away fan might become so aghast at his own club's malfeasance or a manager's ineptitude, that he might forfeit his own zone to access the neutral zone, gaining a respite from the unbearable emotional investment.

Well, a few things about Craven Cottage: it's gorgeous. Its away section offers a grand view of the Thames, of even the current on the Thames, of even the crews rowing along on said current of said Thames. It's expensive in ticket prices and concessions, perhaps gouging people for that view of the Thames and the rowers. It's not really all that loud, befitting a club owned by the owner of a chi-chi department store. And it does have one of the craziest signs of the Premiership, the one that kindly offers directions to those potentially lost neutral fans.

Portsmouth remained in ninth place with 42 points, three behind seventh-place Tottenham but with an advantage in 'goal differential', as I dumbly called it before Hopkins corrected me to the proper 'goal difference'. Fulham had 14th place, with 34 points. While my three new friends went to their section, I went to mine, plopping down about 30 rows behind one of the goals and just to the right of a man named Chris, who said he'd been a Pompey fan for 50 years and had lived his entire life on the Isle of Wight. I said I'd been a Pompey fan for one year, and might've said that during my teen years my school in Virginia had a fierce basketball rivalry with Isle of Wight Academy, which sat just up the highway. I did not say we had a chant about the Isle of Wight Chargers that might just illustrate our national deficiencies in singing and chanting, for it went like this:

> *Chargers are what? Rednecks!*
> *Chargers are what? Rednecks!*
> *Spell it!*
> *R-E-D-N-E-X, rednecks, rednecks, rednecks!*

Then again, I don't tell this to many people.

Chris had travelled alone and seemed so gentle and seemed to get a kick out of some of the inventions that would emerge from our end, particularly the 'Scummer, scummer, scummer' derivations, directed all game long at Antti Niemi, the Fulham goalkeeper. Eventually, at moments when Niemi seemed alone while everybody else played at the other end, I began to figure out that of all the Fulham players, it was Niemi they taunted, and not because of any bias against Finland. He probably once played for Southampton.

Early on, though, there came a jolt, one I still love to call up on YouTube. As the recording begins, you can still hear one group of fans and not the other, and guess which. Yes, the outnumbered. It's one of my favourite songs, to the 'Volare' tune:

> *Benjani, whoaaaaa-oh,*
> *Benjani, whoaaaaa-oh,*
> *He comes from Zimbabwe,*
> *He's gonna score today,*
> *Benjani, whoaaaaa-oh.*

At the other end of the pitch, only four minutes in, it might've been Benjani who played the ball into the middle to Kanu, who headed it out to our left to young Niko Kranjcar, Croatian, aged 22. Kranjcar edged to his right and let fly around the defence a ball that from our angle seemed headed well wide of the right-hand post.

In the next instant, however, that thing crashed into the net. We went absolutely berserk.

I'd dare to say that we were mental.

That ball had headed right and then curled around leftward and left Niemi frozen while it helped itself to the top right corner of the goal. The away stand of Craven Cottage began to shudder utterly, which freaked me out slightly and prompted two disparate thoughts. It made me think of the 6.1 earthquake I'd felt in Los Angeles on 1 October 1987, and how my friends' swimming pool out back had little ripple waves, but how their golden retriever lay there unmoved and unimpressed, as if saying, 'I heard this coming before you did.' And it made me think of old Mile High Stadium in Denver, before it yielded to a new stadium across the way. Occupying the Mountain Time Zone, the least populous of the American mainland's four time zones, the fans of the NFL Denver Broncos don't get a ton of national credit for their passion, but passion they possess, as one of the few professional-fan groups with passion to match England's. Normally, for anything to rival English zeal, one must visit a college stadium or coliseum, even as a neutral fan. The old Mile High Stadium in Denver, though, remains the only American stadium to cause wavelets in my press-box coffee, and when I think of Denver set against the stunning Rocky Mountains, I think of those wavelets.

When the stand stopped shaking and I resumed normal respiration, I foresaw 45 points and maybe even sixth place. That led me toward a terrible bit of education, the terrible strain felt when you care about a match and you hold a one-goal lead through almost its entirety. In all of sport, there might not be another routine scenario so nerve-clattering.

Neighbouring Pompey supporters bitched at the team's

performance for the second half of the first half. They railed that Uncle Harry can't get them to sustain anything. David James made a dazzling save at 42 minutes as he neared the all-time Premiership clean-sheet record of 142. The second half crawled by. I felt almost ill and pleaded for time to hurry. I kept my mobile phone in my right hand and looked at it repeatedly. Portsmouth's Svetoslav Todorov, whom I did not recognize, just missed one good chance and one golden chance for 2–0, but I thought we still might make it. We made it to 70 minutes, to 75, to 80, to 85, 88.

We even made it to 90 minutes, and through a good bit of the four minutes of added time. Added time had begun at 4.51 p.m., but I couldn't be sure how many seconds had passed within that minute, so I felt confused. Play continued mercilessly. I reached that point where you think just one or two more 'stops' – that would be an American-football term – might finish off matters.

Then, in a crowded sequence I couldn't see clearly, Fulham's Ian Pearce struck a prayer of a shot. James shifted to cut it off. The prayer caromed off Linvoy Primus's leg. It hurried back toward the right portion of the goal that James had departed. It wrong-footed James. It dribbled sickly into the goal for Pearce, who had spent five minutes of the match on the sideline with the physio, then hobbled through the next 10. I felt an incomparable thud. I wished they'd equalized at 12 minutes rather than 92. James took the ball and disgustedly punted it over the roof and maybe into the Thames, maybe even whacking some unsuspecting rowers and influencing the outcome of some sanguine crew event. I had my first genuine, galling, what-if defeat, even in a draw. Yes, this supplanted Charlton, even with that a loss. Uncle Harry would call it 'a real opportunity lost'. Sol Campbell and James would walk off looking crestfallen.

I believe that signalled that I'd signed on to caring archly, and I thought a bit about Bostonians and Chicagoans, the United States' most accomplished connoisseurs of last-second pratfalls.

In a hyper-famous case with Boston in 1986, the Red Sox sat one out from their first World Series title in 68 years, in New York against the Mets. They led 5–3. They proceeded to yield three of the most haunted runs ever, giving up looping hits that wandered into unmanned spaces. Then the last run scored when a bubbling little trifle of a ground ball slipped through the legs of a first baseman and, with uncommon harshness, altered his image for ever. Boston's drought would age to 86 years before the quenching. In a staggering case from Chicago in 2003, the sad-sack Cubs sat six outs from reaching their first World Series in 58 years. They led 3–0, in Chicago. A Florida Marlins player popped a fly up the left-field side, ripe for catching by Chicago's left fielder. Just then, a fan extended his hands and attempted to catch the souvenir ball, deflecting it from the left fielder, who freaked out. Within the next several, garish minutes, the Cubs also freaked out, and the Marlins scored *eight* runs, and, with uncommon harshness, the fan grew infamous.

Everybody knows his name.

People in my job always chronicle the fan masses beholding these fateful disasters, but we often don't quite comprehend the feelings. I felt I knew just a little inkling of it when that ball redirected itself past James. Carried to its ultimate definition, it's powerlessness, right? Whatever powerlessness I felt, my more veteran Portsmouth brethren felt it exponentially. The entire stand seemed powerless. What could it do?

As the tepid Fulham fans made their little roar, Pompey decided to lash out in the only direction possible, and in the only vein available, toward the home fans, and with an assessment:

> *Your support is,*
> *Your support is,*
> *Your support is f——ing s——!*
> *Your support is f——ing s——!*

I felt astonished, while gutted.

30

Rather hopeless

A visit from Manchester United on a sunny first Saturday in April probably should resuscitate a fan to the brink of foaming at the mouth, but I felt only glum and peeved. The Fulham fiasco had really taken some starch out of me, to a surprising degree given my 20 years as a detached chronicler allowing myself only fleeting bouts of rooting for somebody-or-other, often only because their opponents practised obnoxiousness. After Fulham, I even wondered why we bother placing such psychological emphasis on something that can hinge on a prayer ricocheting off the leg of a commendable defender.

As the Pompey fans walked out of Craven Cottage in a barely budging blob, the foremost buzz concerned Southampton's concurrent 6–0 win over Wolves, and that illustrated the difference between the seasoned crowd and myself. Where the idea of prayers that ricocheted off the legs of commendable defenders and robbed your club of two points rankled with me, it rankled with them less, some having ventured to the fourth division and back during their lifetimes. And while I thought of Southampton as pretty much just another Championship club trying to elbow toward promotion, they knew it as Lucifer.

One must always keep an eye on Lucifer, but I had no Lucifer with the possible exception of Ben Thatcher, so I reeled. First, we proceeded to a pub, an idea I welcomed because repeated scientific studies show that beer possesses an elixir component that shoos from the cranium that horrid what-if feeling after a goal has ricocheted off a leg. That component is widely believed to be alcohol.

For the next Saturday, 7 April, I plied another time-honoured defence mechanism in the fanatic's repertoire – the downplaying of the next game or match, the grand pooh-poohing, the careful practice of low expectations. The brain suffers greatly from fluke goals ricocheting off legs during injury time, or from ninth-inning home runs that wipe out leads, or from fumbles at the two-yard line on the brink of the Super Bowl. My brain carried it to an extreme in which I not only expected nothing from Portsmouth vs Manchester United, but I began to resent that I had spent time and concern on seeing Portsmouth vs Manchester United or on any of this crud in the United States or its mother, the United Kingdom.

As I walked toward Fratton Park, I pretty much mumbled grumbles. I railed within my own brain against the system that subjected us to such predictability. I counted myself as part of a manipulated public and loathed the dishonour. I did spend a millisecond wondering about the wisdom of Sir Alex Ferguson's comment that he could almost taste the title, but I figured he'd honed a keenness on such matters and knew predictability when he saw it. I just knew the Manchester United match would bear a rote resemblance to the Chelsea match, what with Manchester United in dire need, only three points ahead of Chelsea (78–75) by kick-off.

Really, I just about up and questioned an entire life of following games, and I felt contempt for the tiered Premiership system in which you could have a Big Four that has claimed every single one of the last 10 Premiership and 10 FA Cup titles. The money athletes make, I'd never once resented. I'd always figured it made marketplace sense. If the public wants to resent the salaries, then the public can stop funding the salaries. Besides, better to have the largesse in the hands of, say, a bunch of athletes and one club owner, than in the hands of one club owner. If you spread the money around more, maybe it will trickle down more, as when the athletes give it to, say, needy lap dancers.

Yet the system that allows four or five clubs to outspend the others, then pretend they've achieved something when they finish in the top four . . . I decided I hated that as I ambled up Goldsmith Avenue. The imbalance smacks of Major League Baseball, but even baseball lacks the metronomic predictability of those four finishing one through four in the Premiership. Sure, some baseball clubs serve as perennial plankton, never to surface, and some baseball clubs' payrolls can be more than six times those of others ($200 million–$30 million), and there's no thrill-ride of relegation, and baseball's pretty much a festival of steroid-addled phoniness, but the last seven World Series have featured 11 different franchises and seven different champions.

So, money. Always, always money. I always loved sport, not money. Salary negotiations make me yawn. Contract details, even the lavish accoutrements of athletes, bore me to beige. The NFL and the NBA and rugby have salary caps, and most everyone agrees that's wise, but if you start to get into salary-cap details, I start to tune out and mull more compelling things, which include just about anything else on earth. I love to read a good sports section and can't make it through three paragraphs of a good business section. Yet as long-term members of American sports sections, my cronies and I had become business writers ever more until one day in 2005 I found myself refuting the business logic of George Steinbrenner, shipping magnate and bombastic owner of the spectacularly affluent New York Yankees! The absurdity! And yet, I was right, and Steinbrenner, wrong! The double absurdity! Steinbrenner had argued against NFL-style revenue sharing among baseball clubs by noting that Wal-Mart doesn't share revenues with the Target up the boulevard. That argument is, of course, fallacious, and maybe even devious, because he'd misidentified his product, and surely he knows product. The Wal-Mart and Target brands are Wal-Mart and Target, while the New York Yankees' product is baseball, and if you don't believe it, let the Yankees play alone every night and see how well that draws after a short period of people turning up for intra-squad exhibitions.

Around and around and around we go, we sport people, paying attention to sport and paying for sport and even writing about sport, thus generating money, then reeling from that dulling sense that comes from the proliferation of . . . money.

Sigh.

As I entered the antiquated brick gate at Fratton Park, the powerlessness had grabbed me again, I suppose. Still, once inside, I had to admit the occasion seemed boosted by the presence of star-shine from Wayne Rooney and Cristiano Ronaldo, the Premiership Player of the Year. It just made things seem heavier, more pertinent, with the red of Manchester United fuller and redder than normal red. And on a sunny spring afternoon on the south coast of England, Fratton Park seemed unusually plugged in, even for itself, doubtless because of the presence of Manchester United as opposed to say, Wigan. Many of these souls had probably borne Fratton Park witness to Portsmouth's wins over Manchester United in 2004 and 2005.

So here came Manchester United. Ronaldo's runs up the pitch could take your breath away and dredge a gasp had you any concern for the preservation of the home goal. Rooney's very presence instilled dread. Ferguson had just finished playing a Champions League quarter-final leg at Roma on Wednesday night, so he rested Ryan Giggs for the first half, but his team hadn't lost in the Premiership in seven matches, or since the Sunday before playing Portsmouth in that FA Cup fourth-rounder. At 10 minutes, Kanu headed one into the arms of Manchester United keeper Edwin van der Sar. I had that fore-boding feeling that even such half-opportunities would prove scarce.

Ronaldo began treating us to a recital of his catalogue of dives. He dived often enough that I began to wonder if he missed opportunities that would've come moments after the dive had he merely stayed up and not dived. Other teams like Tottenham and Middlesbrough had complained about his diving, and Ferguson and Ronaldo more or less had accused other teams of envy, when in reality other teams had complained about his diving for a completely different reason: because he had been diving. As he dived at Fratton Park, and the Fratton Park faithful along the North Stand barked their gripes, that the referees rewarded some of the dives with free kicks. Ronaldo sent a 35-yard free kick wide left at 12 minutes, another into a two-man wall at 24 minutes (accuracy check courtesy of the match reports of football.co.uk). In other scary sequences, Ronaldo blew by both Dejan Stefanovic and Linvoy Primus, but sent a shot wide to the right, and Rooney fell at the behest of Primus's sliding tackle and the referee managed to rule it a fair challenge.

The Fratton End got involved.

To the tune of 'If You're Happy and You Know It', there came a charming version we never sang in grade school back in the Colonies. It went:

> *If you really f——ing hate 'em, clap your hands,*
> *If you really f——ing hate 'em, clap your hands,*
> *If you really f——ing hate 'em,*
> *Really f——ing hate 'em,*
> *Really f——ing hate 'em, clap your hands*

I marvelled at how my American schoolteachers shielded us, often not teaching us the real lyrics to songs.

As a special gift to Rooney, the Fratton End sang, to 'Guantanamera':

> *Fat, ugly Scouser,*
> *You're just a fat, ugly Scouser,*
> *Fat, ugly Scouuuuu-ser,*
> *You're just a fat, ugly Scouuuuu-ser.*

That one just struck me as unkind.

At 25 minutes, Manchester United's Kieran Richardson missed a reasonable chance from a Ronaldo free kick, high and wide, and we mocked him, and the match had settled in. It seemed plausible, even with scant knowledge of strategy, that Pompey had opted to challenge Manchester United rather than sticking its proverbial tail betwixt its proverbial legs. Pompey did forge a few more chances than I'd expected in my apprenticeship and my misery. After all, up at Old Trafford in November, Manchester United had won 3–0, and across the winter, Pompey's attack had withered. But even with that, Pompey's chances did seem here-and-there, while Manchester United's suggested the beach, as you could set the waves by your watch. In a here-and-there moment at 30 minutes, Benjani Mwaruwari shot one from, oh, I don't know, maybe 30 yards, and van der Sar saved it but did not quite corral it, at the goal just below the Fratton End and just off to my right.

Just then, Matt Taylor slid into my line of sight, where veteran observers had probably noticed him all along. He beat Rio Ferdinand to the ball and flicked it right back into the net, just like that. It happened so suddenly that it seemed untrue. I waited for a signal that somebody had gone offside or committed some arcane infraction wholly unfamiliar to myself. Pompey led 1–0. There seemed a vacant split second there until the Fratton End heaved in mass mirth. I jumped up and down a bit but felt just as much amazement as joy, plus that twinge of caution because we're at only 30 minutes and the other side still goes by the name Manchester United.

A 1–0 lead against Manchester United presents the terrible spectre of hope, so the brain must counterbalance that by anticipating a sure equalizer. The equalizer's coming, you know. It's coming. When? It's coming. At the distant end, that souped-up red attack believed likewise. Michael Carrick quickly had a chance but sent it wide. A stray ball found Rooney at 35 minutes, worst thing a stray ball can do, but he missed a long shot wide.

Carrick then prised open the defence, giving Fletcher a point-blank shot, but James saved it with his considerable legs. Lauren got a yellow card for fouling Ronaldo.

Pompey had a few mild chances.

Then the whole thing slid into half-time, Portsmouth ahead by that 1–0. Here again came football's peerless precariousness, but in an outsized version. For it's one thing to suffer through a second half with a 1–0 lead at Fulham, wishing time would accelerate, but to do the same against Manchester United, there's a temptation just to refrain from looking – you know, just go ahead and leave the premises.

31

The greatest own goal in history

I didn't leave, of course, just sat there for more spite from the sport beast – what else would I do with my time? – while Pompey and Manchester United emerged to go on with an ominous second half. With every extraction of my pen and little pieces of paper for jotting down notes, I'd find my hands quivering increasingly, until the writing got all wavy and illegible. With every futile extraction of my mobile phone, fixing to extend the grand tradition of text-messaging friends from football stands, I'd find my thumbs too a-twitter to text efficiently. They'd blight the phone screen with an errant letter or numeral and I'd just stop before I committed a semicolon. In this 21st century, a great match means one during which your hands cannot text.

At the mouth of the goal just down below, during the 50-something minutes, Manchester United left James so festooned with shots that I went ahead and conceded the goal. Counted it. Regarded the score as 1–1. As Primus cleaned up a through ball destined eerily for Rooney in the 53rd minute, I remembered with trademark ineptitude that Portsmouth didn't have the unfit Sol Campbell that day, and that I'd been so tremulous that I'd completely blanked out on the absence of a behemoth. The biggest peril came in the 58th minute, when it pretty much turned into Times Square down there in the Portsmouth goalmouth. Seemingly half the population of Manchester took shots at the home goal. James made at least one astounding save, which I believe might've been the one-handed Spider-Man prevention of a Ronaldo bid from a corner from Giggs, a Ferguson half-time substitution. The 36-year-old keeper once dubbed 'Calamity' had upheld a stadium's spirits for just that much longer.

Ole Gunnar Solskjaer followed up that save, and Lauren cleared that rebound.

Pitiless, this match.

Fifty-nine minutes, and Giggs loosed a screaming thing that forced a fingertip save from the taller, dark-haired Spider-Man in goal. Sixty-three minutes, and Rooney and Giggs set up Carrick, who shot wide. Sixty-nine minutes, and dread fear, Rooney, on the loose, corralling a Giggs pass, ready to gut the whole of us, then, suddenly, down went Rooney, courtesy Primus, in the box, and pleading for a penalty I suspected he'd get. Yet it did not come. Primus, once considered insufficiently gifted for the top flight, once more had foiled a 21-year-old star deemed extravagantly gifted since his single-digit years.

So the 20,223 of us lurched into the 70th minute, officially entering the concentric circles of horror. An equalizer in the 70–75 range would smart; an equalizer in the 75–80 range would sting a bit; an equalizer in the 80–85 range would sting for real; and an equalizer in the 85–93 range can make you wonder why you continue to put yourself through this kind of thing. Seventy-one minutes, 72, 73. With every time Portsmouth pushed the ball into the Manchester United end, I'd lop off another 30 seconds we'd no longer have to suffer. I pictured us all clambering to various plateaus – the 75-minute plateau, the 77, the 80.

Almost unbearable, it was. Nobody chatted, because nobody ever does, but nobody even made a sound, as every eye in our section remained fixed upon the pitch. Maybe this represents the positive health effects of sport, the fact you're so diverted from everyday worries, but I just didn't feel all that positively healthy. I'd begun quaking not so much unlike the time at age 10 when I thought I heard a burglar in my grandmother's house.

Ronaldo crossed to Giggs. Giggs sent a header just wide. Benign torture persisted.

The referee booked James for taking too long for a goal kick at 77 minutes, and it barely registered with me, and my lack of concern reiterated the duplicity of fandom just 11 Saturdays after Charlton's stalling had vexed me utterly. Eighty minutes. We made 80. I don't know how. Almost 81, but here came Ronaldo, dashing as if on a horse, getting inside the box but shooting wide. Eighty-one. Help. Please. Help.

This had begun to take the shape of something epic, something that would always stand out from my first Pompey year. Even though I'd spoken personally to nobody around me, and even though none of us had hugged any strangers from what I could tell, I felt us all together in the wretched art of hope. I looked over to my left at the North Stand and felt kindred with those strangers as well. Ronaldo tried something from afar in the 85th minute, and James saved it easily.

Eighty-five, 86, 87, and hyperventilation, and the woozy effects of hyperventilation, and please, put a stop to this. The Fulham débâcle remained entrenched in my mind, and if I'd thought of it, I could've grimaced at a different Fulham débâcle, the one Ronaldo pulled out at the end at Craven Cottage earlier in the season, or maybe Manchester United's added-time win at Liverpool. But I believe my brain blotted out those memories to prevent a dread overflow.

Eighty-eight, and at moments Fratton Park seemed oddly subdued, probably in fret, even with two recent-years wins over Manchester United stashed in these other fans' memories. Those squads, however, lacked the fully formed Ronaldo, and the fully formed Ronaldo added a tier of fear even if he looked sort of, you know, pretty. No one knew where this thing might head, until it headed in exactly the last direction anybody on the Premiership planet would've guessed.

In that 89th minute, the ball rattled around midfield a bit. If you look at a recording, you can see it trickle to Matt Taylor, but I could not see that clearly from my end and in my state. You can see Taylor then try to send it to Lomana LuaLua as the latter darts toward the goal, but too many players stood between myself and the fray for any clear vision of that. Then you can see Rio Ferdinand materialize to outrun LuaLua and clean it up, and then to back-pass the ball to van der Sar and to safety.

Again, from the other end of the park, this all looked muddled.

Then we could see that the ball, having left Ferdinand's foot, began rolling.

It kept rolling.

And it kept rolling.

It seemed to roll for a few minutes even though it didn't, and it seemed to roll right into indelible memory.

I suppose a roll so slow could qualify as sickly were that ball rolling into your team's goal. It probably turns up sometimes in a nightmare similar to one I'd have as a child, in which I'd hit a baseball to the fence but continually trip on the way to first base until they threw me out. Maybe the rolling ball turned up in van der Sar's REM stages soon thereafter, and maybe he could even see himself probably too far out from the goal, moving left to fend off LuaLua's possible charge, then wrong-footed, then seeing the ball slip back to his right, not really so far from his hand as he leaned opposite. Maybe in the nightmare, it went through his fingers. Maybe he could revisit the sight of his feet, which looked so frozen in his alarm that it's possible he might've tried to move them but couldn't. On the recording, it appears he might've caught up to that ball had he wheeled and sprinted.

Suppose, though, that the trickling ball becomes absolutely one of the most gorgeous things you've seen in a lifetime of sport-viewing. It would never seem nightmarish, but first it would seem ... Weird. Seemed just weird. It seemed a whistle must've blown, and play must've stopped, because only in odd circumstances could a ball roll that leisurely for that long without some fleet sort intervening. So only in instant recollection did that ball join my list of the greatest things ever. Only in rethinking did it seem to smile on its way into the Manchester United goal, maybe even giggle. Only in rehash did it come to rival a linebacker tackling a receiver on the one-yard line on the last play of a Super Bowl ending so riveting I couldn't breathe, or the sight of Tiger Woods set against the waters of Pebble Beach winning the 2000 US Open by 15 shots, or the ninth son of Wyoming dairy farmers winning a Graeco-Roman gold medal at Sydney against a god who used to train by pretty much running around Siberia carrying refrigerators.

Right up there with them goes one plucky little ball rolling across the terrain of Hampshire, southern England, rolling away from myself and toward the Milton End and the away supporters, rolling into the 'wrong' goal, indelibly.

So as Fratton Park palpably went from this moment of vague confusion to this moment of grand realization, and as the realization seemed to spend a lagging second creeping up the rows and across the sections and into the top corners and the wigs and the drummers and the buglers and at least one blue bear, and as I began to absorb the truth probably another second after everybody else, something happened to me that I would not confess to just anybody.

I cried.

Ugh, the dubiousness.

But I cried.

Oh, come on, I was new.

Twenty years of proud and relative objectivity, then one year of fandom, and here, near the end, tears streaming down because some ball just inadvertently trickled into some mastodon club's goal. Nobody hugged me, and I didn't hug anybody, and it's clear I happened upon a section of non-huggers in a country full of huggers, but it didn't matter, because I hopped and hopped in disbelief, and the tears rolled. Even in a cramped old rodeo ground, there seemed ample room for hopping, because everybody hopped, and the whole Fratton End of the stadium seemed to come unglued and convulse with relief and exhilaration. Then I scanned as much of the stadium as I could, and found the whole long North Stand convulsing similarly.

The moment soared, Pompey led 2–0, Pompey would get all three points from Manchester United after getting only one at Fulham, this was one of the greatest things I'd seen, and something about the blundering nature of the goal added to its appeal. The best team in the league had got confused; the ruthless order of the table had inverted. Bizarrely, it could not have been any better had that noblest of Portsmouth noblemen, maybe Primus, headed in one *à la* West Ham. The gaffe fed the charm. And injury time began. And injury time would be so much easier than anticipated. And then, at the outset of injury time, Solskjaer shot, and James deflected, and John O'Shea gobbled up the rebound and banged it in, scoring the perfunctory Manchester United goal I'd expected all along. Now it stood at 2–1, with still more horrid injury time remaining, but with my central nervous system almost incapable of reactivating steep worry. Manchester United held another goalmouth convention of keen passers below us; Alan Smith loosed a dangerous shot; Spider-Man saved that. The convention reconvened; Solskjaer fired; that one whizzed over the bar.

James gathered it and punted, and as that ball went up, the whistle sang its long-awaited aria.

A roar filled the ground.

Then, most patrons turned to depart. American fans might behold an upset and stay, making more roars. English fans, I suppose, have seen it all already. As the left edge of the Fratton End began bunching up and leaving, I stayed put, standing there looking out over the pitch, trying to digest the exhilaration. I fielded some texts cleanly, and confessed to some that I had blubbered after that ball finished dribbling into the goal.

But it's strange. It really doesn't make much sense. It's not like Portsmouth's 2–1 win decided the title, helped decide the title or clinched anybody's spot in Europe. It's not like it proved all that much of a downer to Manchester United, who spent the ensuing Wednesday doubling as the Old Trafford symphony in a 7–1 win over Roma.

It's only that I'm certain that for the remainder of my days, I'll be able to recount the feverish 89th minute of 7 April, when the best own goal I'll ever see went trundling into the net at the other end of the pitch like some little trickle of magic.

32

You have to be kidding me

If roaming a town aglow after a landmark win, I highly recommend tagging along with a blue bear, if at all possible. I realize the option may not exist for many people and, in fact, may not exist for 99.9999994 per cent of the global population, given the world's appalling shortage of blue bears. Still, without boasting or anything, I must say that a blue bear simply improves a festive evening in ways you'd never foresee. Indeed, it's possible to forge something approaching a good cry because most people go through their entire lives without ever walking around with a blue bear.

It's not just that children beam and wave from car windows, even though it's pretty damned great that children beam and wave from car windows. It's more the look on people's faces when the pub doors open and a blue bear walks in. You can tell that in a world of hardship, strife, divorce, famine, drought, debts and Floyd Landis, it just lifts people a mite when one of the organisms coming through the door happens to be a blue bear. Even if they already knew a blue bear lived and breathed and bought season tickets in their midst, their expressions still take on a smile or a hint of wonderment that tells you the daily drudgery just subsided for a moment.

What's more, once inside, Charlie's an ursine Pied Piper. He makes everybody feel welcome, a part of things, whether he knows them well or knows them only through a Pompey chat room or doesn't really know them at all. He so obviously improves the spirit of a room.

On the night of 7 April, we lacked Dan (mum's birthday) but had Hopkins plus Dave, an Aston Villa fan I could treat to my tedious account of having almost chosen Aston Villa. We swept through several pubs in the Fratton area, plus one convenience store, and the whole thing seemed some sort of zenith of fun, partly because the memory bank had just annexed that ball trickling across the soil into the Manchester United goal. We reached a pub I'd never visited and would have trouble finding again. We met more Pompey fans, who increasingly to myself had begun to develop specific faces and names and existences. We checked departing-train schedules on mobile-phone screens and repeatedly missed those same departing trains by ordering fresh rounds. We completed the whole merry trek in the pub across the street from the train station, where some wry sort saw the blue bear with Pompey insignia and said, 'Man United fan?' And then somebody else from management asked us to leave, because occasionally there's somebody who can't share billing with a blue bear, who feels rickety within the caste system of the animal kingdom. We see this all the time on David Attenborough.

Whatever lurks in human tissue and makes us crave victory and makes us grin for days over the thought of an own goal rolling in, that thing grabbed me through the rest of the weekend. On the walk home that Saturday night from Waterloo through London, near midnight, I beamed preposterously and yearned to tell people I had been there at Fratton Park, but I refrained because they were standing in lines for clubs and seemed for all the world as if they absolutely would not care. With the Sunday newspapers, I did what fans do. I read the accounts not to plumb my own copy for glaring and career-threatening errors, but to relive the match.

I found the whole thing refreshing, but I didn't have much mirth time. Only 42 hours after David James punted and the referee whistled, the Premier League started up another match involving Portsmouth, at 1 p.m., on the bank holiday the day after Easter. In a world of oddities, there's an official holiday adjacent to Easter in the United Kingdom, a secular country in which it's socially acceptable to be an atheist, while there's no such holiday in the United States, a religious country in which 'atheist' finishes last in those 'Would You Vote For ...' polls. Thus, on to Vicarage Road.

Pompey, sitting newly eighth with 46 points, just two behind Tottenham's 48, would make the relatively short trip to Watford, which sat 20th. With just another break here or there, such as a certain penalty call at Fratton Park, we might've found Watford embroiled in a compelling scrap to avoid the relegation scrap-heap, but with its 20 points fully nine behind next-to-last West Ham, Watford had all but booked the drop. Walking to Euston, I wondered if it were humanly possible to defeat the No. 1 club in the Premiership and lose to the No. 20 within 44 hours.

On the half-hour train ride to Watford, I sat across from a Pompey family, a mother and father with a daughter and younger son. They read about Saturday's glories in the Monday *Guardian*, and I could see, across the train car, on a page, a photograph of that ball rolling into that net, and I decided I might like one framed for future walls. The daughter, maybe eight, and son, maybe six, were completely decked out in Pompey strip, which in the daughter's case included red Pompey knee socks. When I saw those red Pompey knee socks, I thought about how much of life hinges on where we are born. If that girl had started life in my Virginia hometown, then instead of the red socks she might've worn some sort of regalia of the NFL team the Washington Redskins. She might've worn shirts or hats or socks with a likeness of a Native American head, and the people in her hometown would've found this completely normal, but other people elsewhere would've found it thoughtlessly racist, whereupon other people would've defended the logo as an homage to the battlefield valour of Native Americans, whereupon critics would've lambasted these people as rubes, whereupon any people who did not follow sports would've found all of us completely insane.

As the train rolled barely north-west, London seemed vacant and forlorn and depressed as it does on many a holiday, as if it would rather just go to work. I disembarked and walked through a network of pleasant roads to reach Vicarage Road, and the stadium looked wonderful, tucked into the town near a hospital, which would make it convenient in case one player tried to gratuitously maul another. The corner gate for bubonic-plagued away fans came up right away, and I took my seat among many empty seats. Seemed the Pompey fans – including my favourite three – had beheld this match and decided to save money. On a sunny spring day just north-west of London with fine foothills off in the distance, we taunted Ben Foster as he readied himself in the Watford goal:

> *England's number two,*
> *England's, England's number two ...*

Foster turned to us and grinned with this expression that said, *Oh, those Portsmouth fans,* and I cannot tell you how much I loved that. The match began. Nine days prior, Watford had carried Chelsea into added time drawing 0–0 before succumbing 1–0. Two days prior, Watford had looked haggard in losing 4–1 at Middlesbrough. I saw the prevalent yellow of the Vicarage Road seats and actually thought about how a man from the Canary Islands had just told me of yellow's bad-luck status in his culture, but no matter.

No matter, because Watford's defence made a blunder which, thank goodness, didn't involve Jay DeMerit, leaving my cheer undiluted as Matt Taylor curled one into the goal at 16 minutes. Pompey led 1–0, and looked to build upon the incredible momentum of 42 hours and 16 minutes or so prior. I turned to the young man of about 25 to my left, and he turned to me, and we suddenly hugged each other while hopping, even though we barely uttered a diphthong to each other the rest of the match.

We hugged partly because we had no idea that we had come to witness the unleashing of the mighty Watford attack. I had no clue I'd come to wish that Pompey would just go ahead and sign the Algerian international Hameur Bouazza – preferably right after the match – as he ran rings around our complacent squad. He banged a penalty past James at 28 minutes, then helped assist a world-class curving mega-goal from Gavin Mahon at 45 minutes, Mahon's first in the Premiership.

No, I really didn't imagine reaching the Vicarage Road urinals at half-time and hearing Pompey fans bemoan a 'disgrace' to reinforce the place of men's-room urinals as bastions of insight. And I really had not imagined the Watford attack, flying free by the second half, wreaking a beautiful display of fundamental football on our hapless defence for Tamas Priskin's first Premiership goal at 51 minutes, nor Bouazza scoring again at 73 minutes for a 4–1 – 4–1! – lead.

If you dare to look it up, as I did later, you would've seen what you already suspected: Watford had scored four goals only once all autumn–winter–spring, in a 4–1 FA Cup win over Stockport. Watford, in fact, had scored three goals only once, back in October, in a draw with Fulham. Having achieved a watershed victory over Manchester United, Portsmouth had managed an added feat of loosing the potent Watford attack, a feat no other Premiership club had accomplished.

Then again, we always admire those clubs who play hard when they're playing for nothing. Another of the greatest things I've ever seen happened in downtown Detroit on the last Saturday night in September 2003. My bosses had sent me there because the 2003 baseball Detroit Tigers began their four closing games with an imponderable 40–118 record, a rapacious threat upon the New York Mets' legendary record of 120 losses in a season from 1962, the season that launched a legendary American line from the legendary manager Casey Stengel: 'Can't anybody here play this game?' On Thursday night, 25 September,

Detroit won the first game of four against Minnesota to reach 41–118, then lost the second to access 41–119. Before the third game of the series that Saturday, a wee batch of reporters interviewed Alan Trammell, the former great Detroit player and current Detroit manager, and as an incompetent interloper, I asked what he'd pondered driving to the stadium. He replied testily that he walked. I asked what he'd pondered as he walked. He cut off everybody's interview. I apologized to everybody. He put his arm around me a few minutes later and said he understood. Hours later, Detroit trailed in the fifth inning by the insuperable, moribund score of 8–0. The 1962 Mets, long alone in the dungeon, could see company coming up the dungeon hallway.

Just then, for no apparent earthly reason, the Tigers rallied and won 9–8. You can go years watching baseball daily without seeing anybody turn 8–0 against into 9–8 for, and the comeback had intoxicating qualities. I felt as if I'd witnessed something phenomenal even as technically I'd witnessed something trivial. I saw Trammell in the hallway beside the dressing room, and he looked at me, an outright stranger, and I said, 'That was really something,' and he said, 'Thank you.' On Sunday, Detroit beat Minnesota again to reach 43–119 and leave the 1962 Mets alone in the dungeon. Having seen Detroit four times the whole season and having seen them win thrice, I decided they'd actually been a very good team, just misunderstood.

Likewise, I decided Watford must've been very good but misunderstood. A late Portsmouth goal provoked a glorious chant indicating that we were going to win 5–4, but it ended at 4–2, and I felt baffled and texted Charlie, who replied that he'd figured. You know those veteran viewers. And I texted my football guru Tom, who wrote back, 'Oh, the predictable perversity of this game. These 48 hours exemplify the beauty – and pain – of football, surely,' an exhibition of why he's my football guru.

Slightly miffed but more just perplexed, I decided to buy a

newspaper and eat lunch. I walked into a W. H. Smith, and I overheard a little boy and his father meet up with the boy's mother after the match.

'Watford won 4–2!' the little boy exclaimed.

'No,' the mother said.

The son and father persisted with their report.

The mother still thought they kidded her.

The son and father persisted.

The mother finally believed them.

Maybe.

33

Not-taken roads

On a pleasant spring Saturday on the south coast of England, 14 April 2007, five matches to the end of the season, at kick-off, we crooned the old standard to Benjani (tune: 'Volare'):

> *Benjani, whoa-ohhh,*
> *Benjani, whoa-ohhh,*
> *He comes from Zimbabwe,*
> *He's gonna score today ...*

My love for this, I could not overstate. To me, this very song almost justified following the bilge of sport on a regular basis. Here I was an American, joining part of England in expressing our love for an African. Here we were in Hampshire, a crowd of mostly white people who had been to Zimbabwe an aggregate next-to-nil in all our 20,165 lives, some of whom knew it only from media coverage as having a spiteful president, yet we serenaded a Zimbabwean. It reminded me of an old poll that queried white Americans and black Americans for their 10 favourite prime-time television shows, when only one show appeared on both lists: *Monday Night Football*. Only sport seems to construct such bridges.

After sensing – but not getting – victory at Fulham, then assuming – but not getting – defeat against Manchester United, then figuring on – but not getting – victory at Watford, I decided

I'd just stop sensing, assuming or figuring. Then, just seven minutes in at Fratton Park, Benjani Mwaruwari muscled Steven Taylor off the ball, wheeled and blasted one in from 12 yards, perhaps my favourite goal of the month scored by an actual Portsmouth player rather than Rio Ferdinand. He'd come from Zimbabwe; he had just scored today. Pompey led Newcastle, 1–0, and the same attack, so hopeless in the winter, suddenly went Barcelona 2006 on us, with help from Newcastle's indifferent defence. I do love a nice, indifferent defence, for it makes sport so much more entertaining. One night in January 2006, Kobe Bryant of the Los Angeles Lakers scored 81 points, the second most in NBA history, and we all went wow but gave far too little credit to the visiting Toronto Raptors and their invaluable contribution of indifferent defence. In an era in which clubs study each other so intently, learn each other's tendencies so thoroughly, the games have dulled somewhat, a point noted by the iconic North American ice hockey coach Scotty Bowman. Defence impedes pleasure. Defence hampers life.

But Newcastle's defence on 14 April? That one was kind, even cuddly, and much appreciated. It abetted the most entertaining, carefree half of the year. The same Pompey employees who had no chance of scoring at, say, Wigan, pelted the Newcastle goal with so many chances that it could've been 4–0 by half-time. It suggested a spring thaw. Kanu won the unofficial prize for most agonizing, when his strike smacked off the bottom of the crossbar but managed not to cross the line. Newcastle manager Glenn Roeder made a defensive replacement at 30 minutes.

It had been 365 days since I first saw Fratton Park and saw Pompey trip Middlesbrough 1–0 in the rush toward survival. I held my own little observance in the stands by marvelling at how I'd learned so much that I felt almost certain that the goalkeeper could not touch the ball with his hands outside that second, larger box there. Now, with 14 April upon us, all of England would start divvying up the trips to Europe and doling out the relegations during the last five weekends leading to the 13 May finales. The table at breakfast, 14 April, found Manchester United still three points ahead of Chelsea at the top, then Tottenham in seventh with 48, Portsmouth in eighth with 46, Reading in ninth at 45, and Newcastle in 10th with the usual civic melodrama (and impending managerial change), and with 41. The dungeon looked like this:

16. Wigan – 34
17. Charlton – 32
18. Sheffield United – 31
19. West Ham – 29
20. Watford – 23

And in those days, with exceptional irony, Fratton Park occasionally would break into a chant: '*We are staying up! We are staying up!*' It cropped up against Newcastle, and it reminded me of the uncommon brightness of the season into which I'd plopped unawares. Then I saw the faithful all the way down the length of the pitch, in Newcastle black-and-white, thickly packed into the Fratton Park away section. But for a subliminal fear of long train rides, plus my weariness with discussions of 'curses' in the beleaguered baseball cities of Boston (86-year title drought, 1918–2004) and Chicago (99-year title drought for one club, the Cubs, 1908–present), I could've been standing in that visiting crowd, bemoaning the lack of defence. Sitting 10th after finishing seventh in 2005–06, with all-the-rage employee Michael Owen still healing from his World Cup knee agony, Newcastle had lapsed into horrific form since February. Sure, earlier they had won their second cup in 52 years, but the Intertoto Cup, while a fine and hard-won cup, somehow lacks the resonance of other cups. In the UEFA Cup, which you can enter by winning the Intertoto Cup, near as I can tell, Newcastle crashed out to AZ Alkmaar of the Netherlands. What fans, though. Many of the young and middle-aged ones had spent their lives on a crusade for that moment of rapture. Unlike Portsmouth or Southampton or even Torquay, their club had spent every year since 1993–94 in the Premiership, so their expectations tended toward swelling. Many of these same away fans at Fratton Park, I reckoned, had lived minute-to-minute through 1995–96, when Newcastle's 12-point lead in the table over Manchester United suddenly made like a sinkhole. Some of them might've even participated in that early-season fan protest after that galling 1–0 home loss to Sheffield United. Looking across at them, I believed I could see them trudging across the veritable desert, mirages of water in bubbles above their heads. If you can hate fans while they traverse the veritable desert, maybe even revel in their horrendous thirst, then you might just qualify as a sadist.

Their defence improved not much early in the second half, and proved ripe for another Matt Taylor masterpiece. This one, from 30 yards on the left, at 59 minutes, hurried diagonally to the right, all the way to the right corner of the goal, into which it absolutely screamed. And then, so did we (scream). Pompey led, 2–0. To the wondrous season, the club continued to add these little bonuses. It lacked the capability, though, to deliver us from fret, and so at 69 minutes, Dejan Stefanovic either nudged or savaged James Milner in the box, and Emre scored the penalty, and we had to spend the last 24 minutes suffering from the sweat glands.

Take that fret and double it at 82 minutes, when David James had to make a luminous save from Obafemi Martins, but finally, three more points came, and Portsmouth had risen to 49, 11 more than in the entirety of 2005–06, with four matches remaining.

Minus the bear, whose vacation would mark a temporary increase in Portugal's ursine population, Dan and Hopkins and I overcame our shouting lack of fur and had a festive beer outdoors at the Shepherd's Crook. There by the picnic tables, I saw Magpies in their stripes mingling with Pompey fans in their blue. In the United States, we love this sort of thing because it informs us we can have a conversation even with the vile, scum-sucking enemy. We often refer to it proudly because it suggests a reasonable tinge to our frothing contempt. In England, I've heard more people lament the presence of away fans at a pub, as if it dilutes the colours.

I noticed two particular Newcastle fans at the pub, two guys, then noticed them again at Waterloo, then noticed them again boarding the Tube, then noticed they sat across from myself. I decided to strike up a conversation, and told them of their brethren in Boston and Chicago whose support did not deteriorate despite long-held frustration. I had no idea they'd won the Intertoto Cup, mostly because I had no idea of the existence of an Intertoto Cup, and they did not bring up their Intertoto Cup or try to shove their Intertoto Cup in my Intertoto Cup-less face. They seemed excellent company, and we'd just got into good conversation when I had to step off at Tottenham Court Road to return to my shoebox. At the end, though, I believe I breached etiquette when I mentioned like a dope that I'd almost chosen Newcastle as my club.

We shook hands as I disembarked, and then as I moved along the platform one of the guys leaned through the open Tube doors and exclaimed:

'It's not a choice!'

I felt that old pang of guilt as the interloper who'd wandered into his country and treated his profound emotional attachment like some quiz question. I thought about how he'd emerged from the birth canal ever so mildly accursed, destined to follow Newcastle through the cupless years unless he ignored football and decided to follow, say, opera, in which, come to think of it, the endings often bear striking resemblance to Newcastle. I thought he should be more understanding of people from distant birth canals. But it didn't matter what I thought, because the Tube doors had shut and the Northern Line had rolled off toward Goodge Street.

Besides, nobody should belittle choices. Choices are tough. The problem I've noticed with choices is that when you choose one thing, then you don't get to have the others. Eight days after looking down the Fratton Park pitch to find Newcastle fans I might've joined, I looked down the Villa Park pitch at the Holte End I'd once inhabited for as goose-bumpy a day as I'd ever known: Aston Villa vs Birmingham, 16 April 2006, that day of such great and durable noise, plus plucky singing.

Only 22 April 2007 lacked similar fervour. Aston Villa would play Portsmouth in a match involving two fan bases who have never had reason to despise one another. This brings such a downer in sport, this complete lack of scorn, hatred or even appalling condescension. As a result, Villa Park approximated the din of a golf tournament's faraway 14th hole on Thursday, when you might hear mild clapping from next-of-kin, recent one-night stands or people who've happened by while walking to the hamburger tent. Such a hush ruled the day that at one point, a Portsmouth fan shouted at Villa's Gabriel Agbonlahor, 'Diver!' and the criticism resonated such that Agbonlahor looked up at the fan.

This blurt came from the away end of Villa Park, behind the goal opposite the Holte End. With no Birmingham on the premises, I'd walked right up and bought a ticket without giving any identification. I had decided to go early so I could have a beer and watch Chelsea's crucial bout with Newcastle. Well, they have no televisions in the away end, nor do they serve any beer, thereby achieving profound injustice. I figured the away fans of today probably pay for the sins of the away fans of yore, and this felt something like travelling the world with a Colombian passport, always a suspect because of others' transgressions.

So I did the only thing there was to do; I leaned against a wall.

A Pompey fan leaning next to me asked what I expected for the match, but I couldn't understand his question because of his accent.

He asked again, and I couldn't understand his question.

He asked again, and I couldn't understand his question.

It reminded me of that Ultimate Fighting Championship reality show, where the Americans used subtitles for the guy from Liverpool. Finally this guy from Hampshire stammered out the question, and I hemmed and hawed and said I expected very little, and we began a conversation in which he said it might be a bad move for Portsmouth to qualify for the UEFA Cup. The whole operation just wouldn't be ready, he said. The squad just didn't seem deep enough for playing in four competitions rather than three. There would be the issue of Fratton Park's fitness as a ground for European play, he said. I had never once mulled these things while singing blithely about a European tour. Seemingly a nice guy – after all, he'd repeated his question four times – he then made a quick trip through the squad and noted which guys had proved 'useless', and I nodded as if I had the first clue. He said we definitely needed a new left-back, and I couldn't have agreed more, even though I didn't know for sure who played left-back.

Seated in a section short on people, next to a section almost completely empty, I looked across at the Holte End and wondered how my life might've felt different had I stood over there after all these days and all these games doubling as melodramas. (For one thing, I'd know one fewer bear.) I might've been singing that catchy Aston Villa theme song. I might've told people I followed Aston Villa because it's the club with the loveliest name on Earth. I could've routinely witnessed my host from the Birmingham match over there, leaning over during matches, smoking furtively.

But as Aston Villa and Portsmouth played to a goalless draw, I suffered Villa's scary bombardment of our goal, and when David James became the Premier League's all-time leader in clean sheets, I applauded as loudly as I could, as a fan of his club, his play and his astute newspaper column.

34

Adopted

Alan Ball's Blue Army
Alan Ball's Blue Army
Alan Ball's Blue Army ...

The chant echoed through Fratton Park on Saturday, 28 April.

Alan Ball's Blue Army
Alan Ball's Blue Army
Alan Ball's Blue Army ...

It reverberated at kick-off, and in added time, and every so often in between.

Alan Ball's Blue Army
Alan Ball's Blue Army
Alan Ball's Blue Army ...

The cheer never became maudlin or overwrought. I found it both understated and intensely emotional, the latter partly because of the former. It just carried on through the afternoon. Sometimes it would overrun itself, so that one group of people would be on 'Army' while another would be starting up with another 'Alan'. In dealing with the ultimate subject, death, Americans often feel impressed by the English who, as an older culture, treat the subject more as part of life and less as cause for apoplexy. On the Tuesday midnight of April 24–25, Alan Ball, 61, died of a heart attack at his home while trying to contain a greedy backyard fire. Every English football person and most every English non-football person knew him as if a cousin, as the youngest member of the England team that won the 1966 World Cup. Portsmouth fans also knew him well as the manager of Portsmouth from 1984 to 1989 and then again in 1998 for a great escape from relegation into the third division. I thought of him in another vein, for a reason fully trivial. He hired the top division's first American player.

In January of 1987, an American born in Canada to Scottish parents, and just out of Duke University, John Kerr, turned up in London. Through connections, he wound up getting a trial at Harrow Borough in suburban north-west London, where for training the club could use only one set of lights or the neighbours beefed. Harrow Borough started winning and getting some attention, which catapulted Kerr toward a spot in a reserve-team match in March between Portsmouth and Crystal Palace, which led a certain flat-capped Portsmouth manager to the dressing room after said match.

'John, I want to sign you,' Ball said to the staggered American. 'I want you to play here next year.' That happened to coincide with Portsmouth's first promotion to the top flight in 28 years, and so, in a 4–2 loss at Oxford United on 15 August 1987, Kerr debuted, after which, Kerr said, Ball mentioned him in post-match remarks to the team because it had been his first game. Kerr would play four games before joining the reserve team and leading that league in scoring.

As someone who spent my first four decades on earth knowing nothing about Alan Ball, and who lacked the emotion we attach to sports figures we've known for decades, I joined in the chants until my throat hurt on 28 April. And whenever I'd refer to the current Portsmouth squad as 'Alan Ball's Blue Army' in honour of the erstwhile manager, I'd add some oomph because he'd given that chance to a starry-eyed American, whose dream of playing English football would've counted as bizarre had it not actually transpired. By so chanting, I felt as if just an itty-bitty part of England, just as I gained a second indoctrination that came from Portsmouth vs Liverpool. I experienced my first match in which a manager purposely gutted his team in anticipation of a different competition. For an American, it's a bit like learning a foreign language, thereby violating our various social tenets against learning foreign languages.

On a blistering English day on the southern edge of England – 72 degrees! – visiting manager Rafael Benitez did not bring Steven Gerrard. He did not bring Jamie Carragher. He brought neither Peter Crouch, nor Javier Mascherano, nor John Arne Riise, nor Daniel Agger, nor Pepe Reina. In the United States, where teams play for one title per year, we occasionally have managers who show up so bereft of stars, and it's always because of injuries. We feel for them. We write sonnets to them and laud their willingness to carry on in fate's nastiness. We even lend them adjectives we probably ought to reserve for soldiers.

Benitez had not brought these bright lights because Liverpool had to play Chelsea three nights later in the second leg of their Champions League semi-final. So this would be my first experience with a match that would conclude with a manager saying something like, 'It's clear the Champions League is the priority.' So it's a bit weird. You know you're pulling for your club to defeat one of the big four, yet you don't know whether it's really one of the big four, and you don't know enough to know whether what's left of Liverpool would still inhabit the big four. Maybe it would. I did know of one player present at Fratton Park, Craig Bellamy. Any tourist even just changing planes at Heathrow might know of someone who turned up in news reports detailing how, on a team training mission in Portugal, he got irked at a team-mate who refused to sing karaoke, threatening the team-mate with a golf club. It wouldn't take a football savant to know of the central figure in a case so puzzling in this sense: which aspect of the story was more preposterous, the weapon or the motive? I also knew, as a seasoned observer, that Bellamy tried to blame the reports on the golf club and the karaoke on the reporters and lamented that he'd encouraged the media by apparently threatening a team-mate with a golf club in a dispute that began when the team-mate wouldn't sing karaoke.

In most groups of males, however idiotic, golf-club threats would stem from *insistence* upon karaoke rather than from refusal.

With the point at Villa Park, Portsmouth had a whopping 50, sitting eighth, with Tottenham at ninth on the same number of points but having played one fewer match. Reading sat seventh at 51. My worry about an underlings' revolt from 10th had dissipated as Blackburn sat stuck on 44, with Newcastle in 12th with 42. Liverpool sat third with 67 points and figured to remain there unless Arsenal would overtake, in which case Liverpool still would sit fourth. There seemed no reason not to take three points from Liverpool and make it a commendable eight points out of a possible 21 thus far against the big four.

There really seemed no reason after we sang about Zimbabwe and then Benjani Mwaruwari scored in the 27th minute with a bold header in a crowded box for a 1–0 lead, with help from a miscalculation from goalkeeper Jerzy Dudek. There really, really seemed no reason after the young Croatian Niko Kranjcar chested a long ball in the 32nd minute and finished for a 2–0 lead, somewhat fluky but perfectly welcome. The best Portsmouth season in 50 years just went bouncing along, with Manchester United and Liverpool defeated at Fratton Park within the same month.

Of course, Liverpool had not yet been defeated, what with Sami Hyypia's header off a Robbie Fowler corner at 59 minutes, after which the Fratton End showed again something that mystifies me by tying its own world record – 0.01 – for time between adversity on the pitch and cheer in the stands. To earlier cheers of 'We are staying up', and 'We love you, Portsmouth, we do', there came the traditional 'na-na-na-ing' of 'Vindaloo'. The rest of the match would bring the singular agony in which football specializes.

Reading back over my jittery notes afterward, I found this: 'OK, made 70.' That means we made 70 minutes. 'OK, made 75.' 'OK, made 77.' 'I'm a wreck.' Liverpool took all the elan left in its squad – which amounted to plenty, by my estimation – and seemed to unfurl it toward the Portsmouth goal. Fans chanted Alan Ball's name. Some had brought along flat caps as homage to Ball. In the 88th minute, at the goal distant from myself, Fowler looked certain to score, but James saved somehow. What a cruel concept is this football. Then, just when you might exhale, there's added time, the slowest time in life, far slower than even the five minutes before the cinema lights dim, far slower than the unbearable time it takes to unload all the rows in front of you on an aeroplane, far slower than church even while clearly its own form of church.

This added time, though, carried added purpose. Through all the hours in the three minutes of added time, you could hear *Alan Ball's Blue Army . . . Alan Ball's Blue Army . . . Alan Ball's Blue Army . . .* Nobody I saw cried, although I did notice one burly guy with tattoos repeatedly chanting just the name, 'Alan Ball! Alan Ball!' Finally, one of life's kindest acts occurred, the whistle tweeted, and Portsmouth had a 2–1 win over Liverpool to go with the 2–1 win over Newcastle, the 2–1 win over Manchester United, the 2–1 win over Manchester City, the 2–1 win over Wigan in the FA Cup and the 2–1 win over West Ham, the only wins since Boxing Day, to go with five draws. This jacked the total to 53 points, hiked the place to seventh, one behind sixth-place Everton and two behind fifth-place Bolton, with a fixture at that very Everton for the next Saturday.

In order to do as the Romans do while in England, I would have stuck with Portsmouth even through relegation, as the Brentford sages Jak and Chris did teach with their League Two aplomb. Yet I'd alighted onto the best top-flight season, points-wise, in 57 years, and the best top-flight season, placement-wise, in 52 years. Without any knowledge of history earlier than Pedro Mendes against Manchester City or maybe a desolate pitch at Stamford Bridge, I'd happened upon a club that went down to the second division in 1959 for two seasons, then to the third for one, then to the second for 14, then to the third for two, then to the fourth for two, then to the third for three, the second for four, the first for one, the second for 15 and the first for four, with finishes of 13th, 16th, 17th and pending.

A win at Everton might all but secure a UEFA Cup spot. Does an unwitting gatecrasher still count as a gatecrasher?

So, burrowing into the village past the easy readiness of the Shepherd's Crook, Charlie and Hopkins and I persisted toward the Devonshire Arms, the place I'd happened upon ages ago, back on 4 November when Portsmouth played at Old Trafford, when I'd felt like a preposterous impostor. Now, six months and one eternity later, in the same pub, I got to assist when a Pompey bear asked me, 'Could you unzip me a bit' in the back, so he could manoeuvre out of his suit without tearing his fur. This ever-so-slight contribution to the well-being of my club gave me a sense of belonging. It resembled childhood memories of when my mother used to come home from work and ask us to unzip the back of her nurse's uniform, but it did not resemble those memories precisely as, for one thing, my mother made us dinner as opposed to buying us a round.

In between greeting people left and right, Charlie told me that a Pompey friend had told him, 'I'm glad to see you've adopted an American.' It's a unique and welcome experience for an American to feel ancillary after so many years of inflating ourselves with so much preposterous pertinence. This, after joining Fratton Park and stadiums all over England in appreciation of Alan Ball. That had been some day, and we stayed in the Devonshire way too long. I finally galumphed out and went to Brighton for that night, waking sometime after arrival to find myself alone on the motionless train. Hopkins and Charlie left the Devonshire even after I did. They made the last possible train. Hopkins disembarked at Woking, and at Waterloo, a guy cleaning up the train came upon a sleeping blue bear, which simply had to enhance his gruelling work shift.

35

It's really the heart of England

First Saturdays in May resonate in my American cranium because of the Kentucky Derby, the oldest annual sporting event in the United States, for which 100,000 chums convene in the underrated river city of Louisville for a poignant bacchanal of wagering and binge-drinking. It all leads to a two-minute cavalry charge at 6 p.m. that can define the legacies of participants and can make the heart beat outside the chest for observers, even those like myself who find wagering almost as tedious as listening to people rehash their wagering.

Two first Saturdays in May ago, in 2005, I covered the Kentucky Derby and could not have told you the location of Everton Football Club if I'd needed the answer to avoid purgatory or a life sentence of residence in Texas. Now, two first Saturdays in May later, on a hot spring day in Merseyside, I rode the last long train of the season eavesdropping on four people, three men and one woman, all Everton fans. With two matches left in the exhausted season, we all headed for Everton for the potential momentousness of sixth-place Everton vs eighth-place Portsmouth.

As the conversation bubbled along, the woman and one of the men wrangled over whether they followed Everton for the pursuit of trophies or for the love of the club. Shockingly, the man preferred the former, the woman the latter, a point she later bolstered by telling me she'd relinquish her cherished season ticket if Everton dared sign that creepy Joey Barton, who had just finished beating up a team-mate during practice before a group of visiting schoolchildren in a display of Manchester City cohesion. Finally, she agreed to disagree with her friend, and he fell asleep and, as she seemed so keen on football that I began to imagine little footballs coursing through her bloodstream, I consulted her.

I explained my tragic childhood deprival of relegation and promotion, and wondered which match I should attend on Sunday, which was the final day of the Championship. With two promotions assured – Birmingham, Sunderland – and one promotion to go, and with the eventual third- to sixth-place finishers to play off for that, should I go to third-place Derby County, at home against the utterly fascinating football train wreck of Leeds, with its impending second relegation within four seasons? Maybe I should go to still-contending Preston North End for Birmingham's visit? What about Southampton, sitting sixth, with Southend inbound? She ran down the list of pros and cons for the half-dozen pertinent matches. I pined away slightly for the bourbon fumes in the Louisville air, yes, but I also thought I'd found the sporting heart of another country, a weekend of Liverpool plus promotion/relegation fever. Seeking knowledge, I quizzed the four Everton sorts on one of my favourite new-found topics, the idea that Everton and Liverpool might indulge in milder loathing than some rivals, that many families might contain fans of both yet still fight no more than other families, which means just about all the time. I asked if they'd rooted for Liverpool or Chelsea the previous Tuesday night in the Champions League semi-final won by Liverpool on penalties.

They'd all pulled for Chelsea, and so the train arrived at Lime Street, and off we went – they, to their usual pub, and I, to Goodison Park, which I loved straight away. The away section had a wooden charm and great sightlines save for a support post here or there that might block your view at times, but for some eccentric reason I always love craning my neck around old support posts in old stadiums, perhaps because it affords me a hint of suffering. Goodison has this excellent verticality, seeming to rise straight up beside the pitch, ideal for absorbing pivotal proceedings such as Portsmouth (53 points) trying to vault over Everton (54) and maybe even Reading (54) and maybe even sputtering Bolton (55) and into fifth place. With rookie denseness, I'd forgotten that ninth-place Tottenham (53) had three matches remaining to everybody else's two.

I walked in past somebody in a T-shirt reading PORTS-MOUTH IS MY RELIGION, FRATTON PARK IS MY CHURCH, and sat down behind a burly guy who would spend his day in the sun complaining about Pompey's play and the refereeing. I, myself, moaned about the refereeing during the first half when the referee achieved an unquestionable feat of incompetence and gave a yellow card to Portsmouth's Noé Pamarot. I counted this absolute and impenetrable accuracy as progress in my tutelage.

Being in Goodison Park, in the city of Liverpool, I felt stationed at the aorta of English football, what with two huge and heaving fan bases right across a park from each other. We have some arrangements like the mere 10.27 miles between Yankee Stadium in the Bronx and Shea Stadium in Queens, but that's nothing like the Liverpool situation. For one thing, I once walked that path just to amuse myself and to write a column about it, and I learned that when crossing the Triborough Bridge, it's wiser to take a bus or a taxi. For another, the pleasant greenery of Stanley Park stands in contrast to the concrete of Queens, as well as to the couple having a loud spat as I passed them on the sidewalk.

In the pre-match, we observed silence for an Everton fan and soldier killed in Iraq, Alan Jones (1986–2007), and his photograph appeared on the video screen, and it grabbed me as much as has any such story since the war began, something about the confluence of something so vibrant (Premiership football) with something so catastrophic. The Pompey players trotted out, and I realized that even while I don't know Gary O'Neil and sometimes got mad at him for coughing up perfectly good possession, I'd miss him plus the rest once this trail ended eight days hence. The public address read the teamsheets, and my Pompey brethren again showed a Mensa-level grasp of all past Southampton squads by jeering James Beattie.

As the 39,619 of us got under way at Goodison, our thickly packed away section quickly crooned 'You'll Never Walk Alone' to the home fans, many of whom responded with popped blood vessels in bald foreheads as they screamed back chants and songs I found so unintelligible they could not possibly hurt my feelings. I began to think of the two rotten lost points at Fulham, and how we should have 55 points and not 53, and how I'd received permission to use the word 'we' from a blue bear, about as authoritative a figure as exists in the animal kingdom. I marvelled at the astonishing presence of 'Is This the Way to Amarillo?', an American-penned song I'd never once heard until moving to England where it became a hit in both 1971 and 2005, a song sung heartily by English football fans who wouldn't know Amarillo from Lubbock.

I also found it impossible to detest Everton and did not join in the chorus of the semi-popular old hit 'You're the S—— of Merseyside'.

Half-time found us all goalless, but it didn't feel quite right, as our squad posed scant threat, what with Matt Taylor injured and unable to send a 45-yard symphony over Tim Howard's hairless head. Sure enough, things soon veered into the ditch. The wondrous young James Vaughan got loose in the box in the 59th minute, and Glen Johnson attempted to do something to him, perhaps shove him as one would a toilet seat into a cheaper box. Mikel Arteta converted the penalty, and I wondered without griping if I'd ever see David James stop a penalty. Joseph Yobo scored three minutes after that, from a Manuel Fernandes corner, and Everton cemented its European tour, as well as becoming insuperable to *us* with 57 points to our 53. Any trip to Europe for *us* would hinge on the match eight days later against Arsenal.

Still, it says something about the astounding buoyancy of Portsmouth fans that the away section chanted 'scummer' at Beattie during the *89th* minute, when many an American fan long since would've exited to sit in the car listening to the radio or made it home to the couch to assume a state of intractable inertia. Four minutes later, the hosts had an added-time goal, they had 3–0, and they had their home season's end. The players left the pitch, then returned and paraded around the stadium to some of the greatest noise I'd ever heard, having hailed from a country where fifth place seldom draws ovations. Most of my fellow visitors filed out, but I stayed in the empty section for the whole clamorous celebration, listening to their catchy theme song, even discerning some of the lyrics (ellipses indicate lyrics I didn't decipher):

> *Everton, Everton ... Everton ...*
> *Everton ... Everton ... Everton ...*
> *Everton, Everton ... Everton ...*

I felt actually lifted, even at 3–0 down, even as the woman from the train text-messaged me with, 'Take *that*,' proving she might follow Everton also for the trophies. Still, my pilgrimage persisted. It's terribly refreshing to visit a stadium that adorns a real neighbourhood with terraced houses and corner stores and children playing on sidewalks. I'd also decided it's a must when visiting Anfield to walk across Stanley Park to look at Goodison and, when visiting Goodison, to walk across Stanley Park to look at Anfield, especially the memorial for the 96 victims of Hillsborough.

Covering sport, you wind up chronicling death more than you'd think. You'd never expect to see rugged men sob into their meaty hands at Daytona Beach, but then Dale Earnhardt rammed into the wall and died. Probably no event ever teemed with life more than the 1992 Olympic Opening Ceremonies at

Barcelona, but days later a batch of American reporters heard the devastated voice of an American swimmer whose father had died of a heart attack that night in that stadium. You'd never think of sport as providing the backdrop for one of the grandest human gestures you've ever known, but it did so in 1998 in Kentucky, after a macabre single-truck crash involving University of Kentucky American-football players. Two passengers, ages 19 and 21, died. The intoxicated 21-year-old driver survived and served four months in prison for reckless homicide.

The driver's parents came from Florida to visit their son, and they attended the funeral of the 19-year-old victim. The victim's parents, in turn, asked these virtual strangers to join them in the front row, so they would not feel ostracized.

You witness these things, you attend the funerals of sporting figures, you stand in stadiums for moments of silence, and sometimes you hope people won't get so embroiled in life as to forget. That's where, to an outsider, Liverpool fans seem to have taken something unbearable and integrated it into their fandom as a way of giving homage.

So, fully 18 years and three weeks down the line in life, Anfield's Hillsborough memorial teemed with fresh flowers and careful attention. I found myself gazing and reading until I had no idea how much time had passed. At the Vietnam War memorial in Washington, the wall with 58,000 names, I always try to read the notes from soldiers' family members or friends, and at Anfield, I found myself reading a poem typewritten on a full sheet of A4 paper.

It came from the family of Adam Spearitt, who died that day at 14, less than the number of years that have passed since his death. The poem went along for two or three stanzas about the day, 15 April 1989, about the fans going to Sheffield for the FA Cup semi-final:

> They chanted their many footy songs
> They strategized the last game's wrongs

They laughed and they chatted, there was plenty to say
As they eagerly went on their way

As I read more, the poem recollected more about 15 April 1989, but then midway through a stanza, came to a jolt:

Some got there early
Some arrived late
Hard to say more
Pain's too great

Those last two lines just staggered me, even as a foreigner who spent the spring of 1989 living in Los Angeles and hearing about Hillsborough only vaguely. All these years later, they conveyed the loss as sharply as ever.

The poem concluded:

Whistle blew
It's six minutes after three
God bless you all
No victory

36

Elvis and the Beatles

I knew a great soul named Dick Fick, who died at 50 of alcohol-related illness in 2003 after I'd lost touch with him, which I'll regret only for the remainder of my days. He coached American college basketball at Morehead State University in Kentucky during the 1990s, and one famous night in a game at the University of Kentucky, he objected to a referee's call by lying supine on the floor and looking straight up to the rafters as if deceased of shock. He was outstanding company at lunch in Nashville or at coffee in Seattle or walking down Bourbon Street in New Orleans. When he told of his baseball treks to Chicago, he'd wax about how he'd tell his wife April he had to go, and she'd reply that she knew he had to go, and he'd drive and fly to Chicago, and he'd take his seat in the stadium with his newspapers and – I can hear it now – 'I've got my *Sun-Times*, I've got my *Trib*, and I've got my beer, and I'm livin'!'

I thought of him on Sunday, 6 May 2007, because I had my *Sunday Times* and I had my train schedules and I had my scenarios for promotion among the Championship clubs, and I was livin'. After a misspent childhood roaming the barren lands of relegation-less sports, I would see some promotion or some relegation.

As of dawn that morning, the top of the table looked thus:

1. Birmingham – 86

2. Sunderland – 85
3. Derby County – 81
4. West Brom – 73
5. Wolverhampton – 73
6. Southampton – 72
7. Stoke – 72
8. Preston North End – 71

I decided that with Derby County safely into the play-off, I'd try a place whose fate teetered in the balance of the day. I'd never been to Preston. On a dismally dreary Sunday afternoon in the heart of the English May winter period, I disembarked at Preston and slowly found Sir Tom Finney Way and the stadium, Deepdale. I passed the sculpture that replicates a prize-winning photograph of Sir Tom Finney sloshing through water during a match at Stamford Bridge, which to me looked like all Torquay. I'd read that Finney grew up right next to Deepdale and that he remained so loyal to the club that he turned down big offers such as one from Italy, an act that would've led to his incarceration in the United States for failure to engage in remorseless capitalism.

I felt curious to see how people would look if their club did or did not leapfrog into the four-team play-off. As it happened, I did not see much of anything, because they would not sell me a ticket, because I lacked a ticket-buying past at Preston, when in fact I also lacked any sort of past in Preston. I did love the name Preston, though, because I'd had a great-uncle Preston with big arms and a big voice and a penchant for not saddling his recollected stories with the fussy dullness of the truth. I had read that Preston North End won the first football title, in 1889, when they became the only team to go unbeaten in both the league and the FA Cup, which must've gone over well in their Internet chat rooms. I read that the club had almost bobbed into the Premiership in recent years but had kept getting ensnared in the four-team play-off thicket and hadn't cracked the top level since 1961. The stadium apparently has the remarkable capacity of 22,222 and has a gaping open end, so I went over and stood there on the sidewalk in front of somebody's terraced house. Police presence seemed heavy. I could see large chunks of the fans inside and see that at times they held their scarves above their heads en masse in that way Europeans do that we never do but should. The stadium seemed somewhat metallic; the fan noise echoed this tinny sound.

I tried to follow the match by the fans' reactions, and I thought maybe I could threaten the all-time record for most games un-witnessed from just outside forbidden stadiums. When Preston scored at 83 minutes, that goal seemed obvious. When Preston finished its 1–0 win, though, the fans leaving seemed reasonably merry but not giddy. I suppose their mid-range expressions could've told me that Barnsley had not been able to beat fourth-place West Brom (uh, no: 7–0), or that Leicester City couldn't beat fifth-place Wolves (4–1), or that Southend couldn't beat sixth-place Southampton (also 4–1), and that Preston North End had finished seventh, leapfrogging only Stoke.

But what blew me away in the dying moments of a Preston North End season that I had not witnessed, was the song that blared out of the stadium speakers as the players must've made their thank-you parade. Again in the world, Elvis Presley crooned 'Can't Help Falling in Love'. As an American, I just couldn't help falling in love with the concept that Elvis, raised in that two-room house in Tupelo, Mississippi, materialized 30 years posthumously in north-west England on a grey Sunday in May. If you ever toured Graceland, Elvis's home in Memphis, they'd tell you that Elvis lined up those three televisions in the living room because he liked to watch three American-football games at once, yet here he adorned that *other kind of football* as a crowd thanked its players.

I felt pleased we Americans could make a contribution, and I watched people head off into summer down Sir Tom Finney Way, and I saw a group of the most astonishing Birmingham fans walking up a sidewalk singing, 'Bye-bye to the Championship'. One had dressed as a waitress in pink, one as a detective in sunglasses, one as a doctor, one as a nurse, one as, improbably, a can of Spam. For just a moment, some young Preston fans, maybe 11 or 12 years old, railed at these gloaters, and a brief sidewalk-to-sidewalk shouting spree ensued, but we all moved on, and I watched children mass for autographs outside the Preston dressing room before leaving.

Well, on the way back to the train station, I ran across a group of Birmingham fans surrounded by police and those scary police horses that might just feel the urge to kick you at any moment. I wondered what these fans had done, but it dawned on me they'd done nothing except attend the match, and that this would be their police escort back to the station. So I inadvertently wound up walking alongside the police, and even though I had no affiliation save for a club so far south it's just shy of France, they seemed to have a surfeit of officers, so I had six protecting me while traffic stopped and drivers probably seethed.

I, dumb American, had my own police escort out of Preston. To me, it defied all known rationale, and I enjoyed it utterly.

I even felt amazed anew at the train platform, where they steered the Birmingham fans into their own segregated carriages, and one of the police officers said I could sit anywhere by explaining to another, 'He's normal.'

Having seen no promotion, I rode off down the country toward relegation, potentially available way down in The Valley in the south-east of London. On Monday night, 7 May, Charlton would play Tottenham hoping to elude Satan's grasp. On Monday morning, 7 May, the Premiership's cellar dwellers went thus:

16. Sheffield United – 38
17. West Ham – 38
18. Wigan – 35
19. Charlton – 33
20. Watford – 27

That meant that if Charlton did not defeat both Tottenham and Liverpool, it would neither catch West Ham nor spend an eighth straight year in the Premiership, this after gaining routine note as a model lower-money operation. In the last 12 months, Charlton had switched managers thrice, employing one manager for 12 matches and another for eight. Fans had booed the team off the pitch after a Carling Cup loss to Wycombe Wanderers of League Two. Back in February, Charlton had drilled West Ham 4–0 in The Valley and looked upbeat. Come late April, though, West Ham had started hogging wins mainly through the controversially acquired Carlos Tevez, while Charlton had not exactly decomposed, but rather sailed sideways.

I saw that tickets remained available so I called on Monday morning, but they would not sell me one because I lacked a ticket-buying history. I tried the idiot-American-tourist-from-New York routine, but they did not buckle. I refrained from asking if it counted that I had stood outside the stadium during a match with Wigan one Saturday in August 2005 eating fish and chips and cursing myself.

I decided to go anyway, hoping to find another ticket angel whose father couldn't attend. I had no such luck despite 45 pre-match minutes of milling around, and I doubled my lifetime total of matches spent just outside The Valley whilst people absorb a match within. I spent the first half of Charlton vs Tottenham in a pub a good walk away, and the second half outside the stadium under the Sam Bartram statue. The statue depicts the Charlton great with wavy hair, smiling and holding a ball in his right hand, palm upward, and I fretted that in his very statue, Bartram might be committing a handball, but I checked it out and learned Bartram had been a goalkeeper. Whew. As the second half opened with Tottenham 1–0 ahead on a goal from the fabulous Dimitar Berbatov, I could hear the public address imploring the fans, 'Forty-five minutes left in The Valley this season! This is the moment when we really need your support!'

I could see the action through a window on a lounge TV screen, and I could see that Charlton strained mightily, but that things looked bleaker by the minute because even a draw wouldn't suffice. It grew clear I would experience my first relegation, even if tangentially, and so I listened for the sounds. I'd never been a Beatles sort – The Clash moved me and rattled my brain – but I had to credit the wisdom of playing the Beatles' 'Let it Be' during the 80s minutes.

I've never heard it sound better. And, in this pregnant moment that called for worthy songs, a clever sort in Charlton employ played 'Always Look on the Bright Side of Life', from Monty Python. Whimsical. Magical. As the minutes drained off and some of the crowd drained out, a steward let me run into the stadium for the closing, the 2–0 final score, the player parade, the chants to 'Stars and Stripes Forever' of 'We'll be back'.

I had seen relegation, and again I felt astounded by that buoyant creature, the English fan. In the top row, a little band played and people danced. The season had waned and then croaked, but this populace we Americans associate with a crusty realism engaged again in a deathless optimism. I don't want to say all the fans exulted, but many smiled. Many looked like people going home after a regular old 2–0 loss to a big club. Some stopped and did interviews with TV crews. Relegation had occurred, and I saw not one 10-year-old boy crying his eyes purple like I did after the Dallas Cowboys upset the Los Angeles Rams 37–7 in the 1976 NFC Championship Game at Los Angeles.

In fact, I saw something downright marvellous.

On Floyd Road coursing out of The Valley toward the train station, I saw a boy not all that much younger than I was on my purple-eyed day when my mother came to my bedroom and tried to console me even as she must've felt baffled. He skipped along, somewhere in the vicinity of his parents, and the Monty Python heyday long preceded his birth, but he sang, solo:

Always look on the bright side of your life
Always look on the bright side of your life ...

I'd seen relegation for the first time in my life, and it was wonderful. In the train station, throngs waited on both platforms. The opposite platform, headed out of central London, suddenly broke into 'Stars and Stripes':

We'll be back, we'll be back, we'll be back
We'll be back, we'll be back
We'll be baaaaaaaaack ...

A train arrived. The doors opened. They boarded, left behind an empty platform, and rode off toward the Championship, and I had to say that I hoped their ticket was return.

37

One goal from Europe

Consider all the farewells accorded people as they retire. Some get an office party. Some hear other people singing, 'For he's-or-she's a jolly good fellow ...' Some listen to original songs penned by co-workers and chock-a-block with dull or callous inside jokes. Some get a big company lunch. Americans used to receive retirement watches, although I never knew anybody who actually got one. Some get cards, genuine presents or gag gifts such as laxatives. Some get something practical, like a laptop.

My own father got ... happier.

Some, if professional coaches or managers, get the cheers of a grateful stadium or coliseum. Some, if professional coaches or managers, get a contract buy-out and a figurative kick in the rear end. Some, if professional United States congressmen, get an indictment or a matching set of same.

And some, if American professional athletes, make farewell tours through their leagues, receiving gifts in every city, looking mildly embarrassed, and reminding us all that we belong to a ludicrous species which will spot somebody exponentially wealthy and then all but foam at the mouth in the act of lavishing more stuff upon him.

Well, on a chilly but clearing day on the southern edge of England, on Sunday, 13 May 2007, some 20,187 of my dearest friends and I may have witnessed an unparalleled send-off.

An English fellow from Tring named Graham Poll, aged 43

at the time, may or may not have refereed his last Premiership match as Portsmouth played Arsenal. Many suspected yes. Others suspected no. Many didn't care. Others cared deeply, and those hoped for yes.

And so, in fond farewell, the distinctive crooners of Fratton Park serenaded Mr Poll for a solid minute at least. They serenaded him with still 19 minutes plus added time remaining in his Premiership career. They sang a song I'd somehow never heard even though I'm sure I'd seen Poll do a Portsmouth match before. Toning down their usual tempo, they went all Celine Dion, all Streisand, opting for a ballad and for overall lyrical majesty:

> *Oh, Graham Poll,*
> *He's a f——ing a——hole,*
> *He's a f——ing a——hole,*
> *He's a f——ing a——hole …*
> *Oh, Graham Poll,*
> *He's a f——ing a——hole,*
> *He's a f——ing a——hole,*
> *He's a f——ing a——hole …*

As this opus, ever more memorable than a watch, wafted out over the Fratton End, then across to the other stands, I did not participate because I felt too much awe. I thought I'd exhausted my supply of awe at the world's most popular sports league, but apparently I had not. Forgive my rawness, but I had just never had the experience of standing in a stadium listening to people warble about an alleged f——ing a——hole.

Mr Poll had just treated the audience to a turn of refereeing seldom seen on the numerous pitches of planet Earth, for in the 68th minute of a goalless draw, he had shown us a black swan, a white alligator, a retroactive offside call. I confess to having no previous idea that anyone on earth, not even Nelson Mandela, had the authority to make a retroactive offside call. I also confess to a lack of guilt over my lack of knowledge of the retroactive offside call, for those seasoned sorts around me seemed similarly flummoxed.

They stated their flummoxed-ness in such words as: 'f——', 'c——', 'w——', 'mother———', and 'dis——'.

(Oh, sorry, that last one's printable: 'disgrace'.)

It had taken me only about 30 live matches to learn how to greet possible offside infractions by swivelling my head to see whether the linesman raised that gaudy little checkerboard flag. So it came as a jolt in the 68th minute of Portsmouth vs Arsenal to see the linesman's flag arm remain down, then see a bunch of Portsmouth players in the corner of the pitch hugging and celebrating their shiny new 1–0 lead, then see almost the entire Arsenal squad protesting, then hear the public-address announcer confirm Niko Kranjcar's rebound goal . . .

Then realize the play had not ended.

Here's how it had begun: LuaLua had manoeuvred to his right just outside the corner of the box and loosed a shot. It had skittered all the way to a reserve goalkeeper with the great name of Mart Poom, then ricocheted off Poom. It had bounced to Richard Hughes right in front. Hughes had swung at it left-legged but not well enough, and Poom had stopped it, whereupon it had bounced back toward Hughes like a diabolical pinball while Arsenal's Philippe Senderos had hopped over Hughes to help Poom. From there, it had bounced off either Hughes's body or Senderos's leg, but almost certainly Senderos's leg, toward the left, where Kranjcar stood and swept it in. If it touched Hughes's body but not Senderos's leg before it caromed to Kranjcar, it should be offside. If it touched Senderos's leg after or instead of Hughes's body before it rebounded to Kranjcar, it should be a goal. But if you could see any of that from the crowd, you must be, as the great Los Angeles sportswriter Jim Murray once wrote while trying to watch ice hockey, part hawk. I had little idea of the details as I hopped up and down celebrating the goal in front of four seats, including the three to my right, weirdly vacant. I thought *we* might've just finished quite possibly beating Manchester United, Liverpool and Arsenal within six Saturdays. Had I really experienced that in my debut season following this game?

As I came to rest with my heart still scraping my ribs, and all Pompey seemed plugged in and supercharged, Poll scurried over toward Darren Cann, the linesman and assistant referee with the flag still pointed downward.

They conversed, and this might not have been exactly the conversation, but I think I lip-read most of it:

> *Poll*: 'Did the ball come off blue or yellow?'
> *Cann*: 'Green.'
> *Poll*: 'Green?'
> *Cann*: 'Well, green is what you get when you combine blue and yellow.'
> Poll: 'Is it?'
> *Cann*: 'Yes, but if I had to guess, I thought yellow.'
> *Poll*: 'Why?'
> *Cann*: 'Well, it might just be that when I look out on the pitch and see you, I see yellow, because you gave those three yellow cards to a single Croatian player in the Australia–Croatia World Cup match last June, when it's almost humanly impossible to give three yellow cards to one player in one match, so I see you and think yellow.'
> *Poll*: 'Oh, well, then, I say blue.'

In truth, the conversation did seem somewhat shorter than that, but no less substantive. Poll waved off the goal – well, didn't actually wave it off, but just pointed to some spot on the pitch which indicated Arsenal should start from there and the score should remain 0–0.

As a whole stand's resentment showed great endurance for a solid minute, then two minutes, then three, I began to time the unmitigated derision of Poll that overran any attention to the continuing game. The contempt went strong for six minutes. It began with the vehement – *You're not fit to/You're not fit to/You're not fit to referee/You're not fit to ref-uh-ree* – but that seemed tame and impersonal, given that nobody in the human race has ever really been fit to referee, and given that this was quite possibly the guy's last game before moving to another division or out to pasture.

Gathering itself, the crowd dipped into its reservoir of lyrics, and the Ballad of Graham Poll, the F——ing A—hole, swept up apparently from a soul just two seats to the left of one blue bear, proving that one man and one voice indeed can make a difference. Thereby could Fratton Park supply Poll with a more personalized farewell, a send-off that would ring across the fields of time.

The song sustained itself through several verses, each oddly identical to the last, and it seemed to emanate from deep in Fratton's collective diaphragm. I've seldom heard such mission attached to a song since Whitney Houston famously sang 'The Star-Spangled Banner' before Super Bowl XXV in 1991 as the United States commenced a first war with Iraq. At last, the ballad faded, and through the final 20 or so minutes, including the mere two minutes of added time, there remained only residual insults, heckles and bad vibes at Poll. That, and zero goals. When the final whistle blew, Primus began by hugging Poll, a lovely gesture. I thought of one of the cleverer tabloid headlines of the 2006 World Cup: EXIT POLL.

Now, that very morning, I had feared 10th place, again. I had walked in the English May winter to the Brighton train station hoping against 10th place. I understand it's madness for a Portsmouth fan to dread 10th place, Portsmouth never having finished higher than 13th in a Premiership season, and 10th in the top level still representing the best season in the last half-century. But, bloody hell, I'd spent my entire Portsmouth tenure in single-digit places, and I'd rather got used to those single digits, and I just did not want a defeat to Arsenal coupled with a Blackburn victory against Reading consigning ninth-place Pompey to the double digits. That's right: Pompey had stayed at 53 points after Everton, while Blackburn had crept up again to 51, and it dawned on me again that fans often travel to the stadium in fear, and that fear is an integral part of fandom that helps make fandom so appalling. Sure, sportswriters travel to the stadium in fear, but it's a vaguer fear; it's a fear of a stringent deadline, or that somebody might've taken down the buffet already, or that the press parking lot might've filled and we might have to walk an extra 10 blocks. Fans have deeper fears, such as tumbling into an undue 10th place after spending eight months in third and fourth and sixth and seventh and ninth.

Well, turns out, some scenarios can prove even worse than your club falling blithely into 10th. One example: your club could begin the last day in ninth place. It could have 53 points. The club just ahead, in eighth – call it 'Reading' – will have 54. The club just ahead of that, in seventh – call that one 'Bolton' – will have 55. Then, as this nightmare grinds away, the final day will have Bolton drawing 2–2 with Aston Villa, reaching 56 points. It will have Reading drawing 3–3 with Blackburn, reaching 55 points. That means that if your club won, it really would go on a European tour – amazing – because its plus-4 goal difference would have bettered Bolton's minus-5 goal difference. A European tour for your club, by the way, would be the first one ever. It's not like you've been awash in European tours and can shrug off the UEFA Cup as would, say, Arsenal.

So as the nightmare hits its spin cycle and your eyes start wiggling, your club also will draw, 0–0, with Arsenal, but not just any 0–0. This will be that special kind of 0–0 which happens to include a goal, and a goal celebration before a jubilant crowd, and an announcement of the goal over the stadium public address. Then, a referee in his final match will run over to the assistant referee, and you'll just know the goal you saw is about to vanish, and the Pompey fans will feel a profound state of powerlessness as he who has all power rules it's still 0–0. And sport just teems with these things, these near-misses, or near-makes, these narrow passageways of exhilaration or excruciation. Some never abate. Chicagoans lament a single basketball call in New York from 1994 – they still can name the referee – and St Louisans lament a single baseball call in Kansas City from 1985 – they still can name the umpire – and here comes Poll over to Cann, and while this one's not so significant because it costs seventh place and not first place, well, still, imagine Fratton Park beholding a shock seventh place.

Imagine that life experience.

And so as your body starts to heave and you start shouting unintelligible things in the REM hours, as sweat droplets start to materialize, a song will rampage around the head, some sort of chant you've never heard in your life, something like:

> *Oh, Graham Poll,*
> *You're a f——ing a——hole …*

In this unquestionable nightmare, you'll hear some people singing 'He's' a f——ing a——hole, and some people singing 'You're', just for variety. Then, somebody in the dream will run up to you and give you the other scores, activating the dreaded what-if gland as you hanker for Reading or Bolton to have won so as to render this Poll tax less punishing. Your avuncular manager will talk of how much he wanted Europe, and he'll try to bite his lip to avoid a fine from the league, and he'll say of his summer plans, 'If I say anything, Sandra and I will end up on a caravan on Canvey Island when I want to go to Mallorca.' And you'll have never heard of Canvey Island, but you'll learn it's an island in the Thames estuary off the coast of Essex, once fashionable, then not, now somewhere in between in the aeroplane age, the home to the Chapman Lighthouse of Joseph Conrad's *Heart of Darkness*.

And finishing ninth, with seventh so accessible, might have

some people waking yelling, for no apparent reason, with
Conrad words.

'The horror. The horror.'

38

The whole meat raffle of it all

Final days haul some pretty heavy emotions that grip even that insouciant creature, the sportswriter. I remember feeling wells of emotion, preposterously, on Sunday nights after Super Bowls, on Monday nights after the consuming three-week American college basketball tournament in March and April, on Mondays after Olympics closed, especially in Sydney, when I felt very nearly debilitated. *How could they just ... stop?*

The last exam has finished; it's time to say goodbye to all your fellow pupils. Have a good summer. See you next year.

'Have a good summer,' the Fratton Park public address blared as everybody filed out. 'See you next year.'

I knew from the morning that the day came equipped with a sigh. One last time in a remarkable Portsmouth season, I entered 'Fratton' into a train-station ticket machine, and one last time, I learned my route would halt for rail replacement. Again, I would sacrifice mightily for my blue squad.

The train from Brighton to Angmering along the southern coast of the great country stopped 11 times. With that, all changed, and time for a tour. So with the clock ticking, about 20 assorted passengers boarded a rail-replacement bus, and we waited as the bus driver conducted an amiable conversation with one of the train supervisors. We presumed they waited for more passengers. No more passengers came. Then, after the jovial conversation ended, thank you very much, on we went.

Thereby did I lose another 15 minutes off the end of my life, for my club.

Like most of the other rail-replacement double-decker bus drivers, this one knew his machine intricately, but that didn't alter my sensation that the bus may well topple given the speed with which he took turns off roundabouts as he seemingly impersonated Lewis Hamilton. We stopped in Arundel, with its lovely castle perched on the hill. The passenger total thickened, and next to me sat an adorable little boy from India with a Chelsea bag. We proceeded bruisingly through the roads, peering out at the open pastures of the real, green England, until reaching Barnham after seemingly several hours. From Barnham, the train stopped only 11 more times before Fratton.

On a grey day on the southern edge of England, at about a quarter to three, a quarter to kick-off for so many heavy English Saturdays through the years, the train rolled to where the left-side window availed a view of the ancient and majestic stanchions of Fratton Park. There they sprouted from their neighbourhood of warehouses and storage facilities. I noticed the big B&Q store and marvelled at my knowledge that it had not been the same B&Q from which Glen Johnson had tried to steal a toilet seat.

The things I'd learned.

I still didn't quite pronounce 'Pompey' correctly, sometimes stressing the latter syllable, and I still waited for referees to blow the whistle for a five-second violation, à la basketball, whenever players took a long time to throw in a ball. But by the season's game No. 38, I did know a gem when I saw one.

One: in the seventh minute, Arsenal's Gael Clichy fashioned a shot that deflected off Noé Pamarot and flew past goalkeeper James, yet seemed awry and unthreatening as it neared the far post. But just as it passed its last swatch of available goalmouth, it seemed to slow. It seemed to activate its left blinker light. It definitely curled antagonistically to the left. It seemed to hang there. I heard a woman shriek. Just then, a guy wearing Portsmouth No. 6, who turned out to be Djimi Traoré, contorted himself and kicked it back over his own head for a save.

Another: any sight of Arsenal's Cesc Fabulous with a football.

And another: when Poll awarded a penalty to Arsenal in the 38th minute, and when Julio Baptista lined up to take the penalty, I thought again of how I'd seen James try to stop penalties at Watford and against Newcastle and at Everton, but none successfully. Here's an athlete with buckets of decency, I thought. Here's a one-man threat to lower the world's athlete narcissism ratio. Here's Portsmouth's player of the year, just awarded in pre-game. So Baptista struck. And James flew to his right. And James met the shot, which flew up over the corner of the goal. And the Fratton End erupted. And so did the other stands. And the place seemed almost to sway. And I joined with my fellow humankind in a vociferous chorus of, 'England's number one! England's, England's number one!' And I long since knew what that meant.

As will happen in this world, Arsenal seemed faster than Portsmouth, and the idea of winning seemed far-fetched, but time ground on, still 0–0. No Sol Campbell (injury), no Matt Taylor (injury) and no Pedro Mendes until near the end (recovering from injury), but with Arsenal similarly depleted, and the season on its dying fumes, we in the Fratton End implored the Pompey players at about 50 minutes with 'Guantanamera':

> *One goal from Europe,*
> *We're only one goal from Europe,*
> *One goal from Eurrrrroooooppppe . . .*

Pretty soon came the heartfelt song to the prospective retiree, a genteel signal of courtesy and esteem. We all drifted into the late 70s, into the 80s, on past 85. In the final five minutes, the 'Blue Army' chant seemed more urgent than ever, the Pompey chimes felt harder. Even in added time, another 'One goal from Europe' went up.

Then it all stopped, another 38 games in the books, still one goal from Europe, and the applause sounded like rain on a roof. The sky had blued, the sun had come out, the players cleared the pitch, and seemingly half the 20,000 left. I stayed, of course, for the kind of lap of honour I'd seen at Everton and even Charlton.

As the players re-emerged and began their lap by walking to their right, there came none of the major din of the last home match at Everton or even the last home match at Charlton, no boom, no catchy loud song with only the single lyric. They came around the pitch in a little blob, a sort of ragtag parade, and I found it fitting, the subtlety of Fratton as compared with other places, rather emblematic of what first drew me to this old rodeo ground. No frills. Sol Campbell walked in jeans and a coat, Matt Taylor, with jeans and a shirt and a tot. The lap so lacked pomp and the stadium fell so shy of posh that if you'd just landed from a trip to Mars you might've presumed this the second division or the third, when not for one moment in the whole marathon, from Blackburn's visit in August to Arsenal's visit in May, had this team felt the floor of the top division so much as quake. I'd sought the relegation tightrope, and I'd found a club that surpassed its previous season by 16 points, the largest improvement within the Premiership.

So as they came by my corner of the Fratton End, I felt a hint of eye mist at the sight of James, leading the pack, and at Campbell, tucked in behind, as well as for the whole last day of exams, school shuttering for summer, Sydney closing down its Games. I made sure to remember I was an interloping American applauding a Nigerian, a Congolese, a Croatian, at least five Englishmen, and that that might be the best you can say of sport, that somehow we'd converged from all these places on the south edge of England and we'd all got along, save for a few referees here and there. I even had a moment of lunacy when I suspected we'd all been through something together, though neither the Pompey players nor the people who sat around me would know me if I bumped into them at B&Q the next day. It can be such a pain to follow sport, so full of the mental gymnastics of rationalizing, so immersed in the hideous business pages, that at least we can value the shared experience.

That and, of course, the company of a blue bear and mates.

So Charlie and Dan and Hopkins and I met up by the player parking lot and walked the walk to the final-exam pub for the season-closing 'pint' which, when translated into English, means 'pints'. Children marvelled through car windows at the blue bear, reaffirming the intrinsic value of a blue bear, especially one that beams right back at them and waves, about which they probably prattle on until bedtime. We entered the Devonshire Arms, where the patrons' expressions reaffirmed the intrinsic value of walking into a bar with a blue bear. We ordered our familiar array of pints, myself and my adoptive Premiership parents. We got a table and watched footage of Carlos Tevez's marvellous goal for West Ham at Manchester United, even while we unanimously agreed it bothered us that any club could stay up because of a light penalty for an illegal contract with the very player who scored their survival goal (plus a batch of other goals in April–May matches). We even felt for old Neil Warnock at Sheffield United, even admired his sincerity in life, and wondered how that tortured face must look freshly relegated. We talked about the normal things, even the previous night's Eurovision Song Contest, and that brilliant voice that undercuts it with commentary on the BBC broadcast, who I learned was Terry Wogan. Who knows, another year, I might even approach cultural literacy.

We sat through an astonishing pub event, something I'd never imagined upon the face of the planet. A temporary table materialized, and on that table appeared plastic bags bloated with bloody stuff that looked very much like the venison sausage we ate for months in 1978 after my little brother nabbed a long-sought, four-point buck. Astoundingly to myself, a woman began reading off winning raffle numbers. So I saw my first meat raffle.

Who knows, another 10 years, I might even attain cultural literacy.

My three parents shocked me with a birthday present, the sight of which shocked me further: a 2006–07 Portsmouth shirt, complete with 'Oki Printing Solutions', but when I flipped it wondering if it'd be a Campbell or a Primus or a James, I saw a No. 7 on the back and a CULPEPPER. Overwhelmed, I said I did not deserve the shirt because I had not suffered sufficiently and had never been lower than the top 10 in my entire Pompey tenure.

You never know. Get out of the house, board the train and go to the stadium, and you might end up knowing some of the best souls you ever ran across.

Good thing, too, as fandom grows tougher across time, never having been easy in the first place in its woolly, exasperating history. As the news programmes showed Sheffield United fans in tears and Charlie sang, 'Cry on the telly/I saw you cry on the telly,' it seemed four clubs might sue the Premiership because of West Ham. What a lovely closing day, a closing day in which, these days, you can hit the post and lose £35 million, a closing day promising ... lawyers.

Jaw-dropping money, resentment, lawyers: why, it seems downright *American*.

Sometime in that early evening still lit up outside with northern latitude, the larynxes of Pompey reactivated, and the pub sang a rendition of the Pompey chimes, and either before that or after that, the pub rediscovered the ballad of the day:

> *Oh, Graham Poll,*
> *He's a f——ing a——hole,*
> *He's a f——ing a——hole ...*

Moments later, I went to get the round that turned 'pint' into 'pints' – two Fosters, one London Pride, one Stella (that's mine) – and as I waited in front of the taps, I suddenly heard a man in a

Portsmouth shirt to my left on a barstool. He stared at the screen on his mobile phone, as if checking texts or reading the Internet or something. And as he looked down, he warbled softly to himself, 'Graham Poll/He's a f——ing a——hole/He's a f——ing a——hole ...'

This floored me utterly, and later on the dark-of-night rail-replacement bus from Barnham back to Angmering, as the monstrous vehicle raged along the southern edge of England threatening to topple, and as a young couple maybe 18 years old sat across from mc and licked each other's faces, and as I tried to decide whether I found them grotesque or sweet, I thought about that guy warbling into his mobile phone. Sure, I thought about buoyant Portsmouth fans and buoyant Charlton fans and two buoyant Brentford fans and soaring 45-yard goals and own goals that trickled in enchantingly. But I also thought about stolen toilet seats and Ben Thatcher and scary stories about favourite players and the big four and Carlos Tevez and money, money, money, money, money. After a year in the Premiership, I may know a little about a little and not much about much, but I do know one thing.

I think it's hard being a fan.